Praise for *The Completely Revised Handbook of Coaching*

"As a long-time practitioner of organizational change, I welcome this book as a contribution not just to the growing profession of coaching but also to good practice as a manager and practitioner in the broadest sense. As coaching begins to develop its models and defining practices, the revision of this pioneering work offers a foundation for positive practices that is broadly accessible and highly useful to practitioners in many fields of practice."

—Dennis Jaffe, Ph.D., Author, *Stewardship in Your Family Enterprise:*
Developing Responsible Family Leadership Across Generations;
Professor of Organizational Systems and Psychology, Saybrook University

"Anyone working in corporations today knows the power of the coaching movement. Pam McLean and the Hudson Institute have been long-time leaders of this movement. It has become clear that managers and talented employees need coaching in order to be more effective in handling the myriad challenges that they face every day. This is a key text for anyone who doubts the importance of this profession or what it can offer to building the talent needed for the future."

—Beverly Kaye, Founder and CEO of Career Systems International;
author of *Love 'Em or Lose 'Em* and *Love It, Don't Leave It:*
26 Ways to Get What You Want at Work

"*The Completely Revised Handbook of Coaching* provides a powerful and comprehensive approach to coaching and a must-read for any coach and leader. Based on decades of coaching experience and research, McLean has developed a proven methodology that will strengthen, expand, and elevate your coaching and leadership capabilities, and she has integrated this agile methodology with a deeper understanding of the coach's use of self in the important work of change. As a seasoned executive and professional certified coach, I can say that this framework works!"

—Patty Ross, Senior Director,
Global Product Process Innovation, Nike, Inc.

"Pam has thoughtfully captured the essence of what it takes to develop into a successful coach and to continue the development journey to mastery. The book is written in a practical and engaging style with numerous helpful examples that bring the coaching concepts, tools, and methodology alive. She skillfully guides you through both the art and science of becoming a coach with a focus on self as coach, the greatest resource and potential hindrance to the coaching engagement, and the use of a comprehensive and reliable methodology. A must-read resource for any current coach or leader who is contemplating becoming one."

—Steve Milovich, Senior Vice President, Global Human Resources,
Disney ABC Television Group

"The Completely Revised Handbook of Coaching is a masterful contribution to helping people at all stages in their coaching journey. Drawing on over twenty five years of experience in the field of coaching and her purposeful work at the Hudson Institute, Dr. Pam McLean provides an authentic and balanced framework for growing as a coach and for developing others.

"This book doesn't play on the surface and goes beyond the application of tools and techniques to 'fix things.' You are challenged to think and reflect at a deeper level so you will be of true value to the clients you serve. What resonated with me was the crucial topic of truly understanding self as coach—the most important instrument in the work of coaching.

"If you are in, or aspire to be in, a coaching leadership role, I highly recommend you use this book to guide your way. I know I will return to this timeless resource time and again."

—Mark Lindstrom, Vice President of Retail Operation and Chief TQE Officer at the Coffee Bean and Team Leaf and Executive Coach

"The Completely Revised Handbook of Coaching is an indispensable guide for any individual or organization seriously committed to expanding his or her capability to impact human performance through coaching. As the leader of the professional coaching initiative at the TaylorMade Golf Company since 2005, it is impossible for me to imagine the consistent and continuing evolution of our impact without our association with the Hudson Institute of Santa Barbara, whose beliefs, principles, and practices are so richly described in this volume. We understand that to grow our business, we must grow ourselves. The speed of change and the demands of innovation dictate that the development of our people, especially our leadership, must be equally intense and significant. To do that, we need reliable constructs and approaches, ones that stand the test of time, allowing a deepening reliance on what works best and the confidence that they will continue to yield outcomes that matter for every person engaged in real dialogue about meaningful change. You will find those here, and you will learn, as we have, that our continuing investment in human development through professional coaching is both deeply meaningful to our culture and also one of the most powerful strategic advantages we have as a company."

—David Berry, Senior Director, TaylorMade Learning Center

"The Completely Revised Handbook of Coaching is THE reference book for coaches at all levels. The handbook focuses not only on the comprehensive methodology of the coaching engagement from beginning to end, but, as important, it focuses on the self as coach and why it is so critical that coaches develop their own inner landscape to be truly effective in opening our clients' hearts and minds to transformative change. This book is a must-have on my bookshelf!"

—Cyndi Selke, Human Resource Executive Director, Americas & Corporate Staffs, Ford Motor Company

"*The Completely Revised Handbook of Coaching* is another example of the Hudson Institute's track record of providing coaches with practical and relevant perspectives, tools, and processes to enable effective change in us as coaches and our clients. Macro-business trends indicate there is increasing value of human qualities that machines and computers cannot replace: empathy, collaboration, integrity, openness, trust, authenticity, caring, and purpose-driven motivation. Hudson's coaching methodology simplifies the art and science of supporting an individual toward fulfilled and sustainable behavioral change."

—Mona J. Kelly, Group Human Resources Director,
The Coca-Cola Company

"Too few think of the powerful impact that can occur when one is generating an open space for extraordinary transformation with a client. The notion of leading from behind is alive and well in this book, with the important highlighting of the need to be aware of self as coach. Kudos to Pam for another extraordinary contribution to this emerging field."

—Eileen Terry, Chief People Officer,
Panda Restaurant Group

"The Hudson Coaching Methodology developed by Pamela McLean has the power to almost ensure the effectiveness of the coaching process because it examines readiness of the client, coachability issues, and the precontracting stages, and it helps you find the feasibility of helping others in a successful way. This model provides a framework to start working as a coach in a safe environment."

—Patricia Pellicer, Latin America Human Resource Director,
Grupo McGraw-Hill, S.A., de C.V

"*The Completely Revised Handbook of Coaching* provides powerful and pragmatic approaches to the most relevant aspects of coaching leaders. Pamela McLean demonstrates that both frameworks and coaching expertise often fail to deliver their true potential if not combined with a continuous process of self-examination on the part of the coach. Viewing one's self 'from the balcony' is an incredibly tangible process for increasing self-awareness—and ultimately success."

—Penny Handscomb, Senior Vice President Human Resources &
Leadership Development, Provide Commerce Inc.

"In *The Completely Revised Handbook of Coaching*, Pam presents the robust, yet flexible, Hudson revised coaching model, integrating multiple layers of the coaching process in a deep and at the same time accessible and engaging way. As she skillfully integrates and analyzes different authors' contributions to the Hudson model, she helps the reader understand the dynamics of this growing and evolving field. Definitely a must-read for coaches."

—Ana Pliopas, PCC, Founder of Carreira de Propósito, Brazil

"This major revision—focused on the journey to mastery—is a powerful integration of all of the essential elements of masterful coaching, and the final section on developing mastery with a focus on a model for supervision is the capstone! McLean examines many types of supervision both a coach and an organization might consider and simultaneously sends an important message to all of us representing this field of coaching: continued mastery is a must!"

—Monique Connor, Partner, PriceWaterhouseCoopers

"This book is for those who are powerfully committed to developing their insights and capabilities as a coach. Taking the reader from the guided wisdom of courageously 'knowing thyself' to the deep insights and practical instruction on coaching theories and methodology, the depth and knowledge in this book is extraordinary and could only have been created out of the vast experience, integrity, and commitment to coaching of Pam McLean and the Hudson Institute."

—Tricia Naddaff, President, Management Research Group

"Dr. Pamela McLean and the Hudson Institute continue to be the front edge of coaching. The work they are doing for and with organizations to help build an internal coaching culture is a game changer for organizations focused on high performance. The section on coaching in organizations is a must-read with a powerful blend of real-world examples and straightforward guidance essential for any leader responsible for developing other leaders. Mixing timeless principles with modern applications, the next generation of coaching emerges through this handbook!

—Sally Chial, Senior Vice President, Human Resources
and Career Services, Capella Education Company

"In this remarkable book, Pam McLean bridges the all-too-wide gap between individual and organizational coaching and between self (coach) and other (client) through her thoughtful use of case studies and her remarkable insights about life-enhancing interpersonal relationships. She builds this bridge on a very strong foundation—for it is clear to me that Pam McLean and her colleagues at the Hudson Institute provide the strongest and broadest base of theory and research of any coach training program now operating inside or outside the United States."

—Bill Bergquist, Ph.D., coauthor (with Agnes Mura) of *Coachbook: A Guide to Organizational Coaching Strategies and Practices*

"This book is a major contribution to the discipline and practice of coaching. Reading it was like time-lapse photography, watching the emergence from ambiguity to highly differentiated clarity. Individual, self-aware coaches who have the capacity to learn in their relationships make the difference. Pam does an excellent job of illustrating the importance of here-and-now presence and self-awareness in the coaching relationship.

"As a practicing coach, I would want this as a reference, to renew, to reflect, to readjust. As a person aspiring to be a coach, I would read it to get a clear sense not only of the profession, methods, and assumptions but also of the challenging journey that I am embarking on. I cannot imagine a better map."

—Ron Short, Ph.D., author, Learning in Relationship; president,
Learning in Action Technologies

"There are hundreds of books around coaching, but this book is about taking coaching to the next level: a coaching 2.0 trendsetter! Hudson is known for its emphasis on values, self, authenticity, and the richness of content, and this book reflects that image well. A must-read for anyone who wants to take coaching to the next level and for anyone who wants to learn coaching from the leaders in this field."

—Santhosh Babu, author, Coaching:
The Art of Developing Leaders, New Delhi, India

"Almost fifteen years ago, the original Hudson *Handbook of Coaching* was the first to reassure me that coaching was a serious, deep-rooted field, with a proper wealth of resources. To call this book a revision, even a major revision, is inadequate. Sir Isaac Newton said modestly, 'If I see further, it is because I stand on the shoulders of giants.' This book indeed stands on the giant first *Handbook*, but like the great scientist, it is an utterly revolutionary game changer. With this book, business coaching suddenly blazes into light. That searching light will burn out shabby or ill-founded practice and inspire all of us, from thought leaders to daily practitioners around the world, to much better work. It sweeps comprehensively from the inner self of the coach, through all the latest models, calmly and clearly integrated, to the latest complexities of the field. How extraordinary that I was given the privilege of reading it on the New Year's Eve of an old and discredited year; this book opens a new era in business coaching. Explosive, unmissable, scientific-yet-warm, calm, human, and humane. Grab hold of it; it's going to take us all on quite a ride!"

—Anne Scoular, author, Financial Times Guide to Business Coaching;
cofounder and managing director, Meyler-Campbell of London

The Completely Revised Handbook of Coaching

A Developmental Approach

Pamela McLean

with Contributions by Frederic Hudson

Foreword by Greg Honey

JOSSEY-BASS
A Wiley Imprint
www.josseybass.com

Published by Jossey-Bass A Wiley Imprint One Montgomery Street, Suite 1200, San Francisco, CA 94104-4594—www.josseybass.com

Credits appear on p. 261

"Enchanted Owl" by Kenojuak Ashevak Reproduced with the permissions of Dorset Fine Arts

Jossey-Bass books and products are available through most bookstores. To contact Jossey-Bass directly call our Customer Care Department within the U.S. at 800-956-7739, outside the U.S. at 317-572-3986, or fax 317-572-4002.

Wiley publishes in a variety of print and electronic formats and by print-on-demand. Some material included with standard print versions of this book may not be included in e-books or in print-on-demand. If this book refers to media such as a CD or DVD that is not included in the version you purchased, you may download this material at http://booksupport.wiley.com. For more information about Wiley products, visit www.wiley.com.

Originally published as *The Handbook of Coaching: A Comprehensive Resource Guide for Managers, Executives, Consultants, and Human Resource Professionals*

Library of Congress Cataloging-in-Publication Data

McLean, Pamela D.
    The completely revised Handbook of coaching: a developmental approach/Pamela McLean; with contributions by Frederic Hudson; foreword by Greg Honey.—Second edition.
        pages cm.—(The Jossey-Bass business and management series)
    Includes bibliographical references and index.
    ISBN 978-0-470-90674-3; ISBN 978-1-118-22061-0 (ebk); ISBN 978-1-118-23507-2 (ebk); ISBN 978-1-118-25964-1 (ebk)
        1. Employees—Counseling of—Handbooks, manuals, etc.   2. Employees—Coaching of—Handbooks, manuals, etc.   3. Personnel management—Handbooks, manuals, etc.
    4. Mentoring in business—Handbooks, manuals, etc.   I. Hudson, Frederic M., 1934-
    II. Hudson, Frederic M., 1934- Handbook of coaching.   III. Title.
    HF5549.5.C8H83 2012
    658.3'124—dc23

                                                                    2012016811

Printed in the United States of America
SECOND EDITION
HB Printing

SKY10069273_030824

The Jossey-Bass Business and Management Series

To the hundreds of leaders and coaches I have had the privilege of working with over the past two decades. Without each of you, this book would not be possible.

CONTENTS

FOREWORD

I cannot separate the importance of the work described in *The Completely Revised Handbook of Coaching* from the work done by the Hudson Institute of Santa Barbara. Both are transformational.

In today's economy, it is more important than ever before to be able to create a competitive advantage through people. Many promise it, but few can deliver on it. The pressure is on, and the game is all about creating high-performance organizations for the benefit of our customers. If we don't, then someone else will. In order to delight their customers better than competitors do, organizations are waking up to the concepts of creating a deliberate culture on a foundation of exceptional leadership. At the heart of that culture is disciplined leadership behavior based on presence, authenticity, and self-awareness.

Leading organizations and people to transform, one by one, is the work of the Hudson Institute. *The Completely Revised Handbook of Coaching* is a succinct articulation of the process, the approach, and the journey to transforming people and organizations at their core. I entered coaching through the Hudson Institute as an intellectual exercise. I left with the understanding that coaching is more than theory, process, and technique. In order to be a catalyst for changing people and organizations, coaches need to start with themselves. Coaching is something that is done, for sure. But it is not done well unless it becomes a way of being for the coach and the leader. When leaders master authenticity, presence, and self-awareness, they transform themselves from ordinary to inspirational. They connect with their team members in a new way, and team engagement soars. The light of presence shines bright, and it is the role of coaches to help people, leaders, and organizations tap into that light.

Greg Honey
Senior Vice President, Human Resources
Farm Credit Canada
Regina, Saskatchewan

PREFACE

Our entrance at the Hudson Institute into the coaching arena in the late 1980s was distinct from many others: we had deep roots in the domain of academia and a long history of developing experiential adult learning curricula in human and organizational systems and psychology. In 1986, Frederic Hudson left his post as the founding president of the Fielding Graduate University, and I was engaged in a clinical psychology practice and organizational work. Together we embarked on creating an organization that was originally focused on mentoring midlife adult leaders who wanted to craft important changes in their lives.

Frederic brought his background in philosophical studies along with a successful history in building adult learning curricula in human and organizational systems and clinical psychology. He had studied under Reinhold Niebuhr and Paul Tillich and was influenced by the work of Dietrich Bonhoeffer and Walter Rauschenbusch during his doctoral years at Union Theological Seminary and Columbia University. I added my background in clinical and organizational work to our efforts, along with years of training and learning in family systems theory through the Philadelphia Child Guidance Clinic under the leadership of Salvador Minuchin, Gestalt group and team training with Miriam and Irving Polster, transactional analysis training with Robert and Mary Goulding, and extensive neoanalytical work.

During the Fielding years, both Frederic and I had the advantage of knowing and working with some of the great thought leaders in organizational development and the field of psychology. The list included Malcolm

Knowles, father of adult learning; Robert Tannenbaum, professor at the University of California, Los Angeles, organizational guru, and author of several books on change inside organizations; Edgar Schein and his well-known process consultation model; Richard Beckhard, organizational development guru and author; Marjorie Lowenthal Fiske, well-known developmentalist and researcher on intentionality; Robert Goulding, founder of redecision psychotherapy; Art Chickering, professor and author who taught us that learning changes as we develop; social scientist Nevitt Sanford; and so many more influencers, including Vivian McCoy, Carol Gilligan, and Daniel Levinson.

Development throughout the course of our lives as individuals, and in systems and organizations as well, has been researched and understood through the many lenses of psychology, adult development, organizational and leadership development, change theory, and more. Work—from the seminal concept of individuation articulated from the perspectives of Friedrich Nietzsche, Sigmund Freud, Carl Jung, and others, to Erik Erikson's and Daniel Levinson's age and stage theories, Jean Piaget's and Robert Kegan's conception of levels of development, Gerald and Marianne Corey's work on team and group development, and Eric Flamholtz's work on the developmental trajectory of an organization—provides an important window into the developmental process of the human journey in the context of our many human systems.

Maslow developed the hierarchy of needs to accentuate the developmental nature of our wish to strive for more. Erikson taught us about the layers of identity we develop over the life course. Kegan draws our attention to understanding the implications of stages of adult development relative to individuation, and Gilligan focuses attention on the gender differences in our developmental journey. Psychology teaches us a healthy respect for the power of the past when we are working to make changes, and the subfield of positive psychology illuminates areas of particular relevance to coaching in leadership domains, including emotional intelligence, optimism, and engagement factors. The field of neuroscience demonstrates the power of mindfulness in providing the resilience we need to make crucial changes in our daily lives. Systems theory illuminates for us the power of homeostasis in a system of any size and the challenge we have as coaches to fully appreciate and work to uncover the natural underlying resistance to change. Charles Handy teaches us about the paradox involved in any change and the force at which change is hurling itself onto us as a culture today.

Learning theory includes the contributions of David Kolb, Chris Argyris, Malcolm Knowles, and others and teaches us how learning, ranging from deep transformative learning to smaller behavioral shifts, occurs and articulates the ingredients that must be in place for learning to be optimal. As coaches, we know that experientially based learning is one of the most vital elements in developing, growing, and changing during our adult years. Finally, philosophy always continues to be a source of wisdom, and the contemporary postmodern work of Manuel Flores, Ken Wilbur, and others builds on these philosophical roots while seeking to articulate an overarching theory of development that transcends all preexisting conceptualizations and combining the best of Eastern and Western thinking.

At one time in history, the sigmoid curve seemed to do a pretty good job of summing up the story of life as individuals and as businesses. We begin the journey slowly, experimenting, vacillating, and wavering along the way; we wax and then we slow down and inevitably decline and wane. Today it's not that simple. Whether we turn to the well-known developmental and longitudinal work of Erikson or the organizational life cycle articulated by Flamholtz, a thoroughly predictable linear pattern in this late-industrial age is no longer workable as a blueprint for our development. Life is changing too rapidly to hold on to a predictable map with a one-way direction. As Hudson (1999) writes, "Since the industrial revolution, linear thinking has dominated our consciousness until now with its basic notions of progress, perfectionism, success, happiness, and planned change. A linear perspective portrays life as a series of advances from simple to complex, from lower to higher, and from good to better" (p. 30). Luckily life today includes multilayered complexities and possibilities, and choices in our lives exist at all points in the adult journey.

Today change happens at lightning speed within the individual human system and the largest of organizations. Our challenge is not just managing and surviving change; it's learning to live with it, use it to our advantage, and remain fully engaged and alive at all points in the journey. As we orient our lives to this time in history, we shift from a predictable linear paradigm toward a cyclical and developmental one. And this is where the emerging role of coaching gains particular relevance.

At the Hudson Institute, we advocate a holistic model in coaching that encompasses and accounts for the context in which we live while simultaneously acknowledging our individual journey in life. Whether coaching a leader at the peak of his career, an early career person looking to define her own path, or a successful midcareer leader who is burned out and bored, it's essential we understand the developmental terrain in all contexts.

When we wrote the first edition of *The Handbook of Coaching* in 1999, we postulated that this emerging field of coaching seemed to be surfacing in response to the culture crisis of the 1990s that brought about immense change and created anxiety and confusion over how to continue to use old roles that governed our lives so well in the past and seemed increasingly irrelevant.

At that time, we outlined a series of principles that were emerging out of this cultural crisis. Today, over a decade later, these same principles are proving essential for our ability to thrive in this century:

Four Principles for the Twenty-First Century

- *Continuous change.* The long, stable periods of great continuity have been replaced in this new century by constant and rapid change. We can count on this as a fact of life. We can no longer expect to arrive at a steady state when our lives become crystallized and predictable. Coaches work with clients to understand, maximize, and leverage the inevitable changes in one's life and their larger systems.

- *Cycles of self-renewal.* Our lives are in continual, cyclical motion. We all live a chapter and then renew ourselves and move on to the next one. We cycle through the longer stable times in our lives, followed by transitions that allow us to realign and reset our course. Coaches inevitably work with clients to master and manage change; they teach the art of cycling through and practicing self-renewal.

- *Inside-out approach to living.* In today's constant swirl of change, we need to rely most deeply on our own inner sense of self and our values, and this requires continually cultivating our inner landscape. Coaches explore with clients what matters most in their lives and help clients shape their story and their actions based on their sense of purpose in the world at this time.

- *Perpetual learning.* Learning was once relegated to our early years, with the college and graduate school capstones viewed as our final chapter of learning. Today we need to weave significant learning into our lives at each step on our journey. Learning is a requirement if we want to remain fully engaged in a rapidly changing world. Coaching work calls on clients to take on new learning about themselves in the service of developing new behaviors and ways of being that lead to success in their stated goals.

FROM THE FIRST EDITION TO THE COMPLETELY REVISED SECOND EDITION

In our first edition of this book, we regarded coaching as a new skill set and a potential stand-alone field focused on helping individuals and systems develop and sustain resilience and renewal at each step in life's developmental journey. We conceived of coaching as a synthesis of mentoring and guiding—a skill set often combined with consulting, leading, and managing.

Over time the emerging field has refined itself. Skill-based competencies have become more reliably consistent, and best and next practices have developed through study, action research, and practice.

Coaching continues to grow at a rapid pace as a skill set and as an emerging field of study. Growth is strongest in the coaching of leaders at all levels in all varieties of settings, from the large corporate environment, to the entrepreneurial venture, to the family business enterprise. What remains true in this rapidly changing field of coaching is what we wrote about this then new field in our first edition: "A coach helps a client see options for becoming a better version of one's self. The appeal of the profession is in the satisfaction good coaches take in seeing their clients discard the old, fixed, constricting rules and begin to develop new behaviors and ways of being in their world that give them the strength to thrive in whatever situation they find themselves."

Our original view of this emerging field of coaching in 1999 included a much broader view from that which has evolved. Coaching today is primarily focused on leadership challenges and development at all levels in organizations large and small and in key transition work at each stage in the developmental journey that adults take.

PURPOSE AND AUDIENCE

The purpose of this *Completely Revised Handbook* is more ambitious than the first edition, with more focus on the specific elements necessary in supporting masterful coaching and much less attention to resources and bibliographical references. This completely revised edition provides seasoned and novice coaches with an overview of the essential elements required on the journey to mastery, including a thorough understanding of the key role of self as coach; a robust and agile coaching methodology; a review of theories and concepts informing the essential pillars of masterful coaching; a holistic understanding of the client's life through the lens of transitions, values, and human systems; a look at the development of a coaching culture inside today's organizations, as well as the value of a coaching skill set for today's managers; and finally all that's required on the coach's journey to mastery, including the growing role of supervision in a coach's development.

The *Completely Revised Handbook* is written for these audiences:

- Professional coaches interested in continuing to develop their coaching skills on the journey to mastery
- Internal coaches, that is, those inside organizations
- Managers and leaders in any organization or company who wish to add coaching to their leadership skill set

- Professionals in allied fields who may want to add coaching skills to their portfolios
- University professors wanting to create academic courses on coaching
- Persons who are considering the field of coaching and want to examine the essential elements required to attain coach mastery
- Human resource and organizational development professionals who want to gain a deeper understanding of the field of coaching

ORGANIZATION OF THE BOOK

The book begins with a brief examination of the history of coaching and the field as it exists today and the current state of coaching. The heart of the book that follows is divided into seven parts. In Part One, we begin by looking at the changes in the landscape of coaching since the first edition of this book twelve years ago. From nascent to current state, the development of the profession of coaching mirrors changing needs and changing times.

Part Two focuses on what we term self as coach: self-knowledge and the all-important use of self as the essential ingredient without which effective coaching does not exist. Knowledge of self includes awareness and insight into our limits, assumptions, beliefs, biases, and blind spots that guide and restrain us in working with others, understanding and empathizing with others, and more. We introduce the concept of leading from behind in Chapter Five and explore how this perspective is important in creating sustainable change that the client owns.

Part Three, devoted to theories and concepts of coaching, examines the intellectual underpinnings of coaching and provides a brief review of the growing body of research and literature on the current state of the field. These are described in Chapters Six to Nine. We believe it's essential for practitioners to have a sense of the broad intellectual roots of the field of coaching, from psychological and social theories to developmental and systems perspectives, and the newest domains of neuroscience, somatics, positive psychology, and others. We must be well grounded in theories and practices that inform our work.

In Part Four, we provide a broad overview of the work of a coach. We then outline the critical role of an underlying methodology in coaching and examine the details of the methodology overlaying case studies that allow us to put methodology to practice.

In Part Five, we provide a broad holistic and developmental perspective of the client's life through the lenses of transitions, human systems, and values. We examine the role of transition and change in our work as coach, study the relevance of understanding the basic values and sense of purpose in the life of our client, explore the complex human systems at play in our client's lives, and demonstrate the power of a bigger, broader vision in the client's life. We conclude this part with an examination of the adult learning agenda.

Part Six explores the essential elements in the development of a coaching culture, as well as the role of the manager as coach and developer of their people. The chapters in this part include key skills needed for moving from a managing mind-set to a coaching mind-set, as well as a tool kit for how to conduct just-in-time coaching sessions.

Part Seven examines the journey to mastery in the development of a coach. We study coaching practice through the lens of the novice, the mid-stage coach, and the masterful coach and overlay a series of case studies to ground us in the development of a coach that occurs over time and practice combined with continuous learning. We then explore the multilayered role of supervision—self, peer, internal organizational, individual, and group—and present an initial model for group supervision. The final chapter returns to the main models (elements of masterful coaching, self as coach, coaching methodology) and concludes with ten strategies for staying on the journey to mastery.

ACKNOWLEDGMENTS

Writing a book is a solitary and at times lonely undertaking, but it is never created in isolation. This book is the work of many people, and the most important contributors are the hundreds of leaders and coaches I have had the privilege of working with over the past twenty-five years. All that I have learned from each of them in our work is what makes this book possible.

I am deeply appreciative to those colleagues who read part or all of this manuscript and provided me feedback that both challenged and affirmed my thinking along the way. Nathinee Chen has been extraordinary as a development editor from beginning to end, and Kathe Sweeney has been a most supportive editor. Linda Antone has worked tirelessly and meticulously on the manuscript and the very long list of permissions.

Great appreciation to my husband, Frederic, for his early contributions to the field of coaching and original concepts surrounding the whole person as articulated in Part Five; Sandy Smith for her long-term thought partnering that serves to enhance our work in the coaching arena and her generous contribution of a handful of case vignettes throughout this book; our leadership team, whose wisdom over many years has advanced our coaching practices and contributed to this work immeasurably; and Ron Short's wisdom and important contributions to the model for self as coach, based on his lifetime of experience in related fields.

Many wise and experienced professionals have contributed opinions, ideas, and helpful recommendations. Karl Grass, Tom Pollack, and Bill Lindberg have provided valuable thoughts on major portions of this book that have served to shape my thinking. Kathleen Stinnett and Joy Leach have been ready to offer ideas and good thinking whenever I asked. Once again, the wordsmith genius, Barbara D'Amico, is evidenced in portions of the book. Finally the support and good thinking of my colleague and sister, Toni McLean, has been invaluable and enormously appreciated at every step in this writing journey.

June 2012   Pamela McLean
Santa Barbara, California

THE AUTHOR

Pamela McLean, Ph.D., is a leadership coach and the CEO of the Hudson Institute of Santa Barbara, one of the leading coach training programs in the United States. She practiced as a licensed clinical psychology for many years before entering the coaching domain in the early 1990s. She is a Master Coach, a coach supervisor, and a contributor to the emerging field of coaching.

She has wide experience working with leaders in a variety of industries as they seek to deepen their leadership skills. She works regularly with organizations as they add coaching skills to their work as leaders, as well as managers who want to add coaching skills to their managerial tool kit. She regularly supervises experienced coaches working externally and inside organizations.

McLean is the author and coauthor with her colleague and partner Frederic Hudson, of several books, articles, and chapters focused on coaching, human development, and transformational learning. She is the coauthor of the well-known book on transition and change, *LifeLaunch: A Passionate Guide to the Rest of Your Life*. She coedited the winter 2009 edition of the *International Journal for Coaching Inside Organizations* focused on a developmental perspective in coaching.

McLean served on Harvard University's JFK Women's Leadership Board; serves on the advisory board of the Women's Center for Leadership in Portland, Oregon; is an editorial board member of the *International Journal of Coaching in Organization*; and is on the faculty in the Organizational Systems Division of Saybrook University in San Francisco.

PART ONE

AN INTRODUCTION
TO COACHING

The more the world around us is in flux, the more we as individuals must be certain about what matters in our lives: how we spend our time, who we are connected to, and where we are going. A coach is someone who can evoke passion and purpose in others, within the dissolving and reconstituting environments of our time.
—Frederic Hudson

CHAPTER 1

THE EVOLUTION OF COACHING

David Drake (2009) has summoned us to step into a new level of maturity as an emerging profession, examining broad roots, new research, and best practices that continually build new layers of structure to this field of coaching:

> Given the speed and manner in which the field of coaching has grown, it would be risky to assume that the future growth will be either linear or uniform. The field of coaching is, in many ways, an unprecedented phenomenon that requires new levels of thinking about its practices, its nature as a collective, and its priorities as a philosophical and professional force in addressing the unique opportunities of our time. I would contend that the many historical struggles around positioning within coaching must give way to broader and more inclusive approaches to deal with the complex challenges facing our clients, our organizations and our society. If coaching proves unable to adequately meet the rapidly changing needs of our time, it will give way—for better or worse—to other means [p. 138].

Drake's summons is an important one for this growing profession to heed. It's the goal of this book to articulate and explore new layers of maturation and sophistication in the growing field of coaching in the hope that the field continues to professionalize itself through rigor and research. The growth of this emerging field has been nothing short of astounding over the past decade.

A BRIEF EXAMINATION OF EARLY WORK IN COACHING

We begin with a brief examination of what has evolved and changed in this powerful progression toward the professionalization of a new field of study and practice.

Early Conceptions of Coaching and Links to Mentoring

The earliest notion of coaching was closely linked to the concept of mentoring. In our first edition of this book, we used the term *mentor-coaching* and wrote:

> Mentoring is the model for coaching ... but the word mentor is too formal for purposes of a coach training model. I prefer the term coach here. Coach is now applied to a person who facilitates experiential learning that results in future-oriented abilities. This term (coach) refers to a trusted role model, adviser, wise person, friend, mensch, steward or guide—a person who works with emerging human and organizational forces to tap new energy and purpose, to shape new visions and plans, and to generate desired results. A coach is someone trained and devoted to guiding others into increased competence, commitment and confidence [p. 6].

Experience reveals a good deal about the important distinctions and overlaps among the disciplines of coaching, mentoring, consulting, and advising. Mentoring was a natural bridge to coaching, but it offers a limited view of the domain of coaching and the essential elements of the field. Understanding important differences between coaching and mentoring and the distinctions and overlaps relative to the fields of consulting and coaching provides role and boundary clarity for today's coach. Table 1.1 illustrates some key distinctions between coaching and other practices.

From Nascent to Mainstream

Although some track the origins to the mid-twentieth century and earlier, most agree little was heard about *coaching* outside the sports arena until the mid- to late 1980s. Today it is a multimillion-dollar business recognized as an effective way to aid in the development of leaders at all levels in an organization, as well as a means of working with people at normative, predictable life transitions. A quick Web search of the words *executive* or *leadership coaching* easily yields over a million sites.

Today there is a blending and merging of the best of the early thinking and increased clarity about what's essential and what's peripheral to the field. As it should be, research and practice provide the grounds for studying and testing what works and which theories, concepts, and methodologies need refining.

Table 1.1 Coaching, Consulting, Counseling, and Mentoring: Key Distinctions

	Coaching	Consulting	Counseling	Mentoring
Who receives?	Individuals Teams Organizations	Individuals Teams Organizations	Individuals Family systems	Individuals
Focus	Future focus Identifying and achieving a desired future state	Problem-solving focus Fixing a known issue and achieving greater results	Healing the past Examining repeated patterns of behaviors	Advancing in the organization Networking Understanding politics
Role of the helper	Lead from behind: client chooses the direction forward	Lead from in front: offer advice and solutions	Lead the process through questions, feedback, observations, and advice	Share past experiences as they might benefit the recipient
Helper-client relationship	Partners working together to achieve a client's stated goals	Expert (consultant) who helps the organization fix problems and grow	Expert (counselor) who helps the client	Senior, experienced individual who helps the novice
Outcomes	Goals, vision, and plan identified Forward progress on action steps	Opinions, and recommendation provided	Greater insight Healing of past	Understanding of organizational dynamics, networking
Length of relationship	Leader as coach: ongoing relationship External coach: six to twelve months to achieve significant change	Varies, depending on nature of assignment	Depends on approach of counselor; some foster ongoing relationships over years	May last over very long periods of time

Individual Biases to Substantive Research

When the first edition of this book on coaching was written, it was one of only a handful on the market; there were only a few coaching schools, programs, and curricula at the forefront and no professional organizations or alliances. Individual biases and approaches focused on singular perspectives were dominant in the marketplace because little research had been conducted in this new arena. Today these individual biases have given way to important substantive research examining relevant theories and concepts informing this emerging field, as well as a growing body of research studying coaching effectiveness and outcomes in a variety of settings.

Coaching Is Coaching Is Coaching; or Is It?

In earlier days, there was a widespread belief that the essential coaching skills were readily adaptable to any type of coaching in any setting. Furthermore, it was initially thought that the uses for coaching were nearly limitless. Today we view leadership (at all levels, from emerging to executive) and transition coaching as the two main domains in which coaching exists, all the while sufficiently and ethically managing the boundaries of consulting, counseling, and mentoring.

Coaching skills alone are not sufficient for a coach to succeed in any environment. The range of knowledge, experience, and skills sets needs to be matched to the specialty in which the coach operates. Coaches who enter the organizational domain must understand how organizations work and how systems thinking bears on the work of the individual, the team, and the larger parts of the organization. They must also be sophisticated in their understanding of their role in this system in order to maintain boundaries that allow them to operate effectively as coach.

From Corrective to Developmental

Early on, coaching was frequently focused on remedial issues, and this mentality still exists in some organizations. However, coaching that occurs in organizations today is most often focused on facilitating the developmental growth of leaders around specific challenges and natural next steps in their leadership role.

Accountability Matters

At the outset of this emerging field, there was little to guide a coach relative to the impact of the coaching work, and attention wasn't yet focused on accountability, results, and the overall sustainability of the field. It was simply too early in the development of the field for best practices to surface.

Today good coaches are keenly aware that the sustainability of this emerging coaching field is contingent on the positive results created in the work of coaching with individuals, teams, and organizations. In Chapter Eighteen, on building a coaching culture in organizations, we explore a case study in which issues of accountability come keenly into play as a company attempts to integrate coaching into its culture.

Market Realities

Coaching is now widespread and commonplace, particularly within organizations in the leadership and executive domains, as well as in the transition work of individuals. This is clear evidence of the maturation of the field, and this also signals a more sophisticated consumer of coaching services. Today coaches are more skillfully scrutinized and vetted by organizations and individuals through any series of rigorous processes, including live coaching, references from coaching clients, evidence of coach training and certification, and years of relevant experience and background.

The expectation is that coaches will be able to provide evidence of the impact of their work—that is, the return on investment must be clear in today's marketplace. The case vignettes on Sarah in Chapter Eleven highlight this link between client goals and the overall needs of her team and the organization.

WHAT REMAINS THE SAME?

The theme of change has been an important factor in the emergence of this field, and this perspective is even truer today than it was in the 1990s. Today change has become the most dependable reality in our lives and in our world. People and organizations around the globe live with continuous uncertainty, tentativeness, and a sense of growing unpredictably. Many have no long-term expectations and plans and simply strive to keep pace with intense daily and weekly schedules of demands and responsibilities with little sense of a long-range plan for the future.

This reality was not true for most of the twentieth century. The world then seemed fairly dependable, uniform, and evolving, and lives took on those dimensions. The professions were organized around the assumptions of a stable culture of perpetual progress, central authority, and control, and there was a trust and a willingness to follow the overarching cultural rules.

Today's world is turbulent, unpredictable, and increasingly fragile. Organizations are operating in a continual state of change, and workers and leaders alike must be agile and skilled at managing transitions and challenges in order to thrive in the evolving marketplace.

CHAPTER 2

THE FUTURE OF COACHING

I n our first edition of *The Handbook of Coaching*, we noted that coaching was in its infancy; the guidelines for training and education were embryonic and largely informal, and a baseline of relevant theories and research was scant. Today the picture is dramatically different: high-quality training and certificates are being issued from independent organizations and universities, and master's and doctoral programs with coach specialty areas are growing in this emerging field of coaching. The sheer volume of research, writing, and doctoral dissertations dedicated to the topic of coaching is indicative of the meteoric growth of this field in the past few years.

Now it's time for the thoughtful maturation of the field, building on the best thinking, research, and existing theories that will support high-quality integrative approaches to coaching in the development of masterful coaches. The continued maturation of the field requires sustained focus in several areas: broad agreement on the theories and concepts germane to coaching, commitment to continual cultivation of self as coach, use of a reliable coaching methodology, a developmental and holistic perspective on the client's life, and an ability to track measurable results with the client linking to the organization's goals and the individual's needs.

BROAD AGREEMENT ON THEORIES AND CONCEPTS

Since the inception of this emerging field, the dominant emphasis has been on a competency-based set of foundational skills necessary in the development of a coaching approach. Several helpful books have addressed key skill-based competencies, and the International Coach Federation and European Mentoring and Coaching Council have articulated sets of skill-based competencies. Yet until recently, little attention has focused on the knowledge-based competencies that are essential for a coach to possess. As the field of coaching continues to mature, it's essential that it seek a broad and integrative understanding of the key theories and concepts on which this field would benefit from fully understanding and using.

COMMITMENT TO CONTINUAL CULTIVATION OF SELF AS COACH

An understanding of the use of self as a key instrument in the work of coaching is essential and requires continual cultivation of the coach's inner landscape—empathic stance, range of feelings, boundary awareness, somatic awareness, courage to challenge and presence—all buttressed by the foundational theories found in emotional intelligence, reflection in action, psychology, and adult development.

The coach's ability to adeptly use self as the most important instrument in facilitating change will increasingly become the gold standard in masterful coaching.

A RELIABLE COACHING METHODOLOGY

A robust and flexible methodology that maps the coaching engagement from beginning to end, linking the essential elements required to support lasting change, is territory that needs continuous development. The methodology outlined in this book represents a flexible, agile system that can be adapted to changing circumstances and environments. A thorough yet adaptive, rather than prescriptive, methodology will be increasingly important to the future of coaching.

A DEVELOPMENTAL AND HOLISTIC PERSPECTIVE ON THE CLIENT'S LIFE

Coaching is not about fixing people and problems; instead, it is developmental in nature and focused on adults who seek to make changes in their lives.

A coach needs to have a developmental and holistic perspective on each client's life, understanding the many lenses that provide a view of the whole person, including the values, roles, and systems at play; the developmental pathway; and the overall sense of purpose in the client's life in the face of ongoing waves of transition and change.

TRACKING RESULTS

Leadership coaching is currently the dominant coaching specialty in today's marketplace. In order to continue to flourish in this domain, coaches must become adept and proficient at tracking measurable results that closely link to the goals of the coaching engagement and track to what is most important to both the client and the organization.

DOMINANT COACHING ARENAS

Coaching is not a profession for the young and inexperienced. The seasoning that comes with years of experience and personal and professional development provide an important foundation for a professional who wants to become a coach. Great coaches typically possess rich and varied careers that have offered plenty of challenges, successes, failures, and ongoing learning. All of these lead to a complex and varied tapestry of experiences that deepens the inner understanding of self and supports the outer manifestations of a successful coach.

In our first edition, we speculated that the areas of coach specialization would be broad and varied. Today in our work and experience, we view the two most viable areas of coaching as leadership coaching at all levels and transition coaching focused on life's major transitions (see Table 2.1).

Table 2.1 Leadership Coaching Versus Transition Coaching

Leadership Coaching Specialties	Transition Coaching Specialties
Individual contributor to senior leader	From college to work
Team coaching	Return to work
Early leader transition	Career coaching
High-potential leader	Leaving the organization
New chief executive officers	Transition to wellness
Succession development	Retirement
Entrepreneurial enterprise	
Small business operation	
Family business	

CONSCIENTIOUS COMMITMENT TO THE JOURNEY TO MASTERY

The journey to mastery is a never-ending pathway for masterful coaches. It requires commitment to continual cultivation of one's inner landscape, a regular exploration of theories and concepts that support good coaching practices, a practice of staying abreast of current research in the field of coaching, and a steady focus on building new skills in support of masterful coaching that provides sustainable change for clients.

It's the intent of this book to provoke coaches' thinking in each of these areas and guide them through a journey of continuous learning and skill building to mastery, building from the inside out, and starting with self as coach as the core.

PART TWO

SELF AS COACH

*The hardest thing to attend to is that which is
closest to ourselves, that which is most constant
and familiar. And this closest something is,
ourselves, our own habits and ways of doing things.*
—John Dewey

CHAPTER 3

SELF AS COACH: AN INTRODUCTION

A s we explore the coach's journey to mastery, we are compelled to turn to cultivating the greatest, most versatile, and often enigmatic tool that we possess as coaches: the self as coach—that is, the whole, cultivated, managed self that we bring to the coaching experience to inspire and help effect change. Although students of coaching may, in the first instance, look at this as something they should (or must) do for their clients, the truth is that the awareness of self is an ongoing awareness (almost a way of life) that we owe to ourselves and individuals and then to our clients if we are to live our own lives of possibility and be truly effective in opening our clients' hearts and minds to change.

Self as coach is a challenging and sometimes elusive concept somewhere between reality and possibility. It embraces who we are, who we want to be, and who we need to be in order to be of true value to our clients. It requires us to be fiercely aware of our strengths, weaknesses, and tendencies. It demands that we call forth our talents, address ever changing challenges, and constantly self-correct.

Understanding self as coach well is the step in our personal and professional growth that allows us to move beyond simply using learned tools in the way an actor might to play a role and to come to a place that models balance and the ability to change. Without it, we are wildly diminished, personally and professionally.

Consider some examples that we explore in the chapters in Part Two:

- What if our strengths are so overpowering that a client is reluctant to share her real anxieties and concerns?
- What if our own raw edges make it difficult to slow down and build the all-important working alliance with our client?
- What if our own fears make us unwilling to help a client pursue a daring alternative?
- What if our aspirations are so strong that we fail to recognize that our client wants something much simpler, more direct, and more achievable at least in the short term?

Simply thinking about these questions, whether or not these specifics hit the mark for a particular coach, should highlight the possibility that something in the self of a coach can either promote or undermine clients' ability to achieve the changes they so richly desire and deserve. The goal here is simple: to understand our inner landscape with the gifts and the challenges inherent in our particular selves as coaches and to call forth the best, meet the challenges, and, above all, balance our strengths and weaknesses in a way that makes each of us a balanced and unbiased presence in serving our clients and builds our capacity as coaches to deal with the widest possible range of challenges.

To begin, we must start on the most human side: the coach's understanding of her own interior—the inner landscape—and all that is required in this domain to become a great coach. We term this self-as-coach work. It refers to the interior dimension that requires continual cultivation in order to bring our most authentic, agile, and capable self to the work of coaching.

The coach's commitment to working the inner landscape of self is central to building the capacity to masterfully coach a wide variety of clients in a broad spectrum of situations. This self-as-coach work requires us to face our own limitations, blind spots, rough edges, and beliefs in order to strengthen and extend our capacities. This is often experienced as rigorous and challenging work. Early in the coaching journey, it is surprisingly easy to overlook the power of our own capacity (or lack of it) and view the client as our challenge—perhaps we view her as resistant, unwilling to examine difficult issues, or talking in circles—at times making it difficult to bring the engagement to a successful conclusion. Yet, truth be told, in most cases, the coach's own work on the inner terrain is what allows for something very different to occur during the coaching engagement. It takes courage and commitment to true mastery for any coach to work the territory of self in order to engage at the highest levels.

A client needs considerable capacity from us as coaches in order to be fully open to the work of making an important change. Fundamentally an individual approaches coaching because there is something she wants or needs to tackle that is beyond her current understanding and capability. An individual knocks on the coach's door when something in life is unsettled, unknown, in motion, or drifting away. Change naturally stirs anxiety and unease, and the nature of the relationship between the coach and client is pivotal to the success of the engagement. The client's list of needs includes these:

- A need to feel a strong sense of respect and unconditional positive regard
- A need to experience a working alliance and sense of partnership with the coach
- An experience of the coach as a partner in the exploration of new and often difficult or unsettling territory
- A need to feel just enough comfort and ease with the coach to delve into the issues that are most important and often difficult to broach
- A need to experience the coach as fully alive, engaged, committed, and present during each session
- A need to have the coach hold just enough tension around important conversations so that real work can be accomplished
- A need to have a coach adept and skillful in providing feedback, even when it isn't easy to receive
- A need to have a coach accomplished in sharing important observations and patterns that surface in the coaching conversations even when it creates discomfort for the client
- A need for a coach capable of crafting a clear contract that resonates for the client and then hold the client accountable in support of reaching the finish line

This is a formidable list for any coach. In order to attempt to meet these expectations and strive to engage at a masterful level, a coach needs to continually engage in learning about herself from the inside out—strengths, raw edges, fears, and aspirations. Organizational development consultant and psychologist Ron Short (1998) writes about our human challenge in this regard: "Our biggest, yet least visible problem is that we think the world is outside of us, distinct and separate from us, this perspective is a simple human reflex" (p. 22). To operate from the inside out and develop a deeper inner dialogue, coaches need to become highly skilled at observing the inner states that drive their outer actions and responses.

Many of us come to coaching assuming it's all about acquiring tools and techniques to support our work. Instead we find that the most important tool is our self, and this requires a sincere willingness to explore the layers of one's inner landscape. Master Coach Doug Silsbee often says, "We do the work on our 'self' in order that we might be granted the privilege of working with our clients," implying that the coach's work on self provides a deeper empathy and honoring of the challenges of a client given the coach has authentically traveled this road as well.

The exploration of how coaches cultivate the self-as-coach domain in order to build capacity in their work with others is the focus of the balance of chapters in Part Two.

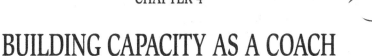

CHAPTER 4

BUILDING CAPACITY AS A COACH

C urrent coaching literature affords surprisingly little attention to an essential dimension of coaching: self as coach, that is, the ongoing inner development of the coach required to build broad capacity and work effectively in an assortment of settings with a variety of clients. This chapter takes a close look at all this entails.

Masterful coaching is a fusion of several essential elements, and no one factor is enough alone. The essentials we are most familiar with include a broad knowledge-based set of competencies in theories and concepts that are both seminal and evidence based, a strong skill-based set of competencies aligned with the work of coaching, and the understanding and ability to operationalize a coaching methodology that spans the first interview to the conclusion of a coaching engagement. Yet this list of basic ingredients is insufficient. A coach must be equally prepared to examine the inner landscape of self-development in order to build capacity. This development work is perhaps the hardest for both coaches in training and coaches in practice because it is forever unfolding, always humbling, and at times quite complex and demanding territory.

The capacity of a coach to practice adeptly is limited and defined by the coach's understanding and development of the inner workings of self and the ability to take full advantage of the use of self (that is, undertaking actions that stem from complete self-awareness). We build capacity as coach when we are able to step back and observe our self in action and open the door to new choices. Robert Kegan (1982) might capture this by posing that "we have object while we are subject" (p. 32). Kegan's use of *subject* refers to ourselves, including our unexamined beliefs and ways of being in the world that we cannot see when operating from this place, while our ability to step back, see, reflect on, and be responsible for all of who we are is "object." The subject prompts us to act, but our way of being is often so ingrained that we cannot observe it or reflect on the action required. The object stance allows us to take a step back and observe and reflect on our self, including our unexamined beliefs and ways of making meaning in our world. This is what we as coaches help our clients do. The fullness of this continually unfolding dance between subject and object in coaching is made richer by how well we, as coaches, cultivate this same ground in our own self-as-coach domain.

As always, we must start with self. A coach can't explore realms of self with a client when she hasn't yet examined this domain for herself. When a coach hasn't accessed her own feelings of anger or explored her sense of inadequacies or other faults, she will find it difficult to notice and create space for this exploration with her client. When a coach has explored little about her own emotions, it follows that her ability to notice the presence or absence of feelings in the client will be limited. The coach's willingness to enter the emotional terrain is limited or served by her own attention to work on self. This means a masterful coach is regularly tilling the soil of self-exploration and developing her own inner landscape, which maximizes her ability to move into important client explorations with agility and ease.

Figure 4.1 portrays self as coach as central and pivotal to masterful coaching with a direct impact on the coach's ability to incorporate skill- and knowledge-based competencies and effectively use a sound coach methodology. The outer rings of coaching practice and journey to mastery are supported by these inner domains, and the upper limits of one's capacity are guided by the innermost circles, which are foundational to the other key elements present in masterful coaching. To date, the field of coaching places notable emphasis on both skill-based competencies and, to a lesser but growing degree, knowledge-based competencies. But it provides insufficient emphasis on understanding the inner dimensions of the self-as-coach domain as central in supporting all of the other key elements.

THE ORIGINS OF SELF AS COACH

Self as coach connotes the work of developing our inner landscape: habits and behaviors, long-held stories, and our ways of making meaning and living in the world. This internal territory has been well researched by the field of psychology and to some extent in the organizational and leadership development arenas. These fields of study provide key models and frameworks shedding light on

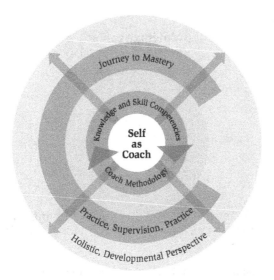

Figure 4.1 The Elements of Masterful Coaching

© Hudson Institute of Santa Barbara.

various aspects of this domain, and the chapters in Part Three provide a more thorough examination of the foundational theories supporting self as coach.

A well-known model that captures the complexities of self as coach can be extrapolated from Karen Horney's (1945) work on the basic neurotic conflict. She conceived of three basic ("neurotic" in her terms) coping strategies for managing conflict. Although her emphasis was on the examination of the more deeply psychological realms of the neurotic, an adaptation of Horney's model of the three coping strategies in normal human beings in Figure 4.2 provides a fascinating perspective into the complexities of the developmental terrain of self as coach. This reworking of Horney's well-known work provides a macrolevel framework for building coaching capacity. While Horney specifically suggested that the neurotic develops a comfort zone and makes a home base in predominantly one corner of the triangle (moving against, moving toward, or moving away), this same pattern of coping strategies is quite adaptable to normal human functioning well in the world, as coaches do.

The three strategies provide the coach with a view of one's most familiar and perhaps dominant stance. In Figure 4.2, each corner represents one's home base likely developed in our early years and supporting our stories about how the world works and how we need to continually adapt in order to live safely in it today. This is self-as-coach terrain at a macrolevel. A coach can't operate at a masterful level unless she is able to exercise agility and shift from one stance to another in order to operate effectively with a client.

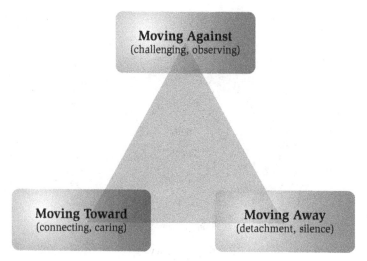

Figure 4.2 An Adaptation of Karen Horney's Triangle of Coping Strategies
Source: Horney (1945).

Consider this adaptation of her three stances as they pertain to the use of self for the coach:

- *Moving toward.* The ability to make a connection with one's client in a manner that creates a trusting, respectful, and caring milieu is essential in coaching. But if moving toward is the dominant stance of the coach, with little access to the two other domains, the coaching is incomplete and the coach finds herself colluding with the client and overcaring in order to ensure a caring environment. The coach who is most at home in this stance may find himself avoiding challenging conversations and feedback when that is what the client most needs.

- *Moving against.* The ability to challenge a client at the right times, sharing observations about patterns and behaviors the client might not be able to fully see. If this is the coach's primary stance, she is at home in provoking new thinking and creating in-the-moment breakthrough events in the coaching sessions. However, when this is home base, there is a risk of being overly aggressive in challenging the client and over-sharing observations without the necessary sense of connectedness, caring, and respect that's essential to the work of coaching.

- *Moving away.* The art of knowing when to step back and allow the client to sit in silence, staying in an important moment and reflecting and deepening the breakthrough experience. Susan Scott (2002) coined the phrase, "Let silence do the heavy lifting," and the coach who uses this as home base does so with ease. Overused, this stance leaves the client feeling disconnected from the coach. Without that all-important connection, a coach risks the possibility of the client's lacking the confidence and security to speak about what's most important.

This adaptation of Horney's model emphasizes the importance to the coach of knowing her own strengths and limitations. Identifying our own comfort zone provides rich information about our own story and potential limitations, creating a launching point from which to extend capacity into all three parts of this triangle.

As we proceed to examine the main goals and target behaviors a coach strives for in developing in the self as coach arena, the broad behavioral groupings and the inherent internal challenges that Horney proposed prove to be important and recurring threads of valuable support to the coach.

CULTIVATING THE SELF-AS-COACH DOMAIN

Most professionals come to the practice of coaching following a long and successful career in leadership and professional practice, from senior leaders and CEOs to executive directors of nonprofits, lawyers, physicians, business owners, career professionals, and more. The predominant belief is that what's required to be a great coach is largely about building a tool kit of techniques, approaches, assessments, and reading resources that will help the coach solve the client's problems. Most leaders initially find it difficult to understand that the most important tool is their own self. What's more, the work of the coach does not primarily involve solving problems for one's clients. The reality that the work of a coach is fostering transformative change that happens from the inside out and requires the coach to connect the head and heart of the client is counterintuitive for most of us. Yet in order to help clients make the real shifts they desire and create lasting change, coaching requires a much more robust approach than providing advice. The self-as-coach domain emphasizes the coach's ability to use self as an instrument of change. This is central to delivering lasting change and demands a continual examination of the intrapsychic workings of the coach.

Most of us can likely scan the past few days and identify a conversation or two where something didn't go as we had intended. Often our conclusion is that it was someone else's fault. We typically look outside ourselves before reflecting on our own role. Now consider a client who does this consistently: every difficulty in the client's life is someone else's fault. To notice this pattern requires careful listening and full presence; to use self as instrument requires the coach to share this observation and challenge the client's thinking. Consider another client who wants to develop the trust and respect of his team, and each time he comes to coaching, he arrives frazzled, apologizing profusely about being ten or fifteen minutes late for the session yet again. The coach skilled in using self as instrument is adept in bringing this up with the client by sharing how it affects the coach and finding out if the client is aware of this impact and if this behavior may in fact show up with others, especially members of his team.

The coach's ability to use self as instrument in this way creates the possibility of powerful breakthrough moments that connect the client's head and heart to some of the very changes he wants to make. This experience anchors a deepened awareness of the change.

Truly masterful coaches routinely engage in examining their own inner landscape, exposing and understanding their feelings, and sharing their struggles and questions with other peers. There is not a sense that "I've arrived" with a master coach; instead there is a fierce commitment to staying on a development path that seeks to continually expand one's capacity as coach and engage one's compassion and respect for how challenging it is for anyone to tackle an important change.

The framework that follows offers a sense of what constitutes this self-as-coach dimension, the pathway for a coach in this domain, as well as some of the models, tools, and resources that can support this development.

WHAT SELF AS COACH ENTAILS

Our inner landscape is complex territory, and while the areas of personality development and intrapsychic dynamics are beyond the scope of this book, it is important in coaching to focus on a basic framework of key elements that comprise the domain of self as coach. This framework (Figure 4.3) is where we start in building our capacity to work with any variety of human challenges using our self with intention and maximum effectiveness and maximize use of coaching skills and techniques.

The domains (resources and exercises for each of these domains will be examined at the end of this chapter, in "Six Reflective Practices to Strengthen Self-as-Coach Capacity") in the self-as-coach framework are presence, empathic stance, range of feelings, boundary awareness, somatic awareness, and courage to challenge. Of course, no one will be able to operate with full awareness in each of these domains at all times. Life doesn't happen this way; even the most skillful coaches will experience a loss of boundaries, a lack of empathy at the right time, a loss of awareness of their somatic being, or the courage to challenge when it's most important. Yet this model provides a way of scanning the inner landscape to determine what's most needed with

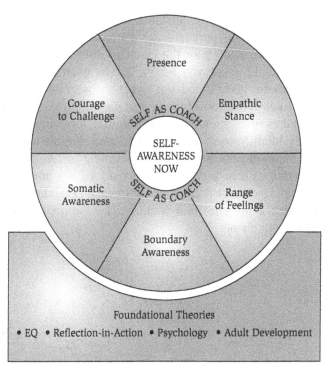

Figure 4.3 Self-as-Coach Domains
© Hudson Institute of Santa Barbara.

the client and with one's self at any given time, and it provides a map for the coach's own developmental journey toward mastery.

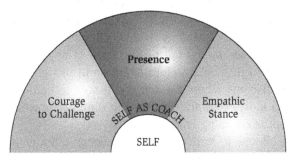

Presence

Tolbert and Hanafin (2006) describe *presence*, a complex blend of unique qualities, as "the use of self with intention—selectively using one's awareness to advance the work with the client" (p. 72). Halpern and Lubar (2003) offer a definition equally well suited to the coach: "the ability to be completely in the moment, and flexible enough to handle the unexpected" (p. 9).

There are many nuances to understanding precisely what this concept of presence entails, but for our purposes, what's most essential is the ability to be fully present and engaged with the client in the moment and alert to all that is happening in the session at several levels: what's being said, what's not being said, what's being acted out, what's observable somatically, and what's a pattern that you've observed before, for example. Full presence is a practice that requires time, attention, and continual development.

We can easily identify signs of the coach who doesn't exhibit presence: the coach who slips into the session just a moment or two after completing an important phone call, or a coach who arrives with a burning unresolved issue, or an unmanaged inner critic at work. In each case, the coach is operating with a diminished presence that compromises the quality of what's possible in the work with clients.

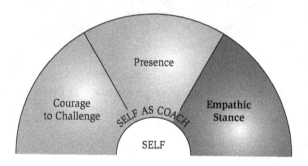

Empathic Stance

The coach's ability to experience and convey empathy is a pivotal element in this work. One's capacity to walk in the shoes of another and experience the feelings of another defines empathy. It doesn't require a lot of words, but it does necessitate that we notice the feeling state of another and convey that we see him or her in this state and are at home in this space with the client. A client quickly discerns when a coach is not able to connect with a feeling state and see the individual, and this rapidly diminishes what's possible and what surfaces in the coaching engagement.

A coach can choose to notice and acknowledge tears or quickly move to get the box of tissues and "help the client feel better." Empathy and noticing the tears is helpful to the client, whereas rushing to the client's aid in an effort to help the client "feel better" or sympathizing and soothing the client results in entering the client's system, losing effectiveness as coach, and, most important, missing the power of the moment for the client. Boundaries are important in this domain as well. If the coach's boundaries are too diffuse, the empathy will likely bleed into sympathy, and the coach's ability to fully observe will be diminished.

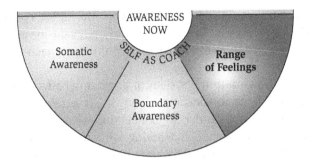

Range of Feelings

A coach needs to have access to a wide range of feelings and ease in exploring and experiencing a full scope of emotions in order to allow the client's emotions to surface and get used effectively in coaching. The coach who is at ease with her own feelings will notice them in the client and make space for these feelings in the coaching work.

The coach who is uncomfortable with a particular feeling will likely move away from it or avoid it entirely if it surfaces in the coaching work. The coach who has a limited range of feelings will likely miss the opportunity to attend to the client's feeling states when it's important. Whatever the client's emotional reaction or state might be, a masterful coach wants to be able to create a safe place for a range of feelings and use them on behalf of the client when appropriate. This ability to connect to the client's feelings and create a space in which the client is comfortable exploring the emotional terrain and developing new insights leading to new actions is essential in coaching.

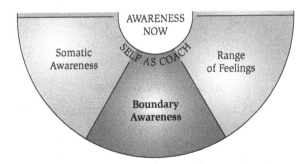

Boundary Awareness

The work of Murray Bowen (1978), a psychiatrist and early family systems therapist, is seminal to understanding the concept of differentiation and boundary awareness in our lives. He taught us that the less differentiated we are as human beings, the more likely we are to engage in an endless stream of third-person conversations in order to avoid the direct conversations we need to have with someone. This is particularly relevant for a coach because the tendency to discuss a third person within the coaching engagement almost always arises.

It's easy to get drawn into the system of another, whether it's an individual client, a team, or a larger organizational system. It requires a coach's careful attention to boundaries in order to notice this dynamic, manage himself, and attend to it effectively. When working with coaches, we often draw an imaginary line on the floor with very tight boundary management at one end and diffuse and highly permeable boundaries at the other end. We ask coaches to place themselves on this continuum and then talk about the upsides and downsides of their location. Coaches on the diffuse and permeable end notice that it's easy to get drawn into the client's world, the client's needs, and the client's feeling state and render it difficult to step back sufficiently to allow clients to notice their own dynamics. Those with tight boundaries notice they may be too hard to penetrate at times, and it may be difficult for the client to feel fully connected and safe with the coach. Boundary awareness and management requires an astute and highly observant coach to walk this line and remain fully effective in the work.

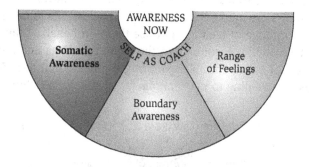

Somatic Awareness

Experts in somatic work remind us that every action originates in the body, and when we fully engage the body in supporting changes we want to make, we increase the likelihood of lasting change. Noticing how we physically hold ourselves shapes our presence and our state of mind, and this level of somatic awareness can help shift a coach to a more effective stance. A coaching colleague reflects on somatic awareness in this way: "I notice that when I reach down and rub my lower legs or squeeze my knees together, I am feeling like I'm in uncomfortable territory and I start to become more tentative with my client. When I hold my posture steady, keeping my feet on the floor and relaxing my hands, I am more present and focused with my client." If a coach wants her clients to experience her as warm and inviting and yet her face is almost always stern with a frown and furrowed brow, her facial expression can be the starting point for a deeper shift. Noticing how our clients present themselves somatically can allow us to make observations that become helpful and meaningful to those clients relative to their coaching goals. For example, if a high-level leader wants to feel confident about his abilities and yet his posture is noticeably slumped, the coach's ability to share this observation can result in a shift in posture, which will create a somatic trigger to support a much bigger change.

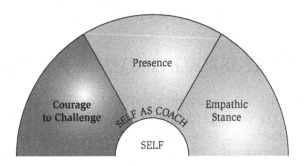

Courage to Challenge

This domain is paramount in coaching. Clients don't come to us looking for a friendly chat or an agreeable shoulder; instead they arrive wanting to make a change they have been unable to attain on their own. And like all of us, even when the client is seemingly committed and clear about the change, obstacles quickly and predictably surface. The skill of challenging a client at the right time is vital in masterful coaching, and the strength to share an observation even when it's a little uncomfortable is essential. Yet many coaches find this territory personally onerous. It may be a wish to stay on the positive side, a desire to remain on the supportive side, or a general uneasiness with more difficult conversations that keeps a coach from entering this important territory. In reality, the coach's ability to view challenging, sharing observations, and providing feedback as critical to facilitating the change the client wants is the hallmark of mastery when coupled with deep trust and respect.

Consider the client who comes to a coach with a goal of strengthening her leadership presence among peers, direct reports, and the senior team. Session after session, the coach observes that this client routinely apologizes to the coach for her smallest comments, using a voice that is almost difficult to hear at times and exhibiting a posture that exudes a lack of confidence. Or the client who wants to create stronger relationships with members of her new team, and you observe a facial expression that includes an almost continually furrowed brow and a slight frown. Or the client who wants desperately to figure out how to get into the job market, and every other sentence is, "I just have bad luck." In most coaching situations, there is a strong connection between how the client appears during sessions and the goals he or she is working on. It's the work of a coach to surface these observations, link them to the goals of coaching, and help create enough awareness that the client is able to make important choices that may have a big impact on next steps.

The coach who fails to address these in-the-moment opportunities, or as Doug Silsbee (2008) aptly phrases it, "catch a habit in the act," does the client no favor. Instead, the coach is likely bypassing the opportunity because she has not built sufficient capacity in the self-as-coach domain.

COMMON SELF-AS-COACH CHALLENGES FOR THE COACH

The situations that follow present a series of common coaching vignettes and challenges. The vignettes are meant to nudge your own self-examination more than provide an exhaustive inventory of coaching challenges. Chances are some of these scenarios will resonate more or less with any coach and provide ample ground for further exploration.

Uneasy with Conflict (Courage to Challenge)

Jane has operated a successful business for many years but admits that she has always found conflict uncomfortable. She works to help people feel at ease and does what is required to lighten up a situation when it gets heated. This has been her modus operandi for thirty years. Now she is moving into the world of coaching, and this dynamic becomes a limiting factor. She notices that when her clients begin to express anger or get upset, she is quick to try to soothe the client or divert the conversation to more comfortable territory. In the past, Jane hasn't paid much attention to the conflict-averse habit she has, but now, as a coach, she understands how important it is to build her capacity on this front.

Conflict naturally shows up in the coaching engagement; sometimes there is tension between coach and client that needs to be surfaced and explored, and at other times conflict arises for the client relative to the changes he or she is committing to. It's hard to avoid this: conflict is a part of life, and if Jane is unwilling or unable to enter that space, she limits her capacity as a coach to fully explore all of the dynamics at play in an engagement.

Uncomfortable Giving Feedback (Courage to Challenge)

Bob has been a successful member of several senior leadership teams over the years, and his track record is impressive. However, as he enters the work of coaching, he admits that feedback has always made him uneasy. He has a tendency to sugarcoat, glossing over areas that others might address and to overlook some behaviors because of his own discomfort. Now he finds himself in coaching engagements where providing clear feedback and sharing observations with the client are clearly important in order for clients to make the changes they want.

Feedback is an integral part of coaching throughout the process. A coach needs to elicit feedback from others (boss–coach–human resource partner and client conversations, and in stakeholder interviews, for instance) in order to work effectively with leaders inside organizations. A coach needs to deftly and routinely provide observations and feedback to clients about behaviors, patterns, and observations that will be helpful, albeit temporarily uncomfortable for the client. Unless Bob works his inner terrain and unpacks his obstacles to providing feedback, this will be an enormously limiting element in his coaching.

Fearful of Feelings (Range of Feelings)

Mary has a stellar track record as a strategic thinker in the world of mergers and acquisitions. She comes to the work of coaching with a strong understanding of what it takes to be a great leader and a clear grasp of the intricacies of organizational systems. But Mary is the first to admit that feelings are uncomfortable territory for her. She isn't well versed in her own feelings and works to stay out of others' feelings. In fact, when she came to coaching, she didn't see feelings as the work of a coach. Yet over and over in coaching engagements with healthy, committed clients, feelings show up, and she knows she needs to make adjustments in herself in order to meet these feelings, hold them with a client, and open the door to exploration of the feelings.

Feelings are a natural part of a whole person. Whether coaching a leader who wants to strengthen her presence, a manager who wants to learn how to delegate, or an individual building a postwork chapter, feelings are an important dimension of the coaching work. Change happens in the melting pot of emotion, cognition, and relationship. Mary needs to start by exploring the inner terrain of her own feelings before she can be comfortable working with a client's feelings.

Unaware of Impact (Presence, Somatic Awareness)

John has been a fast-moving, successful executive for years, with plenty of accolades and a hefty track record to prove it. He comes to coaching believing this will be an easy transition. Yet he has a certain intensity about him that manifests in a strong, sometimes loud voice, a tight torso that is always leaning forward, and a rapid pace that is almost palpable for anyone in his vicinity. All of this likely worked in his previous career, but it's now an impediment in the work of coaching.

Understanding one's impact on others is central in working with clients. It's hard for a client to connect with a coach if the pace and intensity are barriers. An inability to fully connect with the client will be enormously limiting for a coach and the prospect of building a coaching practice. John will need to elicit feedback from others on his impact and then build some methodical practices that will support him in changing some of these long-standing habits.

One Speed Only—Fast (Presence, Somatic Awareness)

Laurie came to coaching with a long list of accomplishments as a leader in the nonprofit sector. She has been in the role of executive director in more than one organization and is sought after by many boards. She's now ready to shift gears and provide much-needed coaching services to leaders in the nonprofit realm. Laurie has a no-nonsense approach to life and admits that work has been the primary driver in her world for the past thirty years. Her biggest challenge (when she's willing to examine it) is slowing down and creating space for something other than work in her life. She's had only a modicum of success on this front, and it has been in small fits and starts. As she moves into coaching, it is becoming clear that her well-honed rapid-fire pace is an obstacle to deep listening and full presence with her clients. Her style of interrupting conversations, talking over clients, and watching the clock shows up in her coaching and creates barriers she needs to address.

Laurie wants to get from start to finish as quickly as possible in an effort to deliver value to the client. But this approach does not allow the client to do the deeper work that builds a foundation for meaningful and sustainable change to unfold. When Laurie had the experience of three clients canceling and discontinuing the coaching work with her, she knew it was a signal about her, not her clients.

Our pace is a way of being that is hard for most of us to notice, and it's an area that others are often reluctant to provide candid feedback about. Laurie needs to slow down and take the time to become perceptive to her clients' needs so she can make the important connections they need her to make. She can take on practices and routines in her personal life that provide more grounding and calming and involve greater reflection. She can begin by gaining feedback from those close to her in order to make adjustments where it's most important for her.

Caring Too Much (Boundary Awareness, Empathic Stance)

Marcia admits she gets uncomfortable when a client seems unhappy, ill at ease, or near tears, and her first response is reassurance. She believes this has worked well in her long list of impressive leadership roles, and she brings this same perspective to coaching. Yet through both peer and supervision feedback, she begins to notice that her quick move to reassure a client, grab the box of tissues, or give the proverbial pat on the back robs the client of important moments of exploration.

Reassurance promotes comfort, not change, and while there is a time and place for it, reassurance is seldom the dominant approach that will facilitate lasting change. In fact, reassurance ill timed will prevent the client from facing important work in coaching. If a client tells the coach he received some tough feedback from his boss that felt hurtful and the coach moves to reassure the client, the real work of unpacking the interaction and examining how the client wants to address this are lost. Marcia can begin by noticing how often she moves into caring mode in her conversations. Journaling or creating a daily log may be a support. Gaining feedback from those close to her will also provide important perspective about the impact her singular approach has on others.

Inner Judging (Presence)

Mike is a pro. He has headed up successful sales teams at the highest levels in a series of prominent organizations, and his track record is one that others covet. He's passionate about coaching sales leaders and knows he can make a difference, but each time he sits down to engage in a coaching conversation, he can hear a voice on his shoulder second-guessing him, doubting his abilities and making it difficult to be at home in his own skin as a coach. He finds himself getting nervous before each coaching session and conducting a postmortem analysis about every little thing he might have done better as a coach.

The inner critic that Mike carries with him will limit his ability to be fully present with the client and coach effectively. Mike is aware of the critic, and that's a great first step; now he needs to attend to his work on self and develop a practice that will allow him to shed enough of the inner critic and develop sufficient compassion and support for himself to be fully present and powerful as a coach.

DEEPENING THE SELF-AS-COACH DOMAIN

It's impossible for a coach to uncover the intrapsychic dynamics or the inner landscape of self without the support of others, accompanied by a regular practice heightening awareness of what's at play inside that is contributing to behaviors that show up outside. The coach committed to this pathway needs to invest in both approaches: building a regular practice that cultivates an inner dialogue and engaging with others in seeking candid feedback, input, and support on this path.

Armed with a regular practice and the support of trusted coach colleagues on this journey, where does a coach begin? The areas of exploration for our own growth and development are endless, and it's important to remember it's a journey. We engage in continual development of our self in order to build capacity to be sufficient as a coach and deserving of the opportunity to sit in this role with another human being. Cultivation of the inner landscape ought to be one of the most important precepts in coaching.

Table 4.1 provides a starting point for the coach to examine the self-as-coach domains, highlighting the desired stance of a masterful coach, the natural

Table 4.1 Self-as-Coach Continuum of Learning

The Optimal Stance	The Trap
Full presence	Sidetracked, distracted, absent
• In the moment • Centered, engaged • Present to notice patterns	• Distracted • Unbalanced • Mechanical and rigid • Unable to discern patterns
Empathic stance	Sympathetic or disconnected
• Empathic listening • Unconditional positive regard	• Listening to solve • Missing important client signals
Range of feelings	Moves away from feelings or overindulges in emotions
• Access to full range of feelings	• Limited awareness of feelings • Inappropriate response to emotional context
Boundary awareness	Fusion or collusion
• Maintains independence • Discerns important boundaries • Understands systems thinking	• Plays role of go-between • Does work that belongs to client • Becomes mediator
Somatic awareness	Misses using body cues
• Uses own physical self to support effective coaching • Notices revealing patterns of client	• Inadvertently projects inconsistent messages • Misses internal signals • Overlooks important client signals (for example, sitting on hands, tapping fingers, frowning, laughing when sad)
Courage to challenge	Plays it nice, polite, or safe
• Challenges thinking patterns • Shares observations • Shares feedback	• Holds back for fear of offending • Holds back because it's uncomfortable • Unwittingly supports status quo

traps, and a closer look at some of the nuances of each domain. In addition, a thorough set of practices and resources for supporting development in each self-as-coach area follows.

The contents of Table 4.1 represent a continuum of learning rather than an either-or dichotomy; setbacks are predictable and typically lead us to greater advancement of goals with awareness and a willingness to change. The goal is what a great coach continually strives for but can never expect to fully attain because there is always something to be learned. The trap is what a coach seeks to avoid and what leads to coaching work that remains less effective and sustainable over time.

SIX REFLECTIVE PRACTICES TO STRENGTHEN SELF-AS-COACH CAPACITY

Reflection practices are pivotal in the pathway to change. They help a coach gain a new level of awareness about a specific way of being or a behavior that is crucial in the pathway to change. The self-as-coach stances outlined in Table 4.1 are within reach when the coach spends time linking helpful models and tools to regular practice. In the sections that follow, each self-as-coach domain is linked to theories and models that provide more understanding of the stance, followed by practices a coach may consider in strengthening one of the areas of development.

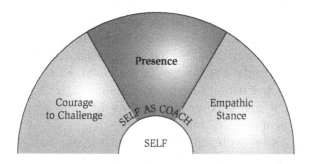

Reflective Practices for Strengthening Presence

Doug Silsbee (2008) defines *presence* as "the most resourceful, ready, resilient inner state available to us at every moment" (p. 13). Halpern and Lubar (2003) define this concept as "the ability to connect authentically with the thoughts and feelings of another" (p. 3). In both definitions there is an emphasis on the quality and readiness of one's inner state that allows one to be authentically present in the here and now with a client.

Good coaches know that what sounds simple takes a lot of attention to cultivate, and nowhere is that truer than in the development of presence. The impediments to our full presence are mighty forces: our habits, our ego, the board of directors in our head directing us, and more. Full presence is intimately linked to cultivating our inner landscape. Without an inner dialogue and an awareness of the internal chatter, presence is impossible to achieve.

An important by-product of full presence is the heightened ability of the coach to view the larger context of the client and hear the nuances of patterns and stories that the client is living in. The fully present coach hears, reads, and perceives the client on many levels, including the literal words, the metaphors, the emotional terrain, and the somatic manifestations. Halpern and Lubar (2003) also emphasize flexibility as a key element in presence: our ability to respond in the moment relative to what the client is presenting us.

Consider this coach's situation. Janet combines her coaching work with consulting and spends about 60 percent of her time on the road for her work. That means a lot of time on planes, in airports, and in hotels and constantly shifting time zones. Her life is fast paced, and it's not uncommon to find herself managing travel delays and shifting schedule challenges. Although it's not impossible for Janet to hone her ability to be present at any given moment in the midst of her day-to-day work routines, it surely requires a fierce commitment and practice on her part. Otherwise the demands of her lifestyle will inevitably intrude on her ability to authentically connect with a client in the midst of one of her fast-paced days.

Noticing patterns and themes is an ability heightened by the full presence of the coach. Books have been written on this important topic, so this brief description and examination only skims what's important. In the early stages of development as a coach it's easy to get drawn into the details of a client's story and believe the work of a coach is in understanding all of the details. In fact, the real work of the coach is not in the sordid details of a situation, but in the ability to notice patterns in the client's stories, pay attention to the language of the client, and uncover the world as the client sees it and the limiting stories the client exists within.

Otto Laske (2006b) writes of the "FoR," that is, the frame of reference of the client that ultimately determines his or her behavior: "Behavior is shaped by how one makes meaning and sense of the world and this defines their 'FoR.' The work of noticing the client's FoR requires a well-honed ability to listen to and pay attention to the patterns, stories and essence of the client's words and the courage to surface this deeper layer of the coaching conversation" (p. 45). James Flaherty (2010) provides a similar perspective in his use of the concept of the structure of interpretation and writes, "Each person's actions are fully consistent with the interpretation he brought, an interpretation that persists across time, across events and across circumstances" (p. 8).

What is required in order for a coach to pay attention and tease out the client's story, frame of reference, or structure of interpretation is presence to one's client and presence to one's self. As always, a coach must start with work on self that uncovers one's own stories, one's own particular structure of interpretation. Once a coach has begun to uncover this for herself and is able to observe how this bears on her own life, she becomes attuned to noticing this in others.

Doing Your Work: Practice for Deepening Presence. Building presence as a coach includes multiple layers, and the first step is the work of managing distractions before, during, and after a coaching session. Consider using the following three steps with each of your coaching engagements over a thirty-day period, and pay attention to how deliberate reflection supports and deepens your presence as a coach:

1. *Preserve time before a coaching session.* There is a big difference between sliding into a coaching session with barely a break from one appointment to another and the practice of creating reflective time prior to a coaching session to prepare yourself, review your work with this client, and check inside yourself to make sure everything but your work with this client is on the shelf and you are fully present.

2. *Remain fully present throughout the coaching session.* The coach who finds herself distracted during the session, thinking about other things, limits the full range of work that can occur with the client. A practice of noticing when intrusions enter your thoughts and allowing them to simply pass through and recenter on the client is important in cultivating full presence.

3. *Create reflective space as coach following the session.* The temptation is often to move from a coaching session to the next item on the work agenda without creating reflective space to notice and log the themes of the session reduces the power of the coaching work. A postsession reflective practice allows you to harvest the highlights and themes of the actual session and reflect on your own learning journey as well.

Exercises for Deepening the Ability to Notice Patterns.

1. Take a step back and consider what your own frame of reference or your unique view of the world is and how this guides your behavior.

2. Explore what might be unavailable to you because of your own view of the world.

3. Engage in an exploration with a fellow coach and see if you can discern differences in your view of the world and the impact that has on each of you.

Reading on Presence

Flaherty, J. *Coaching: Evoking Excellence in Others*. Burlington, Mass.: Elsevier, 2010.

Halpern, B. L., and Lubar, K. *Leadership Presence*. New York: Gotham Books, 2003.

Horney, K. *Our Inner Conflicts*. New York: Norton, 1945.

Laske, O. *Measuring Hidden Dimensions*. Gloucester, Mass.: IDM Press, 2006.

Laske, O. "From Coach Training to Coach Education." *International Journal of Evidence-Based Coaching and Mentoring*, 2006, 4(1), 45–57.

Moss, R. *The Mandala of Being: Discovering the Power of Awareness*. Novato, Calif.: New World Library, 2007.

Silsbee, D. *Presence-Based Coaching*. San Francisco: Jossey-Bass, 2008.

Tolbert, M.A.R., and Hanafin, J. *The NTL Handbook of Organization Development and Change*. San Francisco: Jossey-Bass/Pfeiffer, 2006.

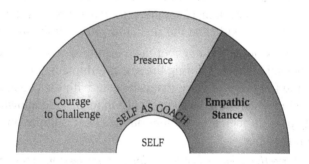

Reflective Practices for Empathy Building

Empathy, the ability to perceive the feelings and experiences of a client and communicate this to the client, requires skill, practice, and awareness.

One of the big challenges for coaches is caring too much and wanting one's client to feel better now or wanting to spare the client needless suffering. It may seem counterintuitive, but it's a well-documented fact that one thing a client needs is just enough tension and discomfort in the coaching engagement to create new awareness that will lead to exploring new ways of being. If a client expresses sadness and hurt during a session and begins to cry, the coach can send an empathic signal that demonstrates a connection and caring through a word or two or perhaps a facial signal. If instead the coach moves toward the client with tissue in hand, it conveys a message, "Oh, how can I make you feel better right now so that feeling goes away?" The urge to be sympathetic and soothing moves toward colluding with the client in an effort to protect the client from something uncomfortable that's emerging, often in the form of feelings. To the extent that the coach has a limited range of feelings that are comfortable, this has a direct impact on the client.

Bill, a client, shares his deep fear of standing up in front of a large group and making a presentation and his coach, John, responds with an empathic stance: "I get that; it can be a tough challenge." If instead he moves to a sympathetic response, he might say, "Boy, do I understand this one. I've struggled with it myself, and I have a lot of memories of a whole lot of anxiety and perspiring before those sorts of presentations. I learned a few things I think could be helpful for you." Once John shifts from the empathic stance to the sympathetic one, he loses his ability to view the client's needs, feelings, and experience objectively.

The pull to collude with the client is often prompted by a coach's unaware desire to please the client, be liked by the client, care for the client, or manage his or her own discomfort with certain feelings and situations. When this collusion occurs, the boundaries of the coach become blurred, and the coach enters into the system of the client instead of observing the client's system, holding a firm boundary and conveying the empathic message, "I care, I see you, I am here," without getting entangled and playing a part in the client's well practiced story.

Empathic listening is another element in the empathic stance. The work for any coach in developing empathy requires an ability to self-manage her own internal dialogue as a conversation develops, suspend judgments and solutions, and listen to what this means to the client. This requires the coach to notice her own emotional cues and states. Given what we understand today about how our limbic systems work, the coach's emotional cues provide clues about the client's state as well. Second, an empathic stance demands deep listening on the coach's part in order to fully understand what the client's story means to the client, all the while resisting the urge to shift to one's own interpretations, judgments, or potential solution-building efforts.

Chris Argyris's (1982) well-known model, the ladder of inference (Figure 4.4), provides a helpful map into the intricacies of our fast-paced internal dialogue. He provides an illustration of how quickly a coach can shift from listening and empathizing with the client's experience to instead responding and reacting through her own set of assumptions and biases. The ladder of inference provides an easy way for a coach to track her own thinking and inner experience and make it more conscious. Choice comes from awareness, so once we've become conscious of biases, assumptions, and meanings that limit our ability to connect with another and hear another, we can more freely make new choices.

One of Argyris's (1982) interesting findings is that the more experience we have in life, the more likely we are to hasten the speed of each successive trip up the ladder of inference. In other words, the well-practiced individual relies

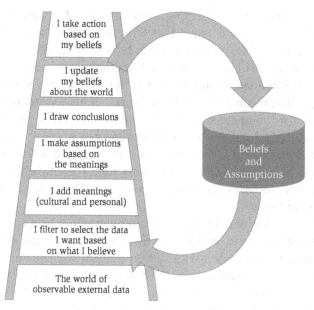

Figure 4.4 Argyris's Ladder of Inference
Source: Argyris (1982).

on certain assumptions based on years of experience. These assumptions cut one off from critical information and likely decrease our empathic response.

Translate a "quick run up the ladder of inference" to the work of a coach, and it quickly becomes problematic. John, the coach, meets a client for the first time and throughout the exploratory conversation notices that the client is quite quiet and a little passive. Based on some experiences with clients who weren't very engaged in the coaching work, John quickly leaps to the conclusion that this client isn't ready to engage in the serious work of coaching. Judy is working with a client who is constantly fidgeting during the coaching session: moving and tapping his feet, clicking his writing utensil, at times tapping his fingers. She makes a rapid trip up the ladder assuming (without checking) that he is impatient and restless about their coaching work. In fact, when Judy finally musters the courage to share her observations, her client gets a little teary and tells her about his long-fought challenges with attention deficit disorder. Our empathy is ignited when we connect with our client, and ultimately this requires managing our own stories, life experiences, biases, and assumptions.

Argyris's model is a helpful tool for coaches to track their own ability to stay close to the bottom of the ladder where their biases, experiences, and beliefs are held at bay and self-managed in order that they stay focused on what is observable in the present with the client. When the coach hones in on this important observable territory, it's possible to provide critical information to the client through the sharing of observations in the moment and often creating a powerful breakthrough experience for the client. For example, the coach could notice that her client smiles almost continually throughout their session, whether the conversation is difficult or easy. If the coach climbed up the ladder, she might infer that the client is very uncomfortable with feelings and trying to keep things superficial. But instead she simply shares her observation (bottom-of-the ladder information): "I wonder if I might share an observation I'm having. We've talked about some very difficult situations for the past hour or so, and your facial expression has continually maintained a smile, even when we were discussing some very sad things. I wonder if you have any awareness of this? The impact on me is that I find myself wondering what's happening inside you." Or perhaps she notices that the pace of her client's speech is so rapid that it's hard to discern each word at times. Instead of making assumptions about the rapid-fire approach, she instead shares her observation (bottom of the ladder): "I want to stop you for a moment and share something I'm noticing: your speech pattern is so fast, so rapid, that I have to work very hard to catch each word, and I often miss some. I wonder if you have any awareness of this?"

The ability to stay at the bottom on the ladder overlaps and requires some of the other essential self-as-coach stances, including a deep presence, respect for the client, and courage to share important observations with the client.

Doing Your Work: A Practice for Strengthening Empathy. One of the helpful tools for a coach to strengthen the empathic response and become more aware of any tendency to sympathize is a focused attention on moving from what Whitworth, Kimsey-House, and Sandahl (2007) term "level 1 listening" to "level 2 listening." A reflection practice immediately following a coaching session allows a coach to pay close attention to when the listening was focused on what the words meant to the client and what was happening in cases where the coach slipped into the level 1 listening ("what this means to me"). Mapping the cost of slipping into level 1 listening helps a coach strengthen their empathic stance.

An Empathy-Building Exercise. Think of individuals you interact with most often on a daily basis. Perhaps it's members of your team or a key person in your personal life. Jot down the names of two people you find a little challenging for one reason or another. Ask yourself the following questions (test the ladder of inference on each rung of the ladder):

1. What belief, bias, or judgment do I hold about this individual?
2. What is the basis for this belief, bias, or judgment?

Check yourself from the inside out, trying to notice whether any judgments, beliefs, and biases are coming from you and your story. Then take it a step further and spend the next several days consciously noticing how the change in your approach adjusts the way you view and understand others.

Reading on Empathic Stance

Argyris, C. "Teaching Smart People How to Learn." *Harvard Business Review*, May 1991, pp. 14–28.

Short, R. *Learning in Relationship*. Bellevue, Wash.: Learning in Action, 1998.

Silsbee, D. *Presence-Based Coaching*. San Francisco: Jossey-Bass, 2008.

Whitworth, L., Kimsey-House, H., and Sandahl, P. *Co-Active Coaching*. Mountain View, Calif.: Davies-Black Publishing, 2007.

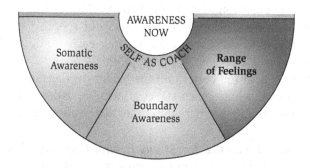

Reflective Practices for Deepening Range of Feelings

A coach needs access to a range of feelings that he is at ease exploring and expressing in his own life in order to provide ample room (a container, in a sense) for a wide range of feelings to emerge within the coaching engagement. The primary feelings of joy, anger, fear, and sadness cascade into more complex feelings of love, hate, betrayal, compassion, admiration, anxiety, and others. Most of us have stories about growing up in families where some feelings were more acceptable than others and, in some cases, in families where feelings were not allowed or where any feeling of any intensity was fair game.

The coach's work in this area includes examining the repertoire of feelings that are in her comfort zone, the feelings that create uneasiness, and her favorite resting spot in the feeling domain. Harkening back to Horney's model, our comfortable feeling range will dictate our capacity as coach and our inclination relative to the three-legged stool of moving toward, moving away, and moving against the client.

Doing Your Work: Practices for Extending Range of Feelings. Start by paying close attention to your current repertoire of daily feelings by trying these two practices:

- Build a simple seven- to ten-day log or journal. Keep it close by—on your desk, in your purse or briefcase, or in your pocket. Make a commitment to log a feeling you notice in yourself three times a day. By the end of ten days, you'll have a view into your default range of feelings.
- Choose one or two feelings you seldom access based on your ten-day experiment, and begin to consciously find low-risk opportunities to express these feelings.

Exercises for Extending Range of Feelings.

- Take an emotional quotient (EQ) assessment, such as EQ in Action (Learning in Action Technologies, n.d.), to understand your own emotional terrain. The EQ in Action assessment is perhaps one of the most powerful tools available for coaches to rapidly learn about their range of feelings and develop practices to build new pathways for broadening the use of their feeling states. There are many others, including the Bar-On EQ-i.
- Consider a daily series of body scans to detect physical clues to emotions you are experiencing. According to Siegel (2001, p. 135), "a disconnect between having emotions and bringing them into consciousness in the body is often the link."

Readings on Range of Feelings

Ekman, P. *Emotions Revealed*. New York: Holt & Company, 2007.

Johnson, J. *The EQ Fitness Handbook*. Seattle, Wash.: Learning in Action, 2010.

Short, R. *Learning in Relationship*. Seattle, Wash.: Learning in Action, 1998.

Siegel, D. *The Developing Mind*. New York: Guilford Press, 2001.

Segal, J. *Raising Your Emotional Intelligence: A Practical Guide*. New York: Holt, 1997.

Stein, S., and Book, H. *The EQ Edge*. Hoboken, N.J.: Wiley, 2011.

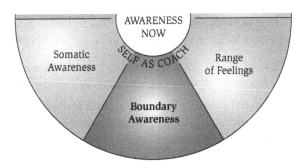

Reflective Practices for Cultivating Boundary Awareness

The work of family systems expert Murray Bowen (1978) examines the concepts of differentiation and triangulation within the framework of the family, but his work on differentiation is particularly relevant to coaches as well. Bowen views differentiation as the personality variable most essential to mature development wherein one is able to balance emotions and intellect (feeling and thinking) in conjunction with important relationships. This ability to make choices about one's behavior in the moment by distinguishing between one's thoughts and feelings builds a foundation for differentiating oneself from another.

For example, a well-differentiated coach who finds herself in a conversation with a client who is overcome with anger (or any other emotion, for that matter) will be able to manage her own feelings and reactions; she will speak calmly in the moment and proceed in a manner that is useful to the client. If the coach is not well differentiated, she may become overrun by her own emotions. Instead of being present for the client, she may move to fuse with the client by overcaring, moving the conversation to a safer topic, or easing tension by bringing up a third party (triangulating) and focusing emotions on that person. When the coach is less differentiated, she is more likely to mistake the client's emotional responses as her own. Her decisions about how to proceed are then driven by a response to her own emotions instead of helping the client find healthy ways to work with their own.

These considerations make the concept of differentiation worthy of examination by the coach:

- The level of differentiation for a human being is on a continuum, and for each of us it is a journey rather than a destination.
- Differentiation allows a coach to remain calm in the midst of a client's storm and maximize the moment in the service of what's best for the client.
- Differentiation provides the coach with the inner strength to manage herself in the face of an important coaching moment and refuse to succumb to easing the moment at the cost of the client's development.

Doing Your Work: A Practice for Developing Boundary Awareness. Bowen's favorite assignment is a useful exercise for the coach: notice how often you triangulate, that is, engage in a conversation with one person about a third person:

- Spend a couple of weeks paying attention to when this happens, under what circumstances, and what the cost is to you or the other individual.
- Test this for yourself on your home front, and see what you learn. Then test it in your coaching engagements, and heighten your awareness of how often you move to triangulate during the coaching session.

Reading on Boundary Awareness

Bowen, M. *Family Therapy in Clinical Practice*. Northvale, N.J.: Jason Aronson, 1978.

Gilbert, R. *The Eight Concepts of Bowen Theory*. Falls Church, Va.: Leading Systems Press, 2006.

Gilbert, R. M., and Gilbert, R. *Extraordinary Relationships: A New Way of Thinking About Human Interaction*. Hoboken, N.J.: Wiley, 1992.

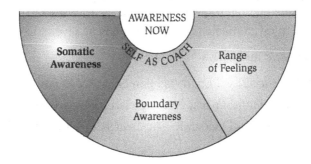

Reflective Practices for Cultivating a Somatic Awareness

We are more than our thoughts and feelings—our head and heart. Our stories, ways of being, and habits are all housed in our body. The body tells a powerful story about each of us if we are alert to noticing these somatic awarenesses. Somatics expert Doug Silsbee (2008) writes, "We store in our tissues (our body) the default habits that form our identity" (p. 154). Strozzi-Heckler (2007), one of the early leaders in somatics work, writes, "Somatic practices allows a leader to literally feel and directly experience one's own patterns of behavior and conditioned tendencies" (p. 33).

As always, a good coach needs to start by gaining a deep awareness of her own somatic story, learning experientially how her habits are stored in the body and how the sensations inside the body are a helpful tool as we seek to make changes in ourselves.

A number of considerations make the concept of somatic awareness worthy of examination by the coach. Silsbee (2008), for example, provides a useful map for a coach who wants to build his somatic literacy and offers four considerations:

1. Our shape perfectly reflects our history.

2. Our body determines our experience.

3. A wealth of sensations is available through our own bodies.

4. Sensation provides an early warning system for our habits.

Siegel (2001) highlights the importance of sensation in developing a heightened awareness of our feelings as well.

Doing Your Work: Exercises for Cultivating a Somatic Awareness

- Learn more about what your unique body communicates to others.
- Watch yourself on video.
- Seek feedback from trusted sources.
- Use Silsbee's (2008) presence-based coaching exercise to conduct a "body scan," moving from the feet through the body to the head, a practice that can be completed in a few seconds or several minutes.

Reading on Somatic Awareness

Silsbee, D. *Presence-Based Coaching*. San Francisco: Jossey-Bass, 2008.

Silsbee, D. *The Mindful Coach*. San Francisco: Jossey-Bass, 2010.

Strozzi-Heckler, R., and Leider, R. *The Leadership DoJo*. Berkeley, Calif.: Frog Books, 2007.

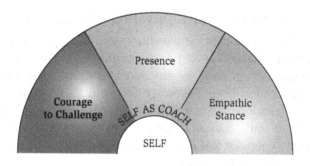

Reflective Practices for Courage to Challenge

Courage to challenge, that is, to share observations and provide feedback to the client, is a hallmark of great coaching. This capacity building begins on the inside. The work of challenging a client to see another view, examine areas that are uncomfortable to explore, or surface a pattern that is out of the client's awareness requires courage combined with a strong working alliance. The working alliance communicates to the client, "We are working this territory together. I am committed to helping you get as close as possible to your goals." This courage to challenge a client's thinking, frame of reference in the world, or self-limiting story is an important part of our value as a coach.

The late Ed Nevis, an organizational development (OD) sage, often talked about two important approaches in creating new awareness with a client:

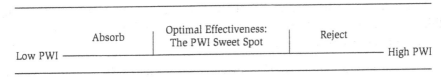

Figure 4.5 Perceived Weirdness Index and Range of Effectiveness
Source: Tolbert and Hanafin (2006).

evocative and provocative. The evocative approach is void of challenge and includes asking good questions that seek to heighten the client's awareness around that which he can't yet see. The provocative approach requires more courage and comes later, when the working alliance is well established. The provocative is more powerful and forceful in bringing something to the client's awareness in the moment through the use of self in sharing observations, providing feedback, and challenging the client's current thinking.

Tolbert and Hanafin (2006) developed the concept of the perceived weirdness index (Figure 4.5) in the OD field to underscore the reality that change takes place for most of us at the edges of what is familiar and what is different. The practitioner with an optimal PWI index is seen as different from the client, able to challenge the client, comfortable taking some risks in sharing observations and providing feedback to the client. In their model, the coach with a very low PWI would likely be focused on the support side without the courage to challenge. Over time this coach likely gets absorbed into the client's system without much awareness that this is happening.

Sharing observations for which a client is often unaware also takes strength and courage for the coach. Observations as they pertain to the overall goals of the coaching work are essential to great coaching. There is often a tendency to shy away from this part of the coaching work in the early stages of becoming a coach, and for all the obvious reasons: it takes keen observational skills, a sense of timing, a thoughtful linking to the coaching goals, and some courage.

Several considerations make this work easier for a coach:

- A clear discussion about sharing observations and providing feedback in the first conversations about what coaching is, how you work as a coach, and how the client reacts to this

- An enduring respect for the client that is discussed early on and easily evidenced by the client throughout the engagement

- A well-honed working alliance—a sense that you as coach are joined with your client to thoroughly explore all areas pertaining to the changes the client has committed to

Doing Your Work: Practice for Strengthening the "Challenging Muscle."
When these important considerations are in place and the coach continues to

find it challenging to provide important observations, the work in deepening this capacity moves to further examination of the coach's inner landscape. Self-inquiry might include exploring these questions:

- What feelings am I aware of inside when I want to share an observation and choose not to?

- How can I become more attuned to my assumptions about what will happen if I decide to share an observation?

- Am I aware of any internal dialogue with myself, in the moment, when the opportunity arises and I choose not to move into it?

- Is there a reflective practice I could take on that would allow me to become aware of missed opportunities and track my inner experiences in the moment?

- When I've logged these reflections long enough to learn more about what's going on inside, can I build a series of easiest early steps where I can practice without doing harm and where the risks for a first step are low?

- Am I stepping back and taking a wide-angle look at the whole person of my client in order to discover and notice patterns in his or her thinking and behaving over time?

- Can I consider metaphors or words that capture the essence of my client and help me to uncover the client's patterns more easily?

Reading on Courage to Challenge

Nevis, E. C. *Organizational Consulting: A Gestalt Approach*. New York: Gardner Press, 1987.

Kegan, R. *In over Our Heads: The Mental Demands of Modern Life*. Cambridge, Mass.: Harvard University Press, 1998.

Laske, O. *Measuring Hidden Dimensions: The Art and Science of Fully Engaging Adults*. Medford, Mass.: Laske and Associates, 2006.

Seashore, C. N., Seashore, E. W., and Weinberg, G. M. *What Did You Say? The Art of Giving and Receiving Feedback*. Columbia, Md.: Bingham House Books, 1997.

CHAPTER 5

LEADING FROM BEHIND

T he work of self as coach is ongoing, and it serves as a necessary prerequisite to an essential stance in masterful coaching: leading from behind. In this chapter, we revisit the concept of leading from behind, developed at the Hudson Institute more than two decades ago, and examine it as a natural progression from deepening self to facilitating change in others.

A leading-from-behind stance is particularly important at specific stages in the coaching engagement. It's a given that the coach is equipped with coaching knowledge and skills along with a coaching methodology and comes to the coaching engagement prepared to lead the way in the unfolding process. However, and most important, when it comes to articulating the change or adjustment the client is committed to making and facilitating the environment wherein the client can attain sustainable results, a leading-from-behind stance is what is called for. Robert Quinn (2004) aptly captures this dance between a step behind and out in front telling and fixing when he writes:

> Telling is not effective in situations requiring significant behavior change because it is based on a narrow, cognitive view of human systems. It fails to incorporate values, attitudes and feelings. While people may understand why they should change, they are often not willing to make the painful changes that are necessary. When the target of change begins to resist, the change agent often becomes frustrated and turns to an even more directive strategy [p. 70].

Today most coaches have spent many years in the role of leader themselves and the general strategy Quinn references of telling is a well-worn habit. Yet in the role of coach, when we are in the heart of the change work in the engagement, the coaching approach must move away from telling and solving problems toward facilitating deep transformative change.

We coined the phrase *leading from behind* as one of the hallmarks of a great coach in order to create a compelling image of the coach's ability to walk slightly behind the client, supporting, challenging, and coaching him or her to facilitate a sustainable and transformative change that tracks to the client goals and acknowledges the multiple layers of systems (team, organization, company) at work. We crafted this provocative phrase in our earliest years of coaching to emphasize a coaching stance that promotes deep and lasting change, understanding that the shelf life of even the soundest of advice is extremely short.

This phrase has surfaced in recent years relative to the role of a leader, and there it's used a bit differently. Nelson Mandela (1994) considers leading from behind to be his style of leadership. For him it means intentionally harnessing the genius of others without abrogating his strength as a leader. It's probably important to acknowledge as well that the phrase has been thoroughly politicized in recent and highly polarized times in the United States as denoting a lack of strength and leadership, quite different from our interpretation and use of the term relative to coaching.

Consider this situation in illustrating a leading-from-behind mind-set. A client wants to be more concise and clearer in his communication style. It would be easy enough for the coach to simply tell the client what to change in order to accomplish this. It might even work, at least over the short term. However, a more lasting and sustainable approach requires leading from behind to jointly surface what the obstacles are to making this change, what the current awareness level is to present behaviors, the benefits that will make this big adjustment in behavior worthwhile, and the competing priorities that might surface along the pathway to change. This is not a passive stance for the coach: it requires strength and courage to challenge at the right times, provide feedback, and share observations that are not self-evident to the client. It also requires the strength of the coach in holding the client accountable for the changes he has committed to making.

The coaching concern may be a shift in one's leadership style, a new way of managing tough conversations, or a pivotal decision. Whatever it is, the stance of leading from behind reminds the coach that our work is in empowering the client to come to terms with the challenges that he or she needs to address in order to fully commit to taking a new step forward in work and life.

For most of us as leaders and professionals, this artful approach of leading from behind initially seems counterintuitive, inefficient, and at times impractical. We ask ourselves: Why not share my wisdom with my client? Why not impart my expertise in order to help the client avert a poor choice? No one would disagree that an efficient short-term solution often emerges from an advisory or consulting approach. However, longer-lasting changes are thwarted when the coach moves ahead of the client and suggests his or her preferred approach or builds the client's solutions for the challenge at hand. This is the essence of the shift from leading the client to the solution to stepping back and leading from behind. The subtle art of restraining the self in order to lead from behind is one that can be cultivated only once the coach has engaged in the practice of deepening the self as outlined in Chapter Four.

Alan Fogel's (2009) work on the psychophysiology of self-awareness provides a deeper view into the leading-from-behind approach that also connects the inner and outer manifestations of self. He describes a process he terms "coregulation" wherein two individuals dynamically coordinate their actions by sensing boundaries between self and other. He uses a powerful example of helping an infant learn to sit up. The adult take the hands of infant as she lies on her back and pulls gently and firmly enough to sense and feel the infant's muscles begin to engage. The adult is leading from behind in order to facilitate the infant's growth and development. If instead the adult fails to consciously engage in Fogel's concept of coregulation, he will pull too quickly or use too much force. The infant may now be sitting up, but the adult has done it for the infant and the young one has been robbed of the opportunity to build muscle and capacity to sit up on her own.

A leading-from-behind stance is in no way implicit permission for the coach to take a position of primarily a supporter and encourager. The coach must continually coregulate and find those moments and opportunities to pull and challenge just enough to promote real growth. The *lead* in *leading from behind* serves to remind us that the coach leads the process by employing a sound methodology. The coach sets the stage to gain clarity and focus in the engagement, and the resulting aspirational goal and behavioral goals to support this are owned by the client. Leading also requires that the coach deftly determine the motivation and commitment of the client, and when the work begins, the coach knows when to challenge, when to share critical observations, and when to confront important areas of discovery with the client. The coach is always leading, but just a step behind the client or at times right alongside, when change is on the plate.

Leading from behind requires restraint and self-management at just the right times while we actively lead the process of coaching. This is a masterful practice that requires emotional agility, deep personal awareness, and the ability to harness the urge to move out ahead of our client. The stance necessitates powerful listening and questioning abilities and a portfolio of coaching tools and techniques that can be easily accessed when the time is right

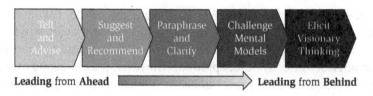

Figure 5.1 Leading from Behind

and they fit the needs of the client. The simple model in Figure 5.1 captures the positions that support either the leading-from-behind stance or the out-in-front approach. Masterful coaches will want to move toward the right, in the direction of leading from behind, particularly when the coaching is focused on facilitating an important change in the client's behavior.

Leading from ahead is what we do when we are in the telling-and-fixing mode. The client arrives at our door with an issue, and before we've taken the time to grapple with the current situation, construct the vision for our work together, the coach believes he sees the client issue clearly and has a strong sense of the next action steps that will be important for the client in order to fix and solve the current dilemma. These are the ways to recognize when you are using a leading-from-ahead stance:

- You strongly influence the contract based on what you determine is best for the client.
- You are often more attached to the contract and goals than the client and don't adequately explore the client's commitment level.
- You view the work of coaching as primarily about problem solving and providing good solutions for the client rather than facilitating deeper sustainable change.
- You get drawn into the client's system because of permeable boundaries, and in so doing, you are unable to help the client step outside herself to see her own story from other vantage points.

Table 5.1 provides some brief vignettes and contrasting approaches.

In each of the examples in Table 5.1, the coach with the leading-from-ahead stance hijacks the client's sense of responsibility for his actions and next steps and misses important opportunities to allow the client to step back and observe self. The coach who embodies the leading-from-behind approach is clear about who needs to be committed to the changes in the behavior and understands how to facilitate deeper awareness and sustainable change through challenging, sharing observations and reflections, and holding the client accountable. Table 5.2 is a descriptive view of these two contrasting approaches.

Table 5.1 Examples of Leading from Ahead Versus Leading from Behind

Client Situation	Leading from Ahead	Leading from Behind
"I've got to get my team behind this initiative now."	"I've got a couple of ideas on how you could do that."	"So what are you doing now that's not working? Any ideas about shifts you could make?"
"I need to find a job now!"	"Okay. Let's put together a list of possibilities that you can start working on this week."	"Okay. I'm thinking it will be useful to look at what's going to be important for you to attend to in order to get a job. Agree?"
"I wish I weren't such a perfectionist; it makes meeting deadlines so darn hard."	"Jack, you've mentioned this before, and I want to recommend a great book that really gets to the heart of perfectionism. Also I have some steps you can start taking now to see if you can curb this."	"Jack, you know when you mention this, it seems like an important part of your goal to meet deadlines, so I'm guessing we ought to take a closer look and see what we can learn about how this gets in your way, when it shows up most, and so on. Can you give me an example or two of this over the past couple of weeks?"
"I really blew up today. I've had it with one of my team members, always making excuses, making light of deadlines. The guy is a jerk."	"I understand that one, and making excuses won't get you any closer to meeting deadlines. I'm thinking it could be helpful to implement a weekly plan with this fellow and hold him more accountable to time lines. You agree?"	"Boy, that sounds hard. I'm also struck by how closely it links to your goal of developing stronger relationships with those on your team. I'm thinking it will be smart for us to step back and take a look at this situation and see what there is to learn about yourself. Agree?"
"I'm sorry I'm late for our appointment today. I just had so many deadlines …"	"Jack. No worries. I know you've got a busy schedule. I might have planned my day a little differently if I knew you were running late, but it's really not a problem."	"Jack, I appreciate your acknowledging that, and I want to explore this a bit with you. You are wanting to be viewed as more reliable and dependable by your team—so I know making commitments matters to you—and at the same time, I can't help noticing that you have cancelled two recent appointments at the very last minute and you are a half-hour late today and no call. What do you make of this?"

Table 5.2 Features of Getting Ahead Versus Leading from Behind

Getting Ahead of Your Client	Leading from Behind
Telling	Asking
Consulting approach	Change agent approach
Sitting in a knowing place	Holding a curious mind
Increased control	Reduced control
Knowing	Wondering
Changing a specific behavior	Inviting insight into behavior
Fixing the problem	Exploring together
Seeing a problem to be fixed	Seeing an opportunity
Imparting your wisdom	Practicing transparency
Hierarchical	Participatory
Prescriptive	Inquiring
"How would you like to fix this?"	"How do you see it?"
"What are the solutions?"	"What are the opportunities?"
Moving directly from problem to solution	"What will the obstacles be?"
Level 1 listening	Levels 2 and 3 listening
Transactional	Transformative

A CLOSER LOOK AT HOW CHANGE HAPPENS

Underlying the leading-from-behind stance is an understanding of the key elements that create the possibility for sustainable change in our clients. Masterful coaches need significant knowledge about how to support change in clients. The body of literature informing this question is considerable, and a brief look at some highlights that link to and support a leading-from-behind posture in coaching are included below. An in-depth review is in Part Three.

Transactional Analysis Paradigm

Transactional analysis (TA), developed by Eric Berne (1964), highlights his model of the three ego states of parent-adult-child that exist internally and externally for each of us. It's a simple, practical model that readily maps to the dynamics of leading from behind versus leading from ahead.

In TA language, each of us has internalized three ego states: parent, adult, and child. The parent state has two parts, the nurturing parent and the critical

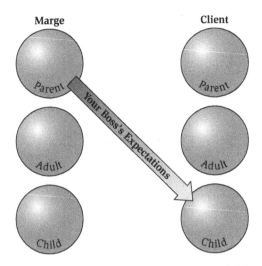

Figure 5.2 Transactional Analysis in Coaching: Eliciting the Child Ego State

parent, an amalgamation of our collective parent. The adult state is the center of logic, reason, and decision making. The child state is the center of feelings, and it includes both a "free child" and an "adaptive child."

When the coach assumes the advice-giving stance, it's likely that a parent-child dynamic gets engaged, and the client finds himself in the role of child accepting the advice of the coach (as parent). The TA model alerts a coach to the dynamic that unfolds when we take on the leading-from-ahead stance of, "I know," "I've got a plan for you," or "Listen to my great advice." Consider this coaching situation. Marge's client comes to the coaching session today feeling pretty ticked off at her boss. She tells Marge, "My boss is really out of line this time. He expects too much of me. I've worked late for the past seven nights, and now at the last minute, with no warning, he drops a big project on my desk that will ruin my plans for a weekend getaway I've planned." If Marge responds, "Boy that's unfortunate, but remember that you are still early on in your new role and your boss expects you to pay your dues and prove yourself. What can you do to make this work for you and perhaps postpone the weekend getaway plans?" In TA parlance, Marge has assumed the parent position and the leading-from-ahead stance, while an unaware or off-guard client can easily assume the child position (Figure 5.2), with the result that little important change ensues.

In short, the TA framework is an easy way to map what our inquiries and observations as a coach will likely elicit in our client. Typically when we get out in front of the client and push our agenda and solutions, we'll pull on the client's child state. If, on the other hand (as in Figure 5.3), you share observations

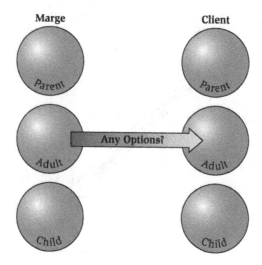

Figure 5.3 Transactional Analysis in Coaching: A Better Path

and make inquiries from a position of curiosity, it will be much easier for the client to consider new possibilities.

While a parent-to-child interaction may lead to a brief change in behavior, it is seldom going to provoke lasting change for the client. The parent-to-child dynamic aligns with a leading-from-ahead approach, whereas an adult-to-adult interaction links to the leading-from-behind stance and factors in the reality that in order to create sustainable change, the client needs to be committed to the change and responsible for taking the action of what is required to achieve deep change: the all-important client ownership that breeds lasting change.

Lewin's Force Field Analysis

Kurt Lewin's field theory is relevant to coaching because he emphasizes the need to expose and understand the forces at play that support or undermine a change an individual (or system) wants to make. In providing this perspective, Lewin (1997) underlines how challenging even the most desired changes are for us. His step-by-step process emphasizes the need to investigate the client's commitment to a change and then examine the many obstacles that might emerge as the client seeks to move forward with this change. His work aligns well with the leading-from-behind stance and reminds the coach that it's impossible to facilitate deep and lasting change by using the fix-and-tell approach.

Consider Lewin's model in the following coaching situation. Mary's organization routinely provides coaching to its more senior leaders, and Mary's boss has recommended coaching for her in order to strengthen her leadership style. In particular, her boss views Mary as needing to strengthen her

Force Field Analysis
Strengthening Leader Presence

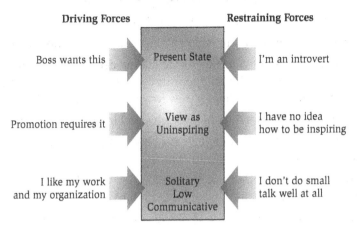

Driving Forces		Restraining Forces
Boss wants this	Present State	I'm an introvert
Promotion requires it	View as Uninspiring	I have no idea how to be inspiring
I like my work and my organization	Solitary Low Communicative	I don't do small talk well at all

Figure 5.4 Lewin's Force Field and the Example of Mary

communication style with her team and ramp up her ability to inspire and motivate the team. In a leading-from-ahead approach, a coach might leap to the rescue and offer Mary some tools and reading resources that could be helpful. Lewin's force field analysis reminds the coach instead of the importance of uncovering of obstacles rather than seeking solutions at this early stage. Some of the restraining forces and driving forces are uncovered with Mary in Figure 5.4, and this becomes an important part of the exploration in the early stages of the coaching engagement.

The TA model underlines the need for a dialogic exchange (adult-to-adult), and Lewin's model highlights the importance of slowly uncovering the competing priorities and natural obstacles that arise whenever a coach is working with a client to make changes in long-held habits and approaches.

There are several key change models that provide powerful confirmation that real change happens when a coach can lead the client to a state of self-revelation that occurs from the inside out. Part Three offers an in-depth review of theories and concepts in this arena.

In Part Four, we examine the stages of the Hudson coaching methodology and look at how some elements of those stages require leading-from-behind strategies. We learn that coaching requires a sound methodology that tracks the process from beginning to end and provides an overall structure that links the contract for change (the aspirational goal and the behaviors goals linked to this) to the work that occurs throughout the engagement and the outcomes that occur as a result of those goals.

The Leading-from-Behind Mind-Set in a Nutshell

- Awareness, understanding, and management of self
- Understanding of the complexities of change
- Underlying understanding of how change happens in the individual
- Viewing the work of coaching as facilitating deep, lasting change and providing the client with an opportunity to gain new perspectives on herself leading to new choices in ways of being in the world
- Exploring and uncovering the obstacles and impediments to change
- Reviewing descriptions of what's happened in the past to help uncover the challenges and obstacles to change
- A willingness to explore and surface feelings with the client because creating lasting change requires more than thinking
- An ability and willingness to challenge the client to consider new vantage points about self and situations
- An ability and willingness to practice transparency and candidly share observations of parallel processes and descriptions of what you, as coach, are noticing and observing in the coaching sessions and in any of the early three-way meetings (boss, human resource partner, coach and client) or in any team observations sessions you, as coach, might join
- Awareness of boundaries and systems at play

Part Four examines in more detail the intersection between elements of a sound coaching methodology and this leading-from-behind stance.

For now, the following case example illustrates the pitfalls of moving into the fix-and-tell stance of leading from ahead.

A Fix-and-Tell Approach: Leading from Ahead

My client enters, and we exchange some initial pleasantries about travel travails, weather, and pace of work. Then we get down to the business of coaching. We have our broad contract, and we've narrowed in on the most important areas of our work. John is determined to become a stronger leader, and he knows that means he's got some work to do in developing stronger relationships with members of the leadership team and creating his own high-performing team.

I've been engaged in leadership coaching for several years in this sector, and I know the territory. John has great technical skills, he has been promoted based on his stellar track record, and now he's being asked to use those same experiences and skills to lead a team to success and interact as a colleague on a senior leadership team that sets the pace and standards for the department going forward. John is somewhere between thrilled and terrified by his advancement, and that's where I come in as his coach.

I query John about his past couple of weeks' experiences with his team and in the leader team domains. I'm not surprised by the frustration he discloses: he tells me about another senior leadership meeting where he's found it difficult to get his voice heard. He feels marginalized by the other members of the team, and this perception seems to make it even more difficult for him to engage as a full member of the team in their discussions.

As I listen to John tell me about the specifics of last week's meeting, my mind wanders to what I know about talented technical folks who lack sufficient emotional intelligence and confidence to engage as leaders. John needs to get up to speed with some skills pretty quickly if he's going to survive and make a place for himself at the leadership table. I quickly scan my experiences for what approaches will work best for him.

I know he needs to get his voice into the conversation at these weekly leadership team meetings, and once I have a good sense of the issues the team is discussing, I suggest to John that he find two contributions he can make to next week's discussion. John agrees and knows this is an important step for going forward. I provide some additional support to John and offer ways to enter the conversation and get his voice heard even when members of the team appear dismissive of his contributions. He seems relieved and appreciative of my suggestions.

Our session is on the right track; we agree to meet in two weeks and say our goodbyes. I'm on my way feeling good about what I've offered to John as a plan for building his strength as a member of this leadership team. I know this is a first step, but we've got to tackle building his confidence and contribution to the leadership team before we move on to his own team.

COACHING FOR LASTING CHANGE

This brief snapshot into a coaching session with John is illustrative of the most fundamental challenge the coaching approach metes out to a coach. The coach wants to add immediate value to his client. He gets out in front of John and moves to action building relying on his knowledge and past experience far more than thoroughly understanding the client's situation and needs.

Yet what we know about how people create sustainable pathways to change runs counter to the fix-and-tell approach. Leading from behind emphasizes a philosophy and an approach to facilitating change in our work with others. It is the artful practice of walking slightly behind the client as she uncovers the obstacles that make her stated goals difficult for her to achieve, while simultaneously leading the coaching process by challenging, observing, providing feedback, and supporting the client as she wrestles down the obstacles and collaboratively builds practices and actions that begin to help her cross the bridge to a new way of being.

PART THREE

THEORIES INFORMING THE ESSENTIALS OF COACHING

He who loves practice without theory is like the sailor who boards a ship without a rudder and compass and never knows where he may cast.
—Leonardo da Vinci

PART THREE

THEORIES INFORMING THE ESSENTIALS OF COACHING

CHAPTER 6

THEORIES: AN INTRODUCTION

In the early stages of the coaching field, little attention was given to the need for knowledge-based competencies, that is, theories and concepts, and a body of evidence-based research didn't yet exist. It's with a sigh of relief that we can safely say much has changed in this regard over the past few years. Today there is growing clarity around the need for both knowledge- and skill-based competencies in this profession connecting science and evidence-based research to coaching practices. Today we understand that if coaches rely strictly on a set of skill-based competencies, they are operating without sufficient depth and connection to the underlying concepts that support our work as coach and the challenges our clients present to us. While theories and concepts are abstract thoughts and ideas, they provide frameworks we can use to understand more complex dynamics in simple terms. In addition, a body of evidence-based research is growing and allowing us to link theories to evidence that provides the basis for best practices in the work of coaching.

The important question now lies in understanding the key areas of knowledge-based competencies essential for a masterful coach. A coach needs to grasp and use linkages between theory and practice in order to provide the highest quality of coaching work possible.

There are numerous coaching books and resources focused on comprehensively reviewing the theories and concepts relevant to the field of coaching, coaching specialty areas, and specific coaching orientations. For that reason, it's not the intent of this book to provide yet another articulation of all relevant theories. Instead, this part's focus links and briefly examines a handful of seminal theories and concepts foundational to masterful coaching. These foundational elements include self as coach, a sound coaching methodology, skill-based competencies, and developmental perspectives in coaching (see Figure 4.1).

An understanding of many of these main theories and concepts foundational to each element offers a baseline for a coach's knowledge competencies. This review is not intended to be exhaustive; instead, it is meant to whet the coach's appetite for further exploration. Well beyond the scope of this part is literature pertaining to specific approaches and specialties or nuanced behavioral issues relevant in our work with clients. Instead, Part Three serves as a launching point for advanced study and exploration.

The elements of masterful coaching represent a dynamic interaction in which the work in the self-as-coach domain lays the foundation for a coach's capacities in developing strong skill-based competencies, working the territory of a sound coaching methodology, while supported by a broad knowledge of sound theories and evidenced-based research that leads to best practices in the field.

CHAPTER 7

THEORIES SUPPORTING THE SELF-AS-COACH DOMAIN

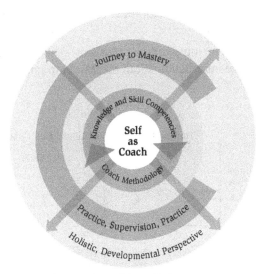

© The Hudson Institute of Santa Barbara

The self-as-coach domain portrayed in the elements of masterful coaching model, the focus of Part Two, is at the heart of coaching. Development and understanding in this area support the range of the coach's abilities and competence in all other parts of the coaching model, starting with the basic skill-based competencies and moving toward mastery. Part Two examined the granular level of self as coach, as well as some of the key theories supporting each of its elements. In this chapter, we highlight some of the broad theoretical foundations informing this central core in masterful coaching.

THEORETICAL FOUNDATIONS FOR SELF AS COACH

Each of the theories explored in this section affects every element of the self as coach: presence, range of feelings, somatic awareness, courage to challenge, empathic stance, and boundary awareness (see Figure 4.3).

Johari Window

The Johari window (Figure 7.1) is a simple model perfect for launching an exploration of theories informing this domain. Joseph Luft and Harry Ingham developed this popular model in 1955 (Luft, 1970). The Johari window provides a snapshot into the essence of the work of self as coach. What we don't know about our self limits our ability to function at a masterful level in our coaching.

The Johari window has four quadrants:

- *Known to all:* The top left quadrant is the arena, where information is known by all parties.

- *Known to others:* The top-right quadrant represents our blind spots: others have and observe information about me, but I am not aware of myself.

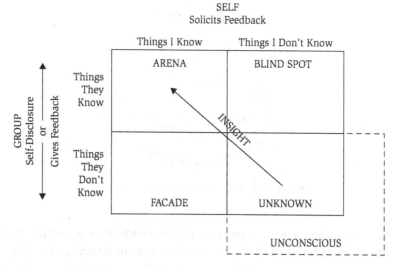

Figure 7.1 Johari Window

Source: http://www.au.af.mil/au/awc/awcgate/sgitc/read5.htm.

- *Known to me:* The bottom-left quadrant, sometimes termed the facade, is where I know things about myself but withhold this information from others or simply choose not to share it, leaving others with an impression that is not entirely accurate (hence the label *facade*).
- *Unknown:* The bottom-right quadrant, sometimes referred to as the unconscious, is that area that is known to none of us at this time.

The quadrant known as the blind spot is what every good coach wants to shrink in order to consciously and intentionally build capacity to use self and minimize unintended impact of self on the client. In short, the impact a coach has on a client who is known to the other but unknown to the coach becomes an impediment in the coaching work. For example, the coach's pace may be quick, with questions that come in rapid-fire fashion, one following another and making it nearly impossible for the client to connect with the coach. But if the coach has no awareness of this blind spot, this markedly limits her capacity to do great work. The Johari window captures a big-picture view of what we mean by the need to build capacity as a coach. Growing capacity requires seeking feedback, gaining new insights and awareness into self, and risking exposing parts of ourselves to fellow colleagues in an effort to shrink the facade and develop the authentic territory of self that is known to oneself and to others with ease.

Two more rigorous and robust theories informing the self-as-coach domain include emotional intelligence and the study of reflection in action. In addition, the broad fields of psychology and adult development serve as further support. Emotional intelligence is a centerpiece in exploring theories foundational to the self-as-coach element of masterful coaching.

Emotional Intelligence

Daniel Goleman (1998) defines *emotional quotient* (EQ) as "the capacity for recognizing our own feelings and those of others, for motivating ourselves, for managing emotions well in ourselves and in our relationships" (p. 3). He and other EQ experts, including, most notably, Howard Gardner (1983), John Mayer and Peter Salovey (1997), and Reuven Bar-On (1997), suggest that truly effective leaders today are those with equal parts of EQ and IQ. It is often said that technical expertise gets one through the door to a new opportunity, but EQ keeps one there. This applies to coaches as well. The technical skills, theories, competencies, tool kits, and extensive leadership experience are all important, but without a well-cultivated and emotionally intelligent self, a coach will have only a limited ability to coach effectively.

Figure 7.2 captures the essence of the development of one's emotional intelligence according to Goleman. Self-awareness is the essential building

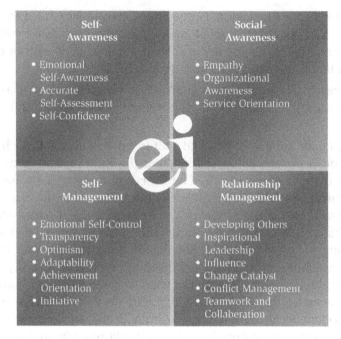

Figure 7.2 Emotional Intelligence
Source: Goleman (1998).

block for all other quadrants. The leader who is challenged to thoroughly engage and inspire her team will need to begin by exploring her own level of awareness relative to how she currently operates and her impact on others. And the coach who is challenged by his drive to solve the client's problems and produce instant solutions needs to return to the first quadrant of self-awareness to uncover what's at play in the inner landscape before adjustments can be made in the outer territory.

Reuven Bar-On (1997) provides another view of emotional and social intelligence and highlights four components: intrapersonal, interpersonal, adaptability, and stress management. He then adds the element of general mood, tracing positive mood to emotional intelligence in each of the other four components. General mood includes a sense of optimism about life and resilience and relative happiness about one's world. The cup is half full for the individual who has good emotional intelligence.

Clearly the mood of a leader affects everyone he or she has contact with (in fact, mood turns out to be almost contagious), and it is both an important outcome of emotional intelligence and a success indicator in life. The sense of optimism and happiness of a coach also affects his or her approach to a coaching engagement (Figure 7.3).

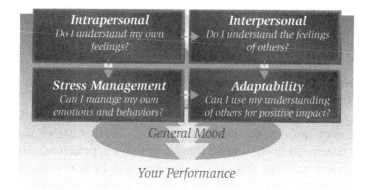

Figure 7.3 Emotional Intelligence Competency Framework
Source: Bar-On (1997).

If John, a coach, carries with him a certain sadness in his life (for which he has little awareness) and a sense that life is not exactly fair, his general mood and disposition relative to his life and the world will quickly impair his ability to coach effectively. The impact may show up in several ways; it might be hard, for example, for him to be fully present and concentrate on the coaching sessions. It's highly likely that his sense that the world isn't fair will change the way he interprets his client's story and challenges, and given that mood is contagious, this may have reverberations for the client. If Mary, a coach, has a stern and demanding internal parent continually second-guessing her ability to effectively coach a particular client, this will automatically restrict her abilities as a coach. It will likely be hard for Mary to be fully in the moment with her client because she is managing the voice in her head critiquing her approach, her questions, and her next steps with the client. In EQ language, Mary needs to start with the intrapersonal quadrant and build awareness of the critical voice in order to quell it. This will allow Mary to be more present and in the moment in the work with her client.

The emotional intelligence models of both Goleman and Bar-On provide a coach with an understanding and a road map of where the work begins.

Reflection-in-Action

Reflection is at the heart of learning and unlearning, and a coach needs to hone the art of reflection in order to cultivate the inner landscape and build capacity in the self-as-coach domain. Recent research in neuropsychology draws our attention to the power of reflection in literally changing the neural pathways of our brain. It also underlines the human challenge we all encounter when we create an intention to sit silently with self for the pure purpose of building awareness of our inner landscape. Daniel Siegel (2007, 2010) provides the coach practitioner with important insights into cultivating one's mind.

Donald Schön. Donald Schön wrote *The Reflective Practitioner* in 1983 and examined the distinct structure of reflection-in-action. His research brings the concept of reflection into the core of what professionals like coaches do in developing their own capacity and working with their clients. Coaches cannot build capacity or coach effectively without using a reflective approach regularly.

Schön's early work in this area draws attention to important distinctions between reflection-in-action and reflection-on-action. *Reflection-in-action* is defined as the ability to think in the moment or think on one's feet; *reflection-on-action* is done after the fact. During the coaching session, it's important to cultivate this capacity as the coach and with one's client. This ability to step back and reflect in the moment by using a reflection-in-action approach urges both coach and client to actively and regularly reflect on the story they have just conveyed or the experience or feeling they have just stumbled on or articulated. In the case of a coach, a continuous cycle of reflection is required, beginning with the preparation phase and ending with postsession reflections that include note taking on one's own behaviors and interventions as the coach as well as the client. This reflection-on-action generates new questions and ideas for the coach's ongoing inquiry about self (Figure 7.4).

David Clutterbuck. David Clutterbuck's (2011) work adds a rich new dimension to the work of Schön and provides a helpful model for an ongoing reflection process occurring throughout the coaching engagement, highlighting the value of reflection before, during, and following the coaching session. Clutterbuck finds that his model supports the coach at each step in the unfolding process in surfacing important self-inquiries in the service of continually building capacity as a coach.

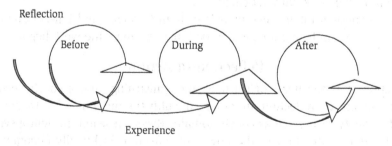

Figure 7.4 Reflection-in-Action
Source: Schön (1983).

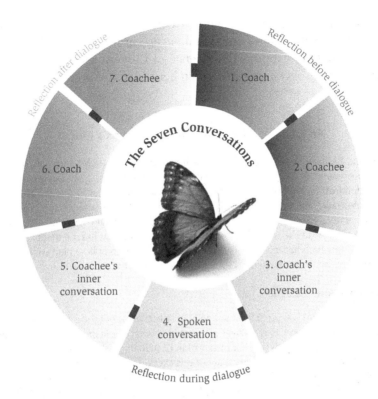

Figure 7.5 Clutterbuck's Seven Conversations
Source: Clutterbuck (2011).

Clutterbuck identifies three phases broken down into seven conversations that are closely aligned with Schön's reflection-in-action and reflection-on-action (Figure 7.5):

- Reflection before the coaching dialogue on the part of both the coach and the coachee
- Reflection during the coaching dialogue, including the coach's internal conversation, the spoken conversation, and the coachee's internal conversation
- Reflection after the dialogue on the part of both the coach and the coachee.

In each phase, there is reflective work for the coach and reflective work to draw the client into as well. While his model broadens this discussion beyond self as coach and into strengthening the reflective practices of both the coach and the client on behalf of the client's success, you'll notice that at each step in his process, an important part of a successful engagement lies in the coach's ability to understand and engage in reflective work. The short vignette that follows captures the essence of Clutterbuck's model as Marlyn coaches Barbara in seeking to strengthen her leadership presence.

An Example of How to Use Clutterbuck's Model

Marlyn and Barbara have launched their coaching engagement with a focus on Barbara's goal of becoming a strong and inspirational leader. The coach has gathered valuable information from a three-way meeting with Barbara's boss, as well as a series of stakeholder interviews, and the theme that emerges is that Barbara is a very smart individual who isn't able to effectively convey her talents through a confident style and a compelling leadership presence. At the last coaching session, Marlyn sat in on a meeting Barbara was conducting with her team in order to observe and help to build a plan with Barbara that will allow her to get started on strengthening her presence.

Reflection Before Dialogue

As the coach, Marlyn will profit from spending a little time prior to the session reviewing where the coaching work is at present with Barbara, what she learned from Barbara in the previous session and during her observation of Barbara as she interacted with her team, and what stands out in general about this client. These questions might prove helpful: What themes stand out for the coach? What are the client's dominant stories? What does Marlyn notice about herself and her own feelings and reactions as she works with her client? And does Marlyn look forward to the upcoming coaching session and enjoy working with this client?

Barbara will be encouraged to engage in a similar reflection prior to arriving at the coaching session. This might be set in motion with a quick e-mail or a regular process that she and Marlyn agree on. The questions for consideration might include these: What stands out as most important from the last session? What threads and themes are becoming more apparent in your coaching work over time? What unexpected feelings are emerging? What aren't you sharing with your coach that might be important to track and surface at point?

Reflection During Dialogue

The Coach's Inner Conversation

As a coach intentionally cultivates the inner landscape of self, it becomes relatively easy to monitor the inner conversation and not only manage it but use it on behalf of the client. For example, if Marlyn regularly observes Barbara qualifying her opinions and comments with an apology like, "I'm sorry. This might not be quite right, but here's how I see this," and observes her own strong reaction to this routine diminishment of herself, this awareness can be used to surface an important conversation in the moment with the client (a great example of self as an instrument of change).

The spoken conversation includes all contents of the conversation. When a coach is engaged in her own inner work of reflecting before the session and attending to the internal conversation while in the session, it will be much easier to maintain a fully present stance with the client.

Encouraging the Coachee's Inner Conversation

This work models the power of a reflective practice in facilitating new choices, new learning, and fresh insights about oneself as client. Questions that will likely encourage these outcomes include: How might someone else view this? If you could get on the balcony of your life, what would you see? Is there another vantage point you haven't considered?

In the case of Barbara's tendency to apologize before she shares her opinion, once the coach has shared this observation, it's important to allow the client space and time to reflect on how this resonates with her, what she is aware of, and how she is feeling.

Reflections After Dialogue

The Coach's Postsession

Immediately following the session, there are insights for the coach to harvest by asking questions that might include these: What did I do that was effective in today's session? What conscious choices did I make during the session? What did I learn about my self as coach? What made me uneasy? What areas did we uncover that link to important elements of the client's goals?

The Client's Postsession

A coach can encourage a client to engage in reflections following the coaching session by suggesting some standard questions: What were my biggest learnings today? What might have made the coaching session even better today? What did I withhold from the coach or resist giving voice to in our session? What new steps will I take based on our session?

Clutterbuck's model is another helpful tool in creating a successful coaching engagement that calls on the coach's capacity in building an internal dialogue and cultivating the inner landscape within himself or herself. Without this skill and without a theoretical understanding of the role of reflection in the work of coaching, a coach will likely veer toward the fix-and-tell, or advisory, approach.

ANALYTICAL THEORIES IN PSYCHOLOGY

Although most coaches do not apply analytical theories directly in their practice, these theories serve to richly inform a coach's thinking and remind us that often what matters most in the coaching work lies well beyond the facts and the words (in other word, what is conscious). Here is a series of descriptions of what the major analytical theorists have contributed to the coaching field.

Sigmund Freud

Freud's psychoanalytical interpretation of personal life became a benchmark for interpretation for all psychotherapy from about 1900 on. Freud believed that the driving forces in people's lives are not conscious (ego driven) but are driven by the unconscious: the id (libido) and the superego (social conscience). Freud thought that these unconscious forces must be considered as symbols and studied indirectly through the clinical interpretation of dreams, free associations, and similar approaches. He taught that in their everyday language, people mask such ego defenses as repression and denial. Therapists still subscribe to the idea that it's important to try to understand the symbolic structure of the patient's mind—a structure that is formed in early childhood experiences. For coaches, Freud's work reminds us that our lives are most often propelled by deeply embedded stories and experiences internal to us rather than by rational external forces.

Applicability to Coaching. Freud's emphasis on defense mechanisms is helpful in reminding coaches that as human beings, we have a natural tendency to protect ourselves. Sometimes our methods of self-protection (defense mechanisms) are useful and at other times destructive. It's helpful to recognize common defense mechanisms in one's self and in one's client (Table 7.1): intellectualization, passive-aggressiveness, projection, denial, and others.

Freud's concept of transference, perhaps one of his most important contributions, is of particular relevance in the coaching relationship. Transference is the process whereby relationship patterns from childhood are transferred to another relationship, most often relationships with a hierarchical or power differential. This means that the coach can observe patterns and parallel processes at play by carefully attending to the dynamics between coach and client. Countertransference represents the coach's reactions to the client's transference (Table 7.2). For example, the helpless client who sees himself as a victim in the world among leaders and people who don't fully appreciate or recognize him will likely recreate this same parallel experience in the coaching engagement.

The astute coach is able to use this in-the-moment experience to heighten the client's awareness, create links to other important relationships, and ultimately generate an opportunity for new choices to emerge. The coach's reaction to a client who feels victimized in the world is helpful information for the coach and client in fully uncovering this dynamic. In self as coach, the use of transference and countertransference requires a good deal of self-awareness on the part of the coach, a knowledge of his or her own inner landscape, and an ease and skill in surfacing these observations and experiences within the coaching engagement.

Table 7.1 Dealing with Defense Mechanisms in Coaching

Defense Mechanism	Client Behavior	Coach Strategies
Projection	A way of managing an uncomfortable internal feeling or desire by ascribing it to another.	Seeking to facilitate the client's self-awareness sufficiently to increase sensitivity to his own inner feelings and desires
Passive-aggressiveness	An indirect way of expressing and managing negative feelings. The individual may agree to do something he doesn't want to do and then resist getting it done in a timely fashion.	Seeking to facilitate the client's comfort in expressing negative feelings directly
Denial	A way of ignoring realities, particularly uncomfortable domains.	Seeking to invite the client to face current realities little by little
Intellectualization	Routinely focusing on the intellectual aspects of a topic and avoiding emotional content.	Seeking to connect the client to his or her feelings about issues

Table 7.2 Transference and Countertransference: A Coaching Example

Transference	Countertransference and Strategies
Richard wants to be heard and understood by others in a role of authority, an experience he never had regularly as a child. Just as in his early years, today he works to overexplain and talk in circular patterns in the hope he'll finally be understood and acknowledged. His boss has told me as coach that Richard needs to work to "be more succinct" and "talk in bullets instead of long paragraphs."	As coach, I notice these same behaviors of overexplaining and circular explanations occurring inside our coaching sessions. What's more, I notice I begin to feel bored and at times impatient with Richard when this occurs. Once I notice and reflect on my internal experience, I'm able to use self as instrument of my own experience in order to create immediacy in our session, sharing my own reactions and working to explore the possibility that others have similar reactions, in particular the possibility this same dynamic occurs in Richard's most important relationships.

Freud also offers the invaluable concept of parallel process, useful in clinical work and invaluable in coaching as well. What the coach experiences inside the coaching session with his client most often mirrors how others experience this individual in the important settings in their lives. If you as a coach feel bothered or annoyed by your client's rapid-fire pace, or bored by your client's slow, methodological, intellectualized descriptions of events, it is highly likely many others have this same experience of your client. This allows you to use self as instrument to deliberately and transparently share your experience of the client in order to maximize the possibility of heightening awareness in-the-moment inside the coaching session.

Alfred Adler

After about ten years of collaboration with Sigmund Freud, Adler left the Vienna Psychoanalytic Society in 1911 and founded the Society for Individual Psychology. Adler preferred to understand human nature as psychosocial rather than as merely biological and deterministic, as Freud had proposed. According to Adler, humans are motivated by social urges. Adult behavior is purposeful and goal directed, meaning that consciousness, rather than the unconscious, is the center of the personality. Adler's was a growth model, stressing what humans do with the possibilities in their lives and environment. His theory focused on personal values, beliefs, attitudes, goals, and interests.

The goal of Adlerian therapy is to reeducate adults to live in society as equals with others. Although Adler believed that much of the therapeutic process was reworking the early childhood formation of personality, he engaged adults directly in goal setting and in reinventing their future, using techniques such as a paradoxical intention, acting "as if," role-playing various options, and task setting.

Applicability to Coaching. Although Adler's ideas are cloaked in the language of psychiatry, he addresses concepts particularly relevant in coaching: the power of purpose, visioning, and personal accountability. His focus on broadening the client's perspective and vision is important in reminding the coach to work with the client to develop an aspirational vision of what he might be truly motivated to work toward rather than adhering to a focused tactical goal that merely solves a problem.

Carl Gustav Jung

The father of modern stage theory is Carl Jung, a Swiss psychiatrist who wrote in the first half of the twentieth century. Jung thought of life as a progression in consciousness or self-awareness, so he viewed the second half of life as an acquisition of deeper human qualities. Like Adler, his friend and colleague for several years, Jung began as a Freudian and then departed into his own way of thinking.

Unlike Freud, who thought of psychology as the study of symbolism grounded in the psychosexual stages of the early childhood years, and Alfred Adler, who thought of psychology as social growth and development, Jung took psychology to be the study of universal symbolism in adult life, revealing lasting values, relationships, and meaning.

Jung's writings concentrate on life after forty. He addresses many of the issues expressed by people in midlife crisis or in midcareer development: issues of spirituality, male-female balance, young-old balance, individuation, and the deeper adventures of the self. He viewed the second half of life as a time when a major progression takes place—from ego to self, from body issues to spirit issues, from differentiation to inclusion. It is during this mature period in life that a person's true identity emerges through a process he called individuation—the spiritual maturation of the self. Our self-centered ego needs become balanced by our self-connecting spiritual feelings, our feminine and masculine qualities find their balance, our love of young finds a balance with a love of old, and our will to kill finds a balance with a will to live and let live.

It is in the second half of life that Jung believed most of us have our full capacities available for recalibrating these polarities to claim our full human imprint. Through the conduct of a life review (this might be a structured series of questions or a long conversation of exploration), we alter our basic commitments to how we will live and be in the balance of each polarity, and we normally choose to increase our self-individuation and our self-connectedness in the context of universal themes.

Applicability to Coaching. Jung made several contributions to the coaching field. First, he proposes that adults experience a profound spiritual awakening in the second half of life. Coaches often experience this themselves and with their clients, and they need to know how to recognize and facilitate the process. "Second half of life" has a different meaning today than in Jung's time, but generally we think of somewhere in the forties as the midway point today. Second, he writes about the importance of myths. Coaches need to discern in their clients what the compelling stories of their lives are about and what they are drawn to in their lives. Third, Jung finds significant meaning in rituals, and coaching often includes ritual-making events that help clients experience their power and rites of passage.

Erik H. Erikson

Next to Carl Jung, no one is more seminal to developmental theory than Erik Erikson, the psychoanalytical (Freudian) child psychologist who expanded

Table 7.3 Erikson's Eight Stages of Development

Stage of Life	Developmental Task
Infancy (ages 0–1)	Basic Trust versus Basic Mistrust
Toddler (ages 1–3)	Autonomy versus Shame
Preschool (ages 3–6)	Initiative versus Guilt
School age (ages 6–11)	Industry versus Inferiority
Adolescence (ages 12–20)	Identity versus Role Confusion
Young adult (ages 20–24)	Intimacy versus Isolation
Adult (ages 25–65)	Generativity versus Stagnation
Old age (ages over 65)	Integrity versus Despair

that field to include adult phases of development. Viewing development as a lifelong process, he hypothesized that a person must successfully resolve a series of eight stages, each involving a crisis between polarities that must be resolved in order to develop as a normal and happy person throughout life. Failure to adequately resolve any polarity in favor of the positive developmental task at hand is to keep the person regressed and arrested at that stage. However, each polarity may reappear later in life, stimulated by crises, by which Erikson means turning points for either maturation or regression. Erikson's eight stages are set out in Table 7.3.

Applicability to Coaching. Erikson's ideas help coaches understand the underlying concerns of clients and to some extent anticipate their issues. The principles of growth and development are critical to successful coaching, and Erikson is foundational for this learning. Erikson writes about the generativity of adults, and this aligns with the need to engage in purposeful living and the continual learning in order to avoid a sense of stagnation and dissatisfaction in the adult years.

CONTEMPORARY THEORIES IN PSYCHOLOGY

The field of psychology provides an important foundation in the realm of self as coach. The fields of analytical and neoanalytical psychology; the contemporary frameworks of gestalt, transactional analysis, neurolinguistic programming (NLP), and family systems; and the cognitive behavioral approaches all provide enormous data and valuable perspectives for further understanding the domains of self as coach. And while it's beyond the scope of coach training to explore all of these domains, it seems essential for a masterful coach to gain a working knowledge in one or two areas of the discipline of psychology. No matter which theoretical frameworks a coach is drawn to, there are immediate applications to the self-as-coach domains. We explore just a few contemporary examples of the use of psychological theories in understanding the underpinnings of the self.

Gestalt Theory

This theory provides a particularly helpful and compassionate perspective on how a coach can most successfully facilitate change. Gestalt theorists postulate that the most efficient way to help an individual make a change is by first attending to what's true now, in the moment, that is, paying attention to what the client is doing now instead of what he wishes to be doing. The underlying belief is that awareness creates the ground for new choices and change, and without a heightened awareness of one's current behaviors, it is difficult for an individual to take on a new behavior or new way of being.

Applicability to Coaching. Marcia wants to speak up and be noticed during meetings, but it's a big leap for her. She has never felt comfortable speaking up, offering her point of view, and taking a stand on issues that matter to her. A coach might be tempted to move into a fast gear and develop action steps for Marcia to start practicing speaking up, but gestalt theory suggests that the essential first step is for Marcia to become highly attuned to what she does at those moments when she might speak up and instead she remains silent.

When Marcia turns up the volume on her inner chatter and becomes aware of how much energy she puts into second-guessing what she might say, she gains new information about herself, and she intensifies her noticing of the inner chatter. According to Gestalt theory, awareness builds the bridge to self-correction through continued practice, reflection, and integration.

Often coaches in training (and, at times, coaches well into their practice) will share with me that it's hard to challenge a client, and when queried about what makes this so hard, the comments are like these: "I feel awkward or uncomfortable," "I don't want to offend my client," "I don't want to make my client uncomfortable," or "I find it uncomfortable being that direct with another human being; it's just not my usual style."

Yet in the role of a coach, challenging a client or sharing an astute observation is a critical skill, so the motivation is high for the coach to change old habits in this regard. The first step for the coach using a gestalt approach is not in building an action plan to become at ease challenging; instead, it is to notice and heighten awareness of what happens inside when he or she doesn't take an opportunity to challenge a client. This repeated in-the-moment magnification helps the coach to understand the forces at work internally that make it difficult to use a challenging style. As the awareness of feelings, thoughts, and bodily triggers intensifies, the power of old fears and reluctance begins to diminish, and the coach is able to deconstruct old habits and deliberately strengthen the ability to challenge another.

Gestalt techniques are enormously helpful in creating in-the-moment experiences where the client is able to experience the power of thinking and feeling coming together and creating a memorable breakthrough experience.

Transactional Analysis Theory

Originally developed by Eric Berne and contemporized by Robert Goulding, Taibi Kahler, Michael Brown, Stephen Karpman, and others, transactional analysis articulates a theory of personality development, a model of communication, and a study of repetitive patterns of behavior. Major contributions include these key concepts: life scripts, the mostly unconscious life plan; rackets, ways of behaving that replicate our early life experiences; and ego states, organized, observable ways of thinking, feeling, and behaving. These are the ego states:

- *Parent ego state*, that is, thoughts, feelings, and behaviors from our early childhood. Often these are the oldest "tapes" from our collective parent. The two elements in this state are the nurturing parent and the critical parent. Each of us has varying degrees of these two elements depending on the particulars of our history.

- *Adult ego state*. Logical, rational, organized, pragmatic, and analytical, this is the state that stores data and information and makes decisions largely independent of old tapes of parent and child.

- *Child ego state*, that is, the feelings and emotions from our early childhood. The two elements in this state are the natural child and the adapted child. The adapted child responds emotionally based on early interactions with parent figures.

Applicability to Coaching. TA's concept of ego states is useful to a coach in the self-as-coach domain, as well as in working with a client. It provides a simple framework for understanding one's internal dialogue and insights into communication patterns. Consider two examples of interactions between coach and client with different ego states at play.

In the first example, the client calls her coach, Jane, with this message: "I am so sorry to cancel yet another coaching appointment. I'm up against another deadline, and I have absolutely no choice in this matter. It's such an awful feeling [with signs of breaking in the voice, the coach wonders if there is tearfulness on the other end of the phone] being in this place. I'm completely stressed out. I know I'm letting you down, and I know I need to take our work seriously. Yikes!"

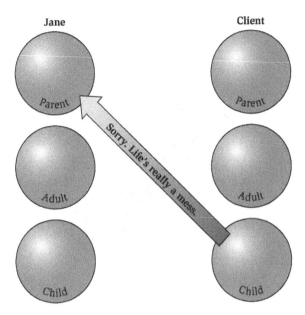

Figure 7.6 Transactional Analysis Client in the Child Ego State

In this interaction the client approaches Jane, the coach, from the child ego state, and this naturally pulls on the parent ego state (Figure 7.6). Jane seems to automatically respond from what's termed the Nurturing Parent territory: "Oh, don't worry about it. You already have a lot on your plate. We can reschedule again. Just take care of yourself."

The problem with this approach is that as the coach, Jane may well be entering the client's system and rescuing her client instead of helping her client gain a perspective about this habit or pattern she might have, as shown in Figure 7.7. So the TA model may prove helpful in providing a map for a coach in order to determine habitual responses and specific communication patterns with a client.

If Jane stepped back and noticed this communication pattern, she might take a very different approach with her client—one that maps to the ego states shown in Figure 7.8. In this example, Jane takes a more deliberate approach. Instead of rescuing her client, she steps into the adult ego state and nonjudgmentally observes this pattern. Then she poses the question of whether there is value in exploring this pattern.

Family Systems Theory

Family systems theory provides an invaluable perspective for the coach in understanding self, and it's a helpful perspective in understanding systems dynamics in the work of the coaching engagement. A review of the key concepts most relevant to the coach is covered in Chapter Eight.

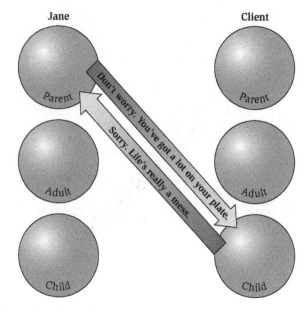

Figure 7.7 Transactional Analysis Coach from the Parent Ego State

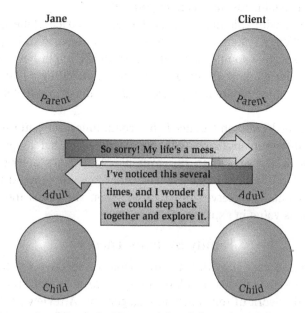

Figure 7.8 Transactional Analysis Client and Coach from the Adult Ego State

FIELD OF ADULT DEVELOPMENT

Context matters, and it's critical for us as coaches to have a keen sense of this. It's about more than settings, histories, geographies, and cultures; it's also about the adult life cycle. No matter what the coaching challenge might be, the work is vastly different when we are coaching a recent college graduate who just landed a great new role in her dream company versus a long-time leader who is about to take a leap outside her organization to launch a new chapter in her life. Among the differences are experience, history, failures, recoveries, perspective, sense of time left, accumulation of roles and responsibilities, freshness that comes from little experience, new hope and endless possibility, last work chapter versus first work chapter, and family waxing versus family waning.

A developmental perspective on the whole person as client is essential for the coach, so knowing how people evolve throughout the life cycle is important information. Even if the client is a whole organization, the development of that organization relies heavily on the human performance and imagination of key people within it. A coach knows how to think developmentally within many contexts.

The humanistic field of adult development grew in the late 1950s as an outgrowth of developmental psychology. In contrast to clinical psychology, which has both theoretical and applied fields for understanding and treating people with mental health problems, developmental psychology began as the study of children and adolescents. Only halfway through the twentieth century did it expand to include adult development: the study of normal and extraordinary growth and development of adults. For years it lacked an applied side while it thrived as a research field. Then people like Vivian McCoy (University of Kansas), Lillian Troll and Nancy Schlossberg (University of Maryland), Alan Entine (Empire State University), Arthur Chickering (University of Memphis), Malcolm Knowles (the Fielding Institute), Frederic Hudson (founding president of the Fielding Institute), and many others began to apply adult developmental research to the lives and organizations of adults. Today thousands of professionals are applying this body of knowledge in career centers, retreat programs, adult education institutes, applied research projects, longevity and health applications, and retirement programs. We look at a handful of relevant theorists here.

Bernice Neugarten

Few have contributed more to the study of adult development than Bernice Neugarten (Neugarten and Neugarten, 1996). She linked theory to empirical testing and added adult study to the already thriving study of children. Unlike Jung and Erikson, Neugarten looks at adult life less from a psychological perspective and more from a social-developmental point of view.

Neugarten's writings on human development form the foundation of that field. Her writings are basic to our understanding of how men and women develop throughout the adult years. She discerned important differences in the lives of men and women.

Applicability to Coaching. Neugarten provides coaches with powerful concepts germane to the adult journey. She coined the term *empty nest*, and this passage for any woman who has been a mother is perhaps one of the most profound life transitions in adulthood. Neugarten also drew our attention to the notion of time left, that invisible line in life when we notice we have less time ahead of us than already lived. Sometimes it is tapped by the passing of a parent, and other times it's the arrival at one of the decade years, likely when turning fifty or sixty. This understanding of the terrain of the adult journey and a series of critical moments that transcend day-to-day issues is essential for a well-grounded coach.

Daniel Levinson

Daniel Levinson wrote a major work on male development during the adult years, *The Seasons of a Man's Life* (1986). He saw male development as proceeding from life structures (periods of stability) to transitions (periods of change) throughout the life cycle. He believed that adult development is age specific and therefore chronologically predictable.

Perhaps the most important feature of Levinson's theory is the role of the midlife crisis in a man's life. To Levinson, the midlife transition is not just another transition. It is qualitatively different. Like Jung and Neugarten, Levinson sees life in two parts: the first half, when a man is achieving, accumulating, procreating, obtaining approval, and gaining security, and (2) the second half, when he is seeking quality (rather than quantity), internal meaning (more than external approval or acquisitions), leaving a contribution, and finding a universal human perspective on the human journey.

Applicability to Coaching. Levinson's concepts of life structure and transition are useful to coaches for understanding the ups and downs of their clients. He also stresses that transitions are times of major growing and learning. Because many coaching clients are in transition from one chapter of their lives to another, coaches can learn the inner workings of transitions from Levinson. Transitions, he says, are normal and inevitable, so we need coaches who understand how to guide people through meaningful and successful transitions. In *The Seasons of a Woman's Life* (Levinson and Levinson, 1997), Levinson reports for women the same general sequence of life structures and transitions, along with more complex themes and patterns.

Robert Kegan

In *The Evolving Self* (1982), Robert Kegan provides a neo-Piagetian model of human development. It is a theory of ongoing interpersonal and intrapsychic reconstruction. The model suggests that all development is in relationship to two fundamental poles: independence and inclusion. Kegan suggests that there are six levels or developmental stages (incorporative, impulsive, imperial, interpersonal, institutional, and interindividual), which move from independence (differentiation, distinctness, decentration) to inclusion (embeddedness, connectedness) and on to a new independence and a new inclusion, and on and on, like a rising spiral or a helix of evolutionary truces throughout the adult years.

Kegan (1982) summarizes his idea this way: "We move from the overincluded, fantasy-embedded impulsive balance to the sealed-up self-sufficiency of the imperial balance; from the over differentiated imperial balance to overincluded interpersonalism; from interpersonalism to the autonomous, self-regulating institutional balance; from the institutional to a new form of openness in the interindividual" (p. 108). When a person enters the interindividual balance, the self senses itself apart from institutions. One no longer is one's career; one has a career. The self is located in one's interiority and has the capacity for intimacy that stems from self-caring. Interdependence, self-surrender, and interdependent self-definition become possible, and maturation reaches its zenith.

Applicability to Coaching. Kegan's concept of the spiral is much like Levinson's life transitions and our cycle of renewal, which I discuss in Chapter Thirteen. Kegan's concern is with what goes on for individuals at times of transitions—growth and development—in their lives. The spiraling progression of self and object over the course of the adult's life provides important opportunities for the client to take a step back, "get on the balcony," and examine and observe one's self, including all of the unexamined beliefs and biases that have influenced one's life. Kegan's work provides a broad contextual pathway for understanding a client's capacity to mature and individuate over the course of their adult journey.

Carol Gilligan

Carol Gilligan provides an alternative developmental pattern for females in her book, *In a Different Voice* (1982), and challenges the theories of Erikson and Levinson. Whereas Erikson hypothesized that intimacy is a stage of development, Gilligan proposed that for women, intimacy is the context of female development. Women grow through their relationships and measure themselves through their inclusion. Men grow through their individuation or autonomy; they push away from inclusion to measure themselves by their personally unique characteristics. Furthermore, Gilligan suggests that there may be a higher stage: working things out through caring relationships. Gilligan's work is underscored by other theorists who have suggested that women construct their identities through connections and spirituality. This is not to suggest that women do not succeed, achieve, wield power, or govern nations as well as men. They can and do. They just do these things differently than men do.

Applicability to Coaching. Coaches work with both men and women and need conceptual tools for understanding both genders. The debate that Gilligan raised in the 1980s is ongoing and is worth coaches' attention. It suggests that a woman's identity is constructed in relation to others much more than a man's is and that important life decisions will require careful attention to how choices bear on the important others in the woman's life.

CHAPTER 8

THEORIES SUPPORTING THE COACHING METHODOLOGY DOMAIN

© The Hudson Institute of Santa Barbara

Several fields of study and research are foundational to this important domain of coaching: the working alliance, change theory, systems thinking, outcome measures, and ethics. This chapter reviews important highlights in these five baseline areas in support of a sound coaching methodology.

THE WORKING ALLIANCE

At first glance, a thorough methodology for the coaching engagement can appear overly structured, linear, and formulaic, but a methodology is simply the scaffolding that supports the coach's work rather than dictating a step-by-step process. While it appears on the surface to be linear, it never is, and a useful methodology ought to always be adaptable, fluid, and flexible enough to accommodate each coaching engagement. Underlying the scaffolding of the methodology is the all-important relationship between the coach and the client—the working alliance. This is a respectful, trusting, safe, and open relationship that a coach builds with the client and creates the foundation for the truly transformative work to occur. Without a working alliance, a methodology is sorely insufficient in facilitating a client's development.

The field of psychology provides valuable research underlining the pivotal nature of this relationship in the therapeutic domain. Researchers in psychology have engaged in extensive studies to determine just what the key ingredients are in a successful therapeutic engagement, and each successive research finding points to one pivotal element: the working alliance between client and therapist. According to Bordin (1979) and Wolfe and Goldfried (1988), this working alliance (the collaborative bond between therapist and patient) affects the therapeutic outcome far more than any specific therapeutic approach that the psychotherapist takes. Whether the approach is behavioral, analytical, psychodynamic, or eclectic, it is the quality of the working alliance, and not the approach, that leads to successful outcomes. Although the field of coaching has not yet researched this dynamic thoroughly, it's quite likely we can extrapolate from the extensive research in psychotherapy and infer that similar dynamics are at play in the coaching engagement.

De Haan (2008) works to extend this research into the coaching domain and defines the working alliance in the coaching relationship as "1) the coachee's experience of the coach being supportive and empathic; and 2) a sense of working together towards the goals of the coaching." (p. 132). Building a working alliance with a client requires all of the elements already outlined in the self-as-coach model. The quality of the alliance is dependent on the coach's mastery of self: the ability to empathize, be present, be comfortable within a wide range of feelings, and to challenge while remaining aligned around the coaching goals and to support at the right times.

At each step in the methodology, the working alliance is at the center of the work, whether it is talking through information obtained through stakeholder interviews, exploring the client's level of commitment to making a change, or examining the obstacles that arise on the path to a new way of being.

In Coaching. In our work training coaches, we require each new coach to receive several months of coaching with an experienced coach over the course of the learning program. We ask the coach in training to interview at least two coaches to determine which might be the best fit given his or her particular needs. Once the trainees have completed their coaching, we ask how they chose their coach, and in each situation, assuming competence and experience are prerequisites, it is the nature of the connection that occurs in that first conversation that lays the ground for the engagement. Good coaches have honed the self-as-coach terrain in order to become fully aware of how they are perceived, how they connect, and what barriers might exist that will make it difficult for clients to feel at ease. Humility, compassion, empathy, access to feelings, humanness, respect, and authenticity: a lofty goal for a great coach to realize.

CHANGE THEORY

Change is at the heart of coaching, and deep change is what a thorough coaching methodology seeks to support. How does a coach help a client become a slightly better version of his or her current self? How does a coach work with a client to make a change that he or she can barely grasp, while others around this person see it so clearly? Perhaps it's an abrupt style, a discounting approach, a diminutive presence, an unapproachable veneer. How does a coach understand change in his own life—those areas that have been on the list to change for some time and yet nothing happens? Understanding the elements that must be present to ensure change is essential for coaches lest we veer toward problem solving and consulting for the client.

There exists a series of well-researched models for supporting change that are particularly useful for the coach, including the work of Kurt Lewin, Robert Kegan and Lisa Lahey, Richard Boyatzis, and Rick Mauer. The work of these theorists and practitioners is reflected in the coaching methodology articulated in Part Four, from framing the aspirational goal, to gaining feedback from key parties in the system, to examining the level of commitment and explicitly uncovering the obstacles to change. Each of these steps in the underlying coach methodology is in support of mapping the way to a meaningful and sustainable change in the client's life. What follows is a brief review of these theorists.

Kurt Lewin

Kurt Lewin, a pioneer in group and organizational psychology, developed a three-stage change model in the 1950s (unfreeze-change-refreeze) in an early

Figure 8.1 Lewin's Change Model
Source: Lewin (1997).

attempt to provide a change process that included a series of progressive steps instead of a sense that change is a random, uncontrollable event (Figure 8.1):

Stage 1: Unfreeze. Examine the motivation to take on the change.

Stage 2: Change. Identify what needs to change and make those changes.

Stage 3: Refreeze. Make the new changes permanent and sustainable.

Lewin's (1997) work provides an important early foundation for understanding the elements in facilitating change. Although his model was focused on organizational change, he highlighted the importance of examining the level of commitment to change and emphasizes the need for clear motivation on the client's part in order for change to occur.

Robert Kegan and Lisa Lahey

Robert Kegan and Lisa Lahey's (2009) recent work on immunity to change affirms Lewin's findings and further uncovers the powerful system of immunity embedded in each of us when change is under consideration (Figure 8.2). Their studies suggest that three ingredients are needed in order to facilitate sustainable change:

- *The gut.* They write, "It's not enough to know one 'should' make a change—in order to build a platform for successful change, the gut must be engaged, a visceral sensation that this change is truly important, the sense of timing is urgent and the cost of self-protection—the impossibility of making progress on a deeply desired goal—has just become too big a price to continue to pay" (2009, p. 210).

- *The head and heart:* In this model. the thinking of the head and the feelings of the heart must come together: "New ways of thinking permit new ways of feeling, and new ways of feeling encourage and validate new ways of thinking" (2009 p. 217).

- *The hand:* We can't think or feel our way in or out of change. We must have a plan of action that starts in small, incremental steps and leads to the bigger goal at hand.

Commitment	Doing/not doing instead	Hidden competing commitments	Big assumptions
To better focus on a few critical things: • Delegate. • Clarify outcomes desired. • Accept different approaches. • Support small failures as learning. • Challenge the thought process and logic.	I let new opportunities distract me, adding to my list. I accept more tasks and sacrifice non-work-related things. I don't consistently balance time commitment to urgent and important rankings. I don't ask people to help me.	(I fear missing a good opportunity. Falling behind.) I'm committed to being independent and capable of anything. (I fear letting my team down. If I put myself first I feel guilty and selfish.) I'm committed to being selfless. (I dislike leaving boxes unchecked—it's harder to drop something than just to do it.) I'm committed to always finding a way to get it done.	If I am dependent on others and unable to do many things well, I lose my self-respect. If I put myself first I'll become what I dislike in others—superficial and trivial. If I don't find a way to get things done, I'll stop being valuable.

Figure 8.2 Kegan and Lahey's Model of Change

In Coaching. Both Lewin's and Kegan and Lahey's research places the spotlight on the importance of gaining the client's commitment to do the work of coaching and taking the time to carefully assess the level of motivation, the urgency of this change, the competing priorities, and underlying beliefs that hinder the path to change and the willingness to do the hard work required by the change. Change may sound sensible and reasonable to both the coach and the client, but without a deep sense of commitment and a clear sense that one's old survival strategies are no longer effective, the work of coaching will fall short of the goals.

Richard Boyatzis

Richard Boyatzis (2011; Boyatzis, Goleman, and McKee, 2002; Boyatzis and McKee, 2005) widens the lens in understanding how change happens and places the spotlight on the ideal self as the most important driver in creating a sustainable change. His step-by-step change model (Figure 8.3) begins with a focus on identifying the ideal self and then moves through the cycle as follows:

- *The ideal self:* Boyatzis's research concludes that if a client doesn't have a real vision for what she is reaching for, little change is possible: "Our findings indicate that coaching students with compassion (focusing on their goals and aspirations), as opposed to more standard methods of coaching (focusing on their academic performance), produces enhanced

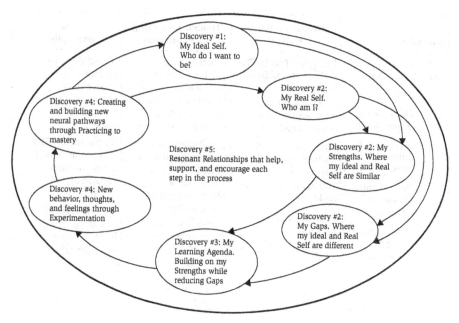

Figure 8.3 Boyatzis's Cycle of Change
Source: Boyatzis (2011).

activation of visual and auditory association areas. We think of this as the neural signature of visioning—the increased perceptual openness that comes from being inspired" (Boyatzis, 2011).

- *The real self:* A careful understanding of the current situation.
- *Strengths:* Areas where the ideal self and real self are similar.
- *Gaps:* Areas where the ideal self and real self are notably different.
- *Learning agenda:* The work of building on the client's strengths while reducing gaps.
- *Experimenting:* The work of testing the learning plan.
- *Practicing:* Putting the new behaviors to work.

In Coaching. The power of an aspirational goal rooted in the heart and mind of the client is essential in order to create sustainable change. Too often coaches develop a coaching agreement tied to a to-do list or a series of behaviors that need improvement. Boyatzis's research confirms the importance of an aspirational goal that resonates at an emotional and cognitive level for the client and inspires him or her with the hope of a slightly better version of self through the coaching work.

Rick Mauer

Finally, Maurer's (2010) contributions highlighting the power of resistance are essential in examining how a coach facilitates change over the course of the entire coaching engagement. He highlights the reality that resistance, a force that slows or stops movement, is a natural, predictable part of any change and a change agent needs to understand this in order to work effectively with this resistance. He outlines three levels of resistance:

- *I don't understand.* When the client doesn't have the necessary information to successfully make a change, the resistance is easily overcome by providing information, resources, and tools for the client. While this simplest level of resistance is seldom what brings someone to coaching, it is often the approach that an early coach attempts to provide— information, resources, and tools—when in fact the resistance is actually more complex, as in the next two levels.

- *I don't like it.* This is an emotional response to a change. The survival instinct surfaces, and the natural inclination to hold on to well-established behaviors surfaces. If, as Boyatzis points out, the coach doesn't do the important work of transforming negative feedback into an aspirational goal, the client will likely remain resistant at a deeply emotional level, and change will be unlikely.

- *I don't like you.* At this level, the client doesn't trust you, the coach. This may be a result of how the relationship boundaries have been established, how the culture of the organization positions coaching, or how the coach approaches the role of coaching with the client. The coach who pushes his or her agenda and gets out in front of the client may easily set resistance in motion because the agenda is being led not by the client but by the coach.

In Coaching. Maurer's work confirms the importance of a clear, visceral aspirational goal that provides hope and inspiration to the client, capturing both the head and the heart. It also underlines the importance of uncovering the natural obstacles that will surface anytime change is afoot. Exposing the obstacles and inevitable resistance helps coach and client build an action plan that includes important practices that build the platform for sustainable change to occur.

Doug Silsbee

Doug Silsbee's book *Presence-Based Coaching* (2008) includes a chapter focused on how humans change in which he explores what is required for a coaching client to become self-generative by moving from automatic to self-generated behaviors, habits, and choices—and change long-held habits and behaviors. The progression of practices he describes provides a helpful framework in supporting the work of building the coaching plan with a client:

- *Self-observation*. The practice of observing oneself in action over a period of time, carefully logging and tracking the behavior or habit one wants to adjust.

- *Realization*. The epiphany or "felt shift" that occurs in head and heart when one has stepped onto the balcony and seen the self. Consider the client who wants to operate in his leadership role with more confidence. This client receives feedback from his boss and peers that his voice is so soft it is often difficult to pick up everything he said. Although the client may want to immediately alter this, making a change is very difficult without adequate awareness of when, how, and where this is happening in both external and internal world. After careful tracking of his voice, the level of volume, the internal experience of it, perhaps seeking more feedback, and recording himself, he is going to develop a heightened awareness that creates the ability to name it and recognize it ("Oh. There's my soft voice again") and create the pathway to new choice.

- *Reorganization*. Silsbee views this as a moment of free choice where, in the example, the client can now choose to use his soft voice or reorganize and develop his stronger voice and use it at will.

- *Stabilization*. The shift from the client's soft voice to a reliably consistent strong voice takes time and regular practice in order to create a stable foundation for this new habit or behavior.

Silsbee's model (Figure 8.4) portrays the pathway of ingrained habit and the self-generative loop that leads to opportunities for new choices.

The link between his work and the latest work in neuroscience articulated by Siegel (2010) lies in the finding that a change in behavior requires enormous focus of attention and mindfulness on the part of the client. This process of becoming mindful and focusing attention on self-observation takes time and is more strenuous than we've previously believed. Building practices to support this ability to self-generate new habits and behaviors is essential.

In Coaching. Silsbee's work in mapping self-generative practices informs the heart of building a coaching plan with a client. In essence, we are working with clients to change habits and behaviors that will allow them to get as close as possible to the goals that matter to them. Robust, thorough practices that support this change and help the client understand the complexities of change are essential to the success of a coaching engagement.

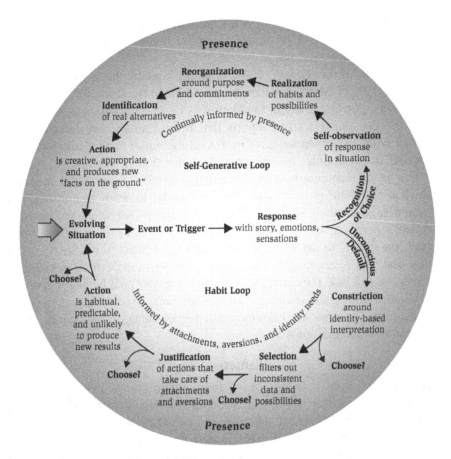

Figure 8.4 Silsbee's Self-Generative Loop

Source: Silsbee, D. (2008). *Presence-based coaching: Cultivating self-generative leaders through mind, body, and heart.* San Francisco: Jossey-Bass. This material is reproduced with permission of John Wiley & Sons, Inc.

SYSTEMS THINKING

Systems thinking provides an invaluable perspective into the complexities of facilitating change throughout the coaching engagement, from the moment you receive a phone call from someone seeking your services until the engagement has fully concluded. Whether you are working with a leader inside a global organization or an individual in a transition outside the organization, an integrative systems perspective is essential for a coach. Systems are at play everywhere, whether we are managing our own complex internal systems, the systems present in any coaching relationship, or the larger context of the client—the team, the organization, and the culture. Organizations can best be understood through the lens of systems thinking, and many of the central elements of family therapy help us understand the systems dynamics of coaching in a business setting.

The work of Murray Bowen (1978) in family systems theory, as well as the systems thinking of Peter Senge (2006) and others in the field of organizational development, provides a useful foundation. A coach might be tempted to take it at face value when a client reports that her teammates are impossible to get along with. But when we have examined the entire system (this might be uncovered in stakeholder interviews and observation in action), we quickly find that team members have a different perspective. Some team members might find the client to be so rigid that they prefer to work around her; others might say that their approach is to simply ignore her whenever possible. A system's perspective teaches the coach that allocating blame is irrelevant; instead, the goal is to determine which interactions inside the system need to change and how to accomplish that change in order to make it more satisfying for everyone and help the client get closer to the bigger goal he or she has set.

A handful of systems thinking concepts are particularly relevant in coaching, including the ones we examine next: homeostasis, triangulation, family roles, and interactional force field.

Homeostasis

Organisms and human beings strive to maintain things just as they are. Whether we are happy about our situation or deeply distressed, our tendency is to remain attached to what we know instead of risking a change that plunges us into the unknown. This is why dysfunctional marriages last so long and why toxic corporate cultures are slow to change: we are more comfortable with what we know than we are with risking change. This concept is particularly important for a coach to grasp relative to how change occurs. To understand the power of homeostasis is to comprehend the profound work involved in helping a coachee make changes she asserts she wants to make.

In Coaching. Early in practice, a coach will often experience frustration with a client who seeks coaching in order to adjust a specific and long-standing behavior—say, a tendency to talk over people and generally talk too much and listen too little. The client seems motivated, her boss believes this is an important area of growth, and the client's team would likely benefit significantly by this change. So when the client repeatedly returns to the coaching sessions reporting no progress but "new fires" to put out, a coach ought not to be surprised. This is homeostasis at work, and it underlines the need for a coach to challenge at the right times, transparently share the observation that the reason the client came to coaching is continually eclipsed by the fire of the week, and spur the client to notice this so that together the coach and client can reflect on what's at play.

Triangulation

The concept of triangulation developed by family therapist Murray Bowen (1978) is of particular relevance in the work of coaching. Bowen found that when tensions rise between two individuals, the most common way to diffuse the stress and tension is to involve a third party. In fact, when Bowen was teaching medical students at the Menninger Clinic in Topeka, Kansas, he would give his medical students an assignment before leaving for the December holidays. He would ask them to notice how often over the family holiday they would observe one member of their family talking to another about a third member of the family in an effort to reduce stress and avoid more personal and direct conversations. Much like Bowen, Mary Beth O'Neill (2007) views triangulation as a mostly unconscious effort to reduce one's stress that typically results in protracting a difficult situation. We all find ourselves in these situations on a regular basis: Jane is upset with the way a member of her team managed a project and, what's more, Jane's boss is now unhappy with Jane about it. Instead of talking directly with her team member, Jane goes to a coworker, or two or three, and vents.

In Coaching. A coach often experiences this dynamic during the coaching session as the client talks to the coach about a third party (not present) instead of talking about herself. As the coach redirects the conversation and focuses solely on the client, the sense of immediacy and the appearance of emotion often surface because the conversation becomes more meaningful, and also riskier, for the client. It's far easier for the client to talk about another person and his or her faults and flaws than to consider what he or she can do and change about a particular interaction or situation. Triangulation can also happen very early in coaching when a coach is contacted to provide coaching for a person referred to as a "difficult leader," only to find out that the leader's boss finds this person difficult but never provides candid feedback to the individual. Hence, as the tension continues to rise for the boss, he calls in a third party to do what he has not done.

Family Roles

Family therapy literature provides several views on the common roles played in families and carried into adult life at work and at home. Virginia Satir (1988) outlined five commonly played family roles, each with a particular communication style:

- The Blamer—always finding fault in others, never in himself
- The Computer—always intellectualizing
- The Distracter—adept at taking the focus away from the important issue

- The Leveler—skilled at engaging in honest and direct communication
- The Placater—apologetic, tentative, and self-effacing

For Satir, the focus is on noticing patterns of behavior and stances in the world that show up at work and in one's adult life that are remnants of old family roles.

In Coaching. It's essential for coaches to understand the roles they are drawn to and the price and benefits of these roles. If a coach is prone to what Satir terms the placater role, this will have important implications for the coach and require a conscious effort to build more confidence and strength in order to meet the client's need for candid feedback, challenging, sharing observations, and continually focusing the work. An understanding of family roles will also prove useful to the coach when working with the client.

The Interactional Force Field

Mary Beth O'Neill (2007) uses this term to describe the power of the web of relationships (systems) at play, whether it is two, fifteen, or one hundred people. O'Neill reminds coaches that it is critical to "recognize how organizational systems affect you, including the ones you are in and the ones you co-create and it's equally important to attend to the system co-created between you and your client" (p. 52).

In Coaching. Every system develops a dance, and inside the coach-client relationship, it's vitally important to recognize this as the coach. In each coaching engagement, the coach is inevitably drawn into the client's repetitive patterns, and to the extent that the coach is able to discern these patterns, it is enormously valuable in the coaching work. The coach who can observe a client's pattern and artfully work to share this with the client creates a powerful in-the-moment shift that combines emotions and thoughts and paves the way for heightened awareness and change. Here is a series of examples. In the first set of examples, the coach inadvertently steps into the client's system without noticing and misses opportunities to address the client's actions and stories:

- The client comes to the session upset and tearful. The coach rushes for a tissue and works to soothe the client.
- The client comes to the session rambling and moving from one topic to another. The coach commiserates and listens.
- The client regularly calls at the last minute to change an appointment time. The coach tolerates it.
- The client continually wants to stay and talk longer than the allotted time. The coach tolerates it.

- The client is routinely late to pay the coaching invoice, and each time the coach needs to ask more than once before the invoice is paid. The coach tolerates this dance.

In this next series, notice how the coach uses the opportunity (and engages his self-as-coach awareness) to help the client access a blind spot or important part of his or her story that might be connected to important elements of the coaching contract:

- The client arrives at a session upset and tearful. The coach steps back, acknowledges the tears, allows the client a moment to reflect, and then asks what the tears are about.

- The client rambles from one topic to another. The coach transparently shares this observation and asks the client if she is aware of this pattern of getting off track.

- The client routinely calls at the last minute to change appointments. When this has occurred two or three times, the coach brings it up with the client, sharing some of her own reaction and wondering if and how this shows up in other parts of the client's life.

- The client regularly wants to extend the coaching session by saving the most important issues for last. The coach is clear about time boundaries at the beginning of coaching, and when this happens on two or three occasions, she shares the observation that the most important issues surface when the time is up and explores the client's awareness of this.

- The client is reticent to pay an invoice. The coach has been clear at the onset of coaching about the arrangement and transparently surfaces the invoice issue for open discussion directly with the client in the session and explores how this same dynamic may be at play in other areas of the client's life.

Systems thinking is foundational to the coaching methodology because it is present in every step of the coaching process. It begins when the first conversation is opened and as the external coach seeks to understand the needs of the organization, the roles of the boss, the human resource partner, and potential clients. It exists when crafting the aspirational and working goals with the client because these are aligned with the larger system, it shows up at an internal level when examining the natural resistance and obstacles to change, and it surfaces when we consider throughout the work how the effectiveness and the impact of the coaching will be evaluated. This requires coaches to manage their own internal system and observe the systems dance at play in each coaching session.

Level	Measurement Focus
Level 1: Reaction, satisfaction, and planned action	What are participant's reactions, and what do they plan to do with the material?
Level 2: Learning	What skills, knowledge, or attitudes have changed, and by how much?
Level 3: Job application and implementation	Was there behavior change, and did the participants apply what they learned on the job?
Level 4: Business impact	Did the on-the-job application produce measurable results?
Level 5: Return on investment	Did the monetary value of the results exceed the cost for the program?

Figure 8.5 Phillips Model for Measuring Outcomes
Source: Phillips (1996, p. 12).

OUTCOME RESEARCH

Outcomes and the measure of the impact and results of effective coaching are essential, and the work that ensures the ability to do this well begins when the first conversations occur with the client or the sponsor engaging a coach in the engagement. They then continue through careful, thorough contracting that focuses on adjustments and changes that the client is committed to and, when internal, that the organization is aligned with.

Jack Phillips (1996) developed a return-on-investment methodology that provides accountability through a measurement focus (Figure 8.5).

ETHICS IN COACHING

Ethical considerations are easy to overlook early in coaching, but it becomes obvious that ethics are at play everywhere in coaching. A short list of ethical issues might include

- Aligning the coach's competence with a particular coach engagement
- Considering arm's-length issues in agreeing to coach a client
- Issues of confidentiality and clear boundaries
- Professional behavior
- Record keeping

The following sources on ethics are useful:

De Jong, A. "Coaching Ethics: Integrity in the Moment of Choice." In J. Passmore (ed.), *Excellence in Coaching*. London: Association for Coaching, 2006.

Institute for Global Ethics, www.globalethics.org. The institute's Web site contains a wealth of resources on ethical issues and challenges.

International Coach Federation. 2005, 2008. Ethics code. http://coach federation.org/about-icf/ethics.

Kantor, R. (ed.). *Best Practice: Ideas and Insights from the World's Foremost Business Thinkers*. New York: Perseus, 2003.

Kidder, R. *How Good People Make Tough Choices: Resolving Dilemmas of Ethical Living*. New York: Fireside Press, 1996.

Maxwell, J. C. *There's No Such Thing as Business Ethics*. New York: Warner Books, 2003.

Zur, O., and Anderson, S. K. "Multiple-Role Relationships in Coaching." In P. Williams and S. K. Anderson (eds.), *Law and Ethics in Coaching: How to Solve and Avoid Difficult Problems in Your Practice*. Hoboken, N.J.: Wiley, 2006.

CHAPTER 9

THEORIES SUPPORTING SKILL-BASED COMPETENCIES

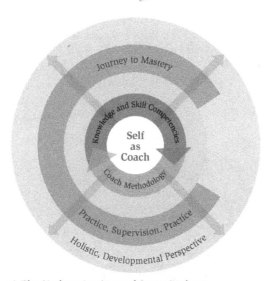

© The Hudson Institute of Santa Barbara

Thehe standard skill-based competencies in coaching are the basics of building a contract, building a trusting relationship, listening, asking good questions that build awareness and insight and create new ways of thinking about things, building action steps, designing plans for supporting change, and measuring results and outcomes. These basics are critical to great coaching and much more complex than a cursory glance might suggest. The tasks of learning to listen at profound levels and ask questions that are provocative and arise from a sense of curiosity are hefty challenges for coaches. And although it is not the purpose of this book to review each of these skills in depth, it is useful to highlight a few resources that are particularly helpful to coaches in the early stages of development:

Egan, G. *The Skilled Helper*. Pacific Grove, Calif.: Brooks/Cole, 2009. This book is specifically designed for helpers and counselors, but it thoroughly addresses many of the skills relevant to a coach and the underlying process that supports change.

Rogers, J. *Coaching Skills: A Handbook*. New York: McGraw-Hill, 2004. This book offers friendly, accessible, and practical tools and skill-building processes for deepening coaching skills.

Kimsey-House, H. *Co-Active Coaching*. Boston: Nicholas Brealey Publishing, 2011. This book is filled with helpful skill-building tools, and the coverage of listening skills is probably one of the best available.

Williams, P., and Menendez, D. S. *Becoming a Professional Life Coach: Lessons from the Institute of Life Coach Training*. New York: Norton, 2007. This book contains thorough coverage of many of the basic coaching skills, complete with useful case examples.

A COMPREHENSIVE METHODOLOGY FOR THE COACHING ENGAGEMENT

Every discourse, even a poetic or oracular sentence, carries with it a system of rules for producing analogous things and thus an outline of methodology.
—Jacques Derrida

PART FOUR

A COMPREHENSIVE
METHODOLOGY FOR THE
COACHING ENGAGEMENT

CHAPTER 10

METHODOLOGY: AN INTRODUCTION

The chapters in Part Four examine the necessity for a thorough coaching methodology based on knowledge-based competencies that inform the work of coaching and support the overall coaching engagement from the first introductory conversation to the final session. The essence of coaching lies in the art of supporting an individual toward an important change that leads to a more fulfilling future and addresses the changes and adjustments required in one's current life as a leader and human being. This sounds straightforward, but in reality, the essential elements needed to achieve this goal are quite complex for the coach. Here are just a few of the questions that are addressed in a sound methodology:

- What does a coach need to understand about herself in order to be effective in coaching another human being?
- How does the coach discern which clients are good fits with her background, approach, and style?
- How does the coaching engagement predictably unfold, and what occurs within each session?
- How does the coach reconcile the goals of the client with the overall goals of the organization in such a way that both are met?
- How does the coach assess the client's circumstances, readiness, learning style, and commitment to the work?

- How does the coach respond to client resistance?
- How does the coach build on the client's strengths?
- How does the coaching plan unfold?
- How are coaching outcomes measured?

All of these questions and more are on the minds of emerging and masterful coaches alike, and each demands careful examination.

Part Four focuses on the importance of a robust and reliable methodology that addresses the complexities of the coaching engagement from beginning to end, whether the goals of a coaching engagement are significant and the changes are deep, or the engagement is short term and highly focused. Several existing fields of study, including organizational development, clinical psychology, and related professions, teach us that a sound and reliable methodology is one of the most important elements in facilitating sustainable and lasting change. A grounded methodology allows a coach to consistently anchor the coaching work in essential ingredients known to be critical to the success of the work. A reliable methodology also provides the basis for studying and analyzing coaching cases within both the organizational and the individual contexts and ensures that best practices prevail. Both of these are essential for the health and sustainability of the field of coaching. Throughout the methodology discussion that follows, attention is given to what's unique in a coaching methodology when coaching a leader within the organizational (large or small) context and when engaging in transitional coaching work that might intersect with entering or departing from a leadership role, along with all of the predictable transitions in life that require the client to make important changes.

CHAPTER 11

A COACHING METHODOLOGY

The work of developing a complete methodology continues to mature in the evolving field of coaching. To date, the field has focused significant attention on understanding the essential skill-based competencies required of a coach, along with some knowledge-based competencies that support the work of a coach. Yet little has been written addressing a thoroughly coach-based methodology for the coaching engagement from beginning to end. Today the field relies on related methodologies that provide important insights into and overlaps with the work of coaching but do not thoroughly address the complexities of an overall coaching engagement; emerging coaching models that focus most thoroughly on the discrete coaching session; and models that fail to address the overall complexities of the coaching engagement or focus on the interface with the organizational system when coaching a leader inside an organization.

Twenty-five years of working with leaders and coaches, training coaches, and engaging in the work of coaching provides ample evidence for us that a thorough coaching methodology is an essential element for a coach in facilitating a successful engagement focused on lasting change for the client. When the field of coaching was in its infancy, there was naturally a heavy reliance on components of process models developed in adjacent fields of study to help understand and illuminate the important ingredients in a coaching methodology. As the field has grown, more models are developing specifically for coach engagements. Although there isn't a single source that currently addresses all of the key elements in great coaching, each model addressed in this chapter has proven invaluable in informing a thorough coaching methodology.

RELATED MODELS INFORMING A SOUND COACH METHODOLOGY

This chapter reviews the main frameworks and methodologies that inform Hudson's development of a comprehensive coach framework, along with an examination of the key concepts that prove most useful to a well-informed and comprehensive coaching methodology.

James Prochaska's Model

James Prochaska's early work in developing a transtheoretical model based on an examination and study of a variety of psychotherapeutic theories provides a broad change methodology that informs elements of an underlying coaching process (see Prochaska, DiClemente, and Norcross, 2002). Prochaska and DiClemente's's model has five stages of change (Figure 11.1): precontemplation (not ready), contemplation (getting ready), preparation (ready), action, and maintenance; sometimes termination (relapse) is added as a sixth stage.

Prochaska's work emphasizes several elements particularly important in a sound coaching methodology. He underscores the complexities at play in understanding the level of commitment the client has when deciding to make a change and underlines the importance of the client's emotional arousal as a prerequisite in gaining true commitment to a specific change. He also offers a core construct of decisional balance—working with the client to thoroughly weigh the pros and cons of a targeted change.

The specific details of Prochaska and DiClemente's (1982) stages of change model are described in Table 11.1, outlining characteristics and techniques of each stage along with techniques relevant to each stage of change.

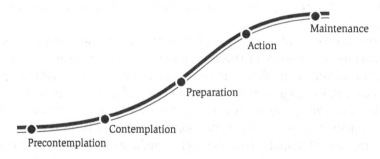

Figure 11.1 Prochaska and DiClemente's Five-Stage Model of Change

Source: Prochaska, DiClemente, and Norcross (2002).

Table 11.1 Features of Prochaska and DiClemente's Stages of Change Model

Stage of Change	Client Characteristics	Techniques
Precontemplation	Not currently considering change: "Ignorance is bliss"	Validate lack of readiness Clarify: decision is theirs Encourage reevaluation of current behavior Encourage self-exploration, not action Explain and personalize the risk
Contemplation	Ambivalent about change ("sitting on the fence") Not considering change within the next month	Validate lack of readiness Clarify: decision is theirs Encourage evaluation of pros and cons of behavior change Identify and promote new, positive outcome expectations
Preparation	Some experience with change and trying to change (testing the waters) Planning to act within one month	Identify and assist in problem solving on obstacles Help individual identify social support Verify that individual has underlying skills for behavior change Encourage small initial steps
Action	Practicing new behavior for three to six months	Focus on restructuring cues and social support Bolster self-efficacy for dealing with obstacles Combat feelings of loss and reiterate long-term benefits
Maintenance	Continued commitment to sustaining new behavior Extends from six months after completion of the coaching engagement to five years	Plan for follow-up support Reinforce internal rewards Discuss coping with relapse
Relapse	Resumption of old behaviors ("fall from grace")	Evaluate trigger for relapse Reassess motivation and barriers Plan stronger coping strategies

Although Prochaska's model is insufficient for a robust coaching methodology, his well-researched model provides powerful evidence that the internal change process of the individual unfolds slowly and requires careful analysis, reflection, practice, and uncovering at the cognitive and emotional levels with the client.

Limitations of Prochaska's Model

- Based solely on the study of psychotherapeutic approaches
- Narrowly focuses attention on the nuances of the change process rather than an overall high-level view of the coaching engagement
- Helpful across time but provides little to guide individual sessions

Concepts Useful in Coaching Methodology

- His attention to what is required in the deep work of change, including his focus on engaging the client in examining the commitment to a change
- His attention to the power of precontemplation and contemplation prior to moving quickly toward action.

Gerard Egan's Model

Throughout the 1990s, Gerard Egan's (2009) counseling methodology proved to be a helpful and practical lens into the unfolding coaching process. While Egan's model (see Figure 11.2) is based on a counseling premise and relies heavily on psychological concepts and language, it provides a thoughtful methodology that informs important elements of an overall coaching process, including an emphasis on establishing a strong working relationship, exploring the client's blind spots, understanding the blocks to change, and examining new possibilities in

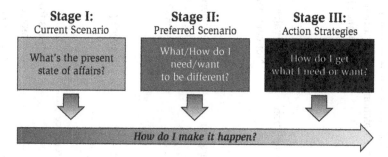

Figure 11.2 Egan's Problem-Based Counseling Approach
Source: Egan (2009).

the action planning phase. Egan also highlights what he terms the shadow-side challenges (common flaws and obstacles in the working alliance) of the counselor throughout the engagement, and this dynamic of understanding the inner work of the practitioner is equally important in the field of coaching.

Two limitations of Egan's approach are found in his emphasis on situation-specific work and problem-management thinking foundational in his approach. Although he also addresses opportunity management, his emphasis on situation-specific work makes it more difficult to set the stage for longer-term developmental work focused on the client's aspirational goals for the future.

The shift from thinking in a problem-solving management framework toward a more aspirational approach highlighting the behaviors and broad goals the client is seeking over a longer period of time turns out to be fundamental to lasting and transformative change.

Consider two very different approaches to a coaching challenge in the example: Bill seeks a coach in order to strengthen his ability to get up in front of his senior team and make a presentation that is compelling.

Two Approaches to a Coaching Challenge

A Problem-Solving Approach

This approach to Bill's challenge focuses on what's occurring on the surface and what Bill needs to change in order to be more successful in delivering a good presentation. The goal is for Bill to make stronger and more compelling presentations, and the work could include examining what Bill includes in his presentation and what he needs to do to make his presentations stronger. The problem-solving approach is focused on fixing a current problem with a focus on the immediate situation.

A Transformational and Developmental Approach

This approach to Bill's challenge focuses first on defining a broader aspirational goal that Bill is committed to living into: How does he want to experience himself in front of his senior team? How does he want others to experience him when he stands up and speaks?

Next, what obstacles might Bill be aware of? What happens as he is standing in front of his team? What is he aware of (for example, critical voices in his head or somatic signals), and where is a starting place that he is committed to working in order to ultimately garner respect and attention of his peers and direct reports in just about any situation? The transformational approach engages the client in a bigger vision of what he wants to aspire to and then examines the deeper obstacles that need to be uncovered in order to create a more lasting change. Throughout the transformative approach, the work is focused on a more enduring change that transcends a particular issue and allows the client to lean into an inspiring aspirational goal for oneself.

Limitations of Egan's Model

- Counseling based
- Problem solving is a dominant part of the model
- Situation-specific orientation
- Based on an individual framework only
- Insufficient attention to organizational dimensions

Concepts Useful to Coaching Methodology

- Building a strong coaching relationship
- Examining the client's blind spots
- Uncovering the client's blocks to making a change
- Exploring new possibilities
- Focusing on the counselor (in our case, the coach)

The GROW Model

Many in the field of coaching today rely heavily on the GROW model, an early articulation of this model by Max Landsberg (1999) of McKinsey and first published by John Whitmore (2009) as a useful coaching methodology. It has four stages:

- Goal (setting)
- Reality (checking)
- Options (and alternatives or courses of action)
- Will (to do it: What, When, Whom)

This model was originally developed as a system for problem solving or goal setting, and it has been modified and adjusted by many over time. There are elements of this model that prove very helpful in a coaching approach; however, much like Egan's approach, the GROW model veers toward a problem-solving stance in the work of coaching.

Perhaps equally important in distinguishing the value and limitations of this model, GROW is principally focused on the work inside individual sessions. This proves enormously helpful to the coach at the ground level but fails to provide the broader context for the work of the engagement.

Limitations of the GROW Model

- Focus is primarily on each discrete, individual coaching session rather than the broad and more complex framework
- Does not address the complexities of an overall coaching engagement
- Insufficient focus on the client's underlying obstacles and resistance

- Insufficient exploration of the client's commitment to the coaching work and agreed-on goals

Concepts Useful in Coaching Methodology

- The broad underlying process linking clear goals to outcomes
- Useful structure for individual coaching sessions

Hawkins's CLEAR Model

Peter Hawkins's CLEAR model, developed in the 1980s, builds on the GROW model and is used as a coaching process and a methodology in training coaches' supervisors as well (see Hawkins and Smith, 2006):

- Contracting
- Listening
- Exploring
- Action
- Review

Although Hawkins places a stronger emphasis on the power of review in the coaching process and the work of contracting, his model is focused on highlighting and examining a process for the individual coaching session without a thorough examination of the intricacies of a long-term engagement.

Limitations of the CLEAR Model

- Too broad and general to provide a detailed map for the work of the overall coaching engagement
- Insufficient focus on the client's underlying commitment and resistance

Concepts Useful in Coaching Methodology

- Emphasizes key elements inside each discrete coaching session
- Emphasizes contracting
- Highlights the importance of review in individual coaching sessions and the supervision process

O'Neill's Systems Model

Mary Beth O'Neill (2007) provides a broad systems model for coaching that is focused on identifying the targeted business results of the organization and then working with the team and individual members to link behavioral changes to the business targets. Her methodology includes these:

- Identifying business results currently needed
- Identifying team behaviors necessary to achieve those results

- Exploring leadership challenges the individual faces in working with the team to achieve the targeted results
- Reflecting on and identifying specific behaviors that individual leaders need to enhance or change in order to get to the target goals

Three factors are at play in O'Neill's model: the business results, the team's actions, and the individual leadership challenges that must be addressed to lead the overall process. The model provides a wider lens for understanding the coaching engagement, and yet it's quite specific to her team-based approach that uses a live action coaching approach.

Limitations of O'Neill's Model

- Largely focused on a systems approach that emphasizes working with the team whenever possible

Concepts Useful in Coaching Methodology

- The systems perspective is valuable to any coach working as an external coach to an organization.
- The focus on the leader's development and the business results is applicable to all coaches working as externals within an organization.
- O'Neill's attention to the complex relationship boundaries in the work of coaching is helpful to any coach working inside organizational systems.

In summary, the field of coaching has been slow to develop a thorough framework for working with individual and organizational clients within the context of their larger systems. The work of Prochaska, Egan, Landsberg, Whitmore, Hawkins, and O'Neill provides an important foundation for understanding many of the essential elements needed in an effective coaching methodology. Egan's work relies heavily on the field of counseling psychology and highlights specific situations, and often inside a problem-management approach. The GROW model provides an important view into the individual coaching sessions but doesn't adequately address the broader coaching methodology spanning from the initial discussion to the final session. O'Neill offers an overall coaching methodology within her team-based live action coaching model, an important expansion on a coaching methodology.

All of these models provide helpful perspectives in the development of a comprehensive coaching framework. What becomes abundantly clear in this review is the need for a comprehensive coaching methodology that is developmentally focused on the aspirational targets of the client within the broader context of the client's systems (team, organization, and others) and able to support both a micro- and macroview of the coaching engagement.

The Hudson model for coaching offers such a methodology that builds on the wisdom of existing research while creating a robust process that addresses the elements needed to provide a comprehensive structure for a coach in a long-term engagement.

THE HUDSON MODEL FOR COACHING: AN OVERVIEW

A short review of our first edition traces Hudson's development in articulating the essential elements in a coaching methodology. We originally proposed a general coaching approach that on the whole remains a strong scaffolding for the work of a coach.

Hudson's Early Model for Coaching

In the formative days of coaching, a stronger emphasis was placed on the coaching conversation in the belief that a sturdy, resonant relationship would be sufficient in helping clients make the changes they were targeting. Although it's clear today that the coaching relationship—the working alliance—is the crucible for facilitating lasting change, we also understand that much more is required to guide the overall engagement. Clear goal setting, development of an aspirational macrogoal along with specific behavioral goals, the client's thorough commitment and coaching readiness, and exploration of obstacles to change and strengths that will support change must be present in the coaching methodology in order to support coaches in facilitating change that is lasting for the client.

Through years of action-based research in the development of thousands of coaches, leaders, and managers around the globe, what has emerged is a robust and thorough methodology that supports the coach in developing a coaching engagement that fosters sustainable, transformative change for today's leader. The methodology has five key stages (Figure 11.3):

1. Establish the coaching contract.
2. Understand the current situation and the inspired future.
3. Build the plan.
4. Execute the plan.
5. Conclude the coaching engagement.

In broad terms, this framework remains quite consistent with the early version outlined in the first edition, and it generally aligns with several dimensions

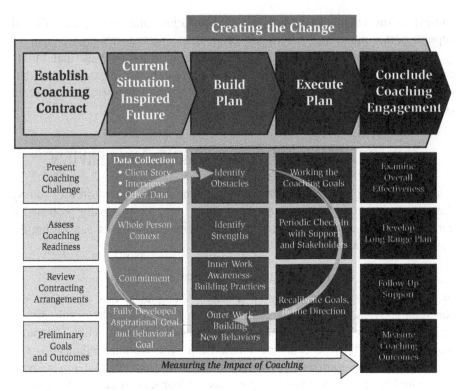

Figure 11.3 Hudson Coaching Methodology
© Hudson Institute of Santa Barbara.

of each of the coaching methodologies already discussed. As the research and literature in the field of coaching continue to grow, it's reassuring to begin to observe significant agreement and overlap in a pragmatic methodology for coaching.

Yet there are key refinements and differences in this framework that seek to provide a deeper layer of structure addressing the complexities of the work of a coach and highlighting the subtleties that must be exposed in order to create deep and lasting change:

- Examining the readiness of the client
- Attending to contracting complexities and essential elements inside a work system
- Conducting stakeholder interviews, particularly inside work systems
- Articulating an aspirational goal that a client is inspired to move toward

- Articulating specific changes the client is committed to addressing in the coaching

- Examining the obstacles that will need to be explored and overcome in order to get to the aspirational goals

- Identifying client strengths that will support the pathway to the over-arching aspirational goals

- Emphasizing the interplay of the inner work of the client that supports the outer work of behavioral change

- Building a thorough plan that supports the client in making the stated changes in behavior and ways of being

- Creating an explicit plan for routinely connecting to key stakeholders in the client's system, particularly when the work is inside an organization

- Building practices in the action phase of coaching that incrementally create a pathway for successful change

- Measuring the impact of the coaching engagement on the overall goals of the organization

Coach practitioners need a thorough yet agile framework that provides ample support in examining each of the necessary steps in the unfolding process. The goal of facilitating lasting change turns out to be a mammoth order that requires more than an overarching gap analysis or a framework for each individual coaching session. Instead, there are important areas of deep exploration and structured tasks and practices along the pathway that set the stage for long-term change to occur.

Our original model covered the enduring basics of a coaching engagement; however, it lacked sufficient consideration of the nuances and complexities in a coaching process that support long-term change. Our updated model expands our original framework by taking the core principle from each step in the coaching process and expanding and strengthening key elements in order to provide a comprehensive methodology that is adaptable and flexible.

Hudson's Updated Coach Methodology

I hope this overview has provided a sense of the evolution of an overall methodology in the field of coaching from the early counseling methodologies (Prochaska, Egan) that provided guidance in the development of our original methodology in 1999 through the review of recent contributions by Landsberg, Whitmore, Hawkins, and O'Neill in this area. This is how sound professional practice emerges, and it is impressive to trace the development in this arena over the past several years.

In a snapshot, the modifications in Hudson's current methodology incorporates these shifts:

From	To
Hudson's original methodology	A more comprehensive methodology that is agile and flexible given the specific needs of a coaching engagement and thoroughly addresses each of the elements of a complex coaching engagement from inception to conclusion
Egan's problem-solving framework	An aspirational approach that highlights the behaviors and goals of a client that transcend a discrete problem
The GROW and CLEAR models' emphasis on problem solving and review within individual sessions	Consideration for the larger scope and the broader context of the coaching engagement
O'Neill's model focusing on the system and using a specific live-action-based methodology with the team and the leader	Consideration for a broader methodology addressing any variety of coaching situations that might not fully engage all members of the team or use a live-action coach approach

Recall the elements of masterful coaching introduced in Chapter Four (and set out in Figure 4.1) highlighting the four essential and integrative elements that novices must grasp in order to become master coach practitioners. One of the foundational building blocks is a solid coaching methodology, an element that interconnects with the others and results in a robust and integrated coaching approach.

Hudson's revised methodology seeks to provide an approach that addresses both the overall coaching process from beginning to end at a high level and the complex and nuanced work that must occur at each stage in the coaching in order to maximize the potential for sustainable change. While the methodology appears as predictable, logical, and linear, it never unfolds in such an organized manner. Instead, it is designed to provide a flexible and agile framework for the coach highlighting essential elements rather than a dogmatic dictum that must be rigidly adhered to with every client in all situations. Moreover, not all portions of the methodology will be relevant to all clients or in all situations. Each element of the methodology, whether being used on its own or in conjunction with other pieces, is adaptable and flexible to each individual coaching situation.

The transition client who wants to explore the territory of the retirement chapter of life represents quite a different engagement from the client inside an organization who needs to learn how to manage a new team and overcome some behaviors others view as problematic. In general, leadership coaching engagements typically incorporate the essential complexities of the system at play from three-way interviews, to stakeholder interviews, and the ongoing work of gleaning support from key parties, along with the continual feedback loop with those individuals. The attention to tracking and measuring outcomes that matter to both the client and the organization is crucial in successful leadership coaching and in an enduring profession. Transition coaching is generally focused on the coach, and the client and work system is typically not a key element in the coaching work. Our revised methodology provides the flexibility and adaptability to work in both of these very different coaching situations.

Whether the coaching engagement is inside an organization or transition coaching work, this methodology supports the important approach of leading from behind, with the coach leading the underlying process of the coaching, holding the client accountable for the specific changes he (and in the case of leadership coaching, the organization) has committed to, facilitating with the client a deepened understanding of the obstacles to the changes, and jointly developing an action plan with the client. However, the coach is always walking slightly behind or alongside the client in this unfolding process rather than getting out ahead of the client and taking a fix-and-tell mode of problem solving and mentoring.

Throughout this methodology, the focus is on the coach who is engaged as an external coach working inside an organization (large or small) or a transition coach working with a client around one of life's natural transitions. The vignettes and examples represent these two quite different coaching engagements. The coaching approach for a manager is examined in depth in Part Six, where the roles of the internal coach and the manager as coach are discussed. Naturally there are many overlaps, but there are also several important distinctions that are explored later in this book.

THE PRECONTRACTING STAGE

Most coaches think of coaching beginning at the first stage with the contracting phase, but in reality there is a precontracting phase that is easy to overlook but essential to acknowledge. This stage precedes the first meeting or two with the prospective client and requires keen attention.

Ethical issues are always at play in the work of a coach and often overlooked at this precontracting phase. Peter Hawkins (2011) has a great caveat: "Beware of the coach who can't see and articulate ethical issues at play in any given coaching engagement." This phase is typically filled with potential ethical dilemmas the coach must examine, including these:

- The arm's-length rule (separate parties without a special relationship)
- The door you enter through (proper channels, back door)
- Alignment of requested work and your areas of expertise
- Your thorough and honest assessment of your availability
- Careful examination of any biases and values clashes relative to this individual or system

Consider these situations:

• *A conflict of interest.* You receive a call from Jack, the leader of a small tech start-up. He received your name from a colleague you had coached. Jack wants to strengthen his presence to be able to be more effective with a prospective investor in his company. During the course of the conversation, you realize that he is describing a situation that is familiar to you. You have heard this same story before, but from the investor—and it's clear that Jack's experience was quite different from what the investor experienced. That you have a work relationship with the investor he wants to influence creates a conflict of interest. You decide the best ethical decision is to explain there may be some dual relationship issues at play here and he is going to be better off working with a coach who does not have these conflicts. You make sure to provide time for Jack to ask any questions and feel clear about your dilemma, and you also provide him with two recommendations of coaches that would be good choices for him.

• *An arm's length.* A good friend and colleague asks if you might be able to coach her son. He's beginning his final year of college, trying to make a good decision about whether to pursue a career track or continue on into graduate school. Her son is well informed about coaching and quite interested in the opportunity to explore his options with an impartial third-party. As you continue to explore the possibility, your colleague shares his frustrations and his hopes for his son relative to next steps. It doesn't take you long to determine that there is insufficient arm's length here, and you could quickly find yourself in a very difficult situation. You decline the opportunity and provide your colleague and friend with two referrals who will serve his son better than you might under these circumstances.

• *A values clash.* You receive a call from the senior vice president of human resources in a global organization. She has heard of your coaching work from a mutual friend and colleague in another organization and wants to talk about your availability for engaging in a series of executive coaching assignments in her organization. The engagements are in your specialty area and entail working with executives in the United States and South America. You have spent a good deal of time in working with leaders in Argentina and Brazil and understand of some of the cultural nuances important in work such as this. What's more, the fee for the work is quite attractive. Now for the dilemma: the entire mission of this organization is at odds with your values and beliefs.

Attention to this early precontracting phase helps the coach set the course, make important decisions about whether to enter the work, and pay close attention to all that leads up to the request for coaching. The referral source, the stated reasons for the coaching, the organization's perception of coaching, the reasons the potential client has reached out, and the way the organization communicates provide important information to the coach. Here is a set of questions that are helpful for a coach to consider before the first face-to-face contracting session with a potential client:

- Have I clearly outlined what coaching is and isn't, what sorts of issues are well suited for coaching, and what the client needs to bring to the work (motivation, time, some clarity) in order to reach success? Have I done this in my materials and over the phone with the potential coachee?
- Have I gained a general sense of the coachable targets and issues and believe these are well within my area of expertise and comfort?
- Have I given the client or client organization an overview of myself as a professional coach, and have I invited the client to ask any questions about me, my coaching experience, approach, background, and so on?
- Have I adequately explained the generalities of how I work by phone, e-mail, or in person—such matters as frequency of meetings, stakeholder interviews, assessments, and tools?
- Have I discussed issues of confidentiality, boundaries, and ethical guidelines?
- Have I outlined general pricing, payment agreements, missed appointment protocol, and other matters?
- Have I briefly spoken with the human resource partner or sponsor to understand his or her desired outcomes and to explain how I work, emphasizing both confidentiality and transparency?
- Have I carefully examined any potential ethical issues?

If a client or organization is surprised by your approach midway into the coaching, it's a clear signal to you that you likely did not do the important pre-work of providing critical information about how you work, what your experience and background bring to the work, and seeking to fully understand their expectations. It's often helpful to include information in your packet of materials on what coaching is and isn't, including the helpful distinctions articulated in Part One of this book relative to coaching, consulting, counseling, and facilitating. Even with this explanation, complexities and surprises arise. Consider this coaching vignette:

Coaching or Consulting?

You've been engaged to provide coaching inside an organization where coaching is new. Its leaders have heard great things about the results colleagues have achieved through coaching work and they are interested in giving it a try. You receive a call because of a mutually respected colleague and you have a short conversation over the phone. You agree to send contact information and your Web site for further information and set up a first meeting.

You arrive at the meeting believing you have provided a clear picture of what coaching is and how it might differ from an experience of using a consultant to tackle a specific problem situation. As you sit in the meeting with the senior vice president of human resources, what surfaces as the most important issue is a growing concern about the organization's declining market share during the current economic downturn. The human resource partner wants you to coach three of the company's top leaders and make recommendations to identify strategies that will increase their sales by 9 percent over the next twelve months.

It's clear to you that this organization needs consulting, not coaching, and perhaps you could not have identified this until you met face-to-face and explored the organization's needs and challenges. You let your contact know that his needs are much more in the consulting domain than the coaching and provide a referral to two consultants she might want to reach out to in this area. You also share your thinking about under what circumstances coaching might prove a useful approach, and you both agree to continue to check in with one another in the coming months.

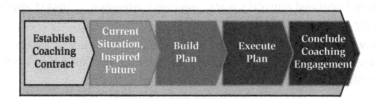

STAGE ONE: ESTABLISH THE COACHING CONTRACT

The real hands-on coaching begins when the first coaching meeting occurs (over the phone or, optimally, in person). This is when the coach and client get acquainted and explore the workability of the relationship—the chemistry of the interaction and the connection around background and experience. They explore together the coachable territory. The mechanics of the coaching agreement are outlined, covering how and when to proceed. It has four essential elements:

1. Present the coaching challenge.
2. Assess coaching readiness.
3. Review contracting arrangements.
4. Come to an understanding of preliminary goals and outcomes.

Present the Coaching Challenge

Most often an urgent issue brings a client to coaching. Perhaps it's been recommended by a superior, or it's the prospect of a promotion or being overlooked for a promotion; sometimes it's developmental feedback that is important to address, or a career dilemma that causes an individual or the sponsor in an organization to reach out and ask you to consider coaching a particular individual. Whether the nudge is an internal prompting felt by the client or an external request relative to a behavior change or area of development, something pressing and important brings a client to the coaching engagement. The earliest conversation begins with an understanding and appreciation for the current situation.

Although the primary coaching challenge will evolve as you are further down the road, it's important to gain an early perspective on what's most important to the client and what challenges bring this individual to you for coaching. There will be ample opportunity later to make necessary adjustments to aspirations and goals once you've completed the work of gathering relevant information (data from the boss and human resource partner, stakeholders, assessment data, and a holistic context) and built a complete picture of the current situation.

Assess Coaching Readiness

The client's readiness for coaching is an important step that allows the coach to discern the client's ability to effectively engage in coaching. Coaching isn't a successful approach for everyone; it requires true motivation, willingness to engage in reflective practices, an ability to invite and entertain feedback on a regular basis, and an innate interest in one's own development as a human being and as a leader.

Key questions and observations on the part of the coach at this early stage yield important information about readiness—for example:

- "Coaching requires both a time commitment to the coaching sessions and a commitment to practices and strategies that will support the changes you are targeting. Are you in a place in your work and your life to carve out the time that's required to do this work now?"
- "Coaching can often be uncomfortable in exploring how others view your current behaviors, your strengths, and your areas of development. How open and comfortable are you in seeking regular feedback from those who work with and for you and those you report to?"
- "Coaching is about developing practices and strategies to make changes in your own behavior that will get you closer to your desired goals. It is not about me, as coach, telling you what you need to do. How prepared are you to explore your own behaviors and motivations?"

It's common for a leader to receive encouragement, a strong recommendation, or at times a requirement from his boss or human resource partner to obtain a coach in order to address new stretch goals or some areas the boss views as critical for the success of the leader. In these situations, coachability factors take time to tease apart. It's natural that a leader might have some initial resistance to the idea of coaching when it is recommended by a superior. In these circumstances, it's important to explore the dynamics with all parties, including a particularly candid conversation with the potential client in order to discern the client's commitment to the work of coaching.

Terry Bacon and Karen Spear make the case in their book *Adaptive Coaching* (2003) that individuals with some psychological issues and disorders render coaching a less viable choice. Examples are serious psychological disorders, including the narcissistic personality, substance abuse, and complex medical issues.

A client's inability to accept feedback, and in many cases actively resist and deflect it, is an important red flag that results in a very low coachability rating on their scale; the unmotivated or complacent client is another signal for the coach that coachability is in question. Table 11.2 provides a good reminder that careful examination of Bacon and Spear's coachability factors will yield critical data about whether to proceed in developing a coaching relationship with a potential client.

The experienced coach will readily discern coachability conflicts, boundary issues, and systemic symptoms that create red flags in the potential workability and success of a coaching engagement. Coaches who are just building their practice and in the early development of their own skills will often find themselves signing on to a coaching contract when there are signals that the

Table 11.2 Bacon and Spear's Coachability Scale

CO	Not coachable at present	Identified psychological issues
C1	Extremely low coachability	Narcissistic personality
C2	Very low coachability	Resists or defies feedback
C3	Fair coachability	Complacent/unmotivated to change
C4	Good coachability	Assessment comes as wake-up call
C5	Very good coachability	Earnest desire to improve
C6	Excellent coachability	Has intrinsic need to grow

coachee is simply not ready for coaching. Novice coaches may be tempted to believe they can create change in the least coachable of clients. It takes time, experience, and transparent and direct conversations with the potential client to thoroughly assess the readiness and coachability factors. The case of John is a good example.

How Motivated Is John?

John had been promoted from an important individual contributor role where he exceeded anyone's expectations in meeting numbers and critical project deadlines in the information technology division of his organization. When it came time to look for a new team leader, John was a natural choice because of his track record on both counts.

Two months into his new role, things weren't going very well, and that's where the coach was called in. Jack, the coach, had worked with others in this organization and knew the HR team quite well. He received a call explaining that John needed to "skill-up quickly" if he was going to survive and thrive in his new leadership role. The HR contact thought that Jack could help coach John to make some key adjustments and asked if he could do an initial interview the following week.

Jack agreed. The work seemed clear, he expected John to be eager to be better positioned as the team leader, and he knew the organization found coaching to be important.

After six weeks of coaching John, the coach realized he had jumped in too quickly without adequately assessing John's interest. John had never managed or led a team in the past, and although his single-minded approach that worked well as an individual contributor was not serving him in his new leadership role, he had little motivation to adjust.

Review Contracting Arrangements

A high-level review at this early stage provides a road map for the work ahead and carefully outlines logistics (meeting arrangements, pricing, timing, and length of engagement, for example) and issues of confidentiality, ethics in coaching, and the overall details of the stages of the engagement. This is the nuts-and-bolts contracting agreement that precedes the heart of the coaching work and the development of coaching goals and sets the stage for clear understandings and expectations. In some cases, much of this information is included in a mailed or electronic packet before the first meeting and covered in more detail in the early conversation. Table 11.3 illustrates the standard areas of discussion and exploration.

Table 11.3 Coaching Contract Details

What coaching is and isn't	Clearly explain how coaching works and how it is different from counseling, consulting, and other professional services. Explore the potential client's understanding of coaching and any past experiences with it.
Confidentiality	Communicate the levels of confidentiality (particularly critical in complex organizational settings) a client can count on. Identify and explore concerns the potential client may have in this important domain.
Frequency	Discuss the optimal frequency of the coaching, and jointly explore what will be most effective in this coaching engagement.
Length of engagement	Discuss broad parameters of the length of the engagement, linking to the complexities of the work and the coaching goals. The length may not be entirely clear until the overall goals of the engagement are examined in depth.
Length of each session	Discuss the typical length of each session and any standard variations that often occur with longer face-to-face sessions at the beginning, somewhere midpoint, and again at the conclusion of the engagement.
Cancellation of session policies	Clarity about cancellation policies strengthens your contract and allows you to freely engage in conversations when cancellations occur. It's standard to ask for a twenty-four- to forty-eight-hour cancellation notice in order to avoid a charge. It's important to provide your client with assurance that you will not cancel an appointment barring a major emergency.
Modality (in person, by phone, or some other means)	The rhythm of face-to-face and over-the-phone sessions varies by coach and by client situation.

Location	Contrary to popular opinion, good coaching does not occur over a cup of coffee in a local coffee shop. It's important to meet in a location that offers privacy.
Pricing	Pricing variables fluctuate according to the level of the leader, the complexity of the challenges, the geographical marketplace, and industry standards. A package fee rather than an individual session rate is common in leadership coaching.
Assessments, stakeholder information, and other relevant client data	Coaching inside an organization is almost always going to benefit from engaging in stakeholder interviews. It's important to lay the groundwork for this at this early stage to normalize this process. Use of assessments is typically customized to meet the needs and the issues the client is facing rather than a standard assessment for all situations. In many cases, assessment data already exist for the client and may prove useful.
Organizational considerations	Gain an understanding of organizational protocol around leadership coaching from your client and human resource sponsor.
Measures of success and outcomes	Briefly provide your client with a sense of how the two of you will measure success and monitor measurable outcomes throughout the coaching engagement.
Feedback and observation styles and preferences	Openly and directly discuss the role of feedback and observations in coaching. Asking, "Do you like the sandpaper or soft blanket approach to feedback?" is useful at the early stage. It allows the client to reflect on how he or she is most comfortable receiving feedback and provides the coach with important information in terms of adjusting his or her style to fit the client's needs.
Explanation of the coach's approach (for example, direct or transparent)	Coaches discuss how they operate inside the coaching sessions and elicit information from clients about how they like to receive feedback from the coach, get challenged by the coach, be held accountable, and so forth.
A caveat to the coach	It may be tempting for the early coach to provide the client with the coaching methodology, but given the reality that it is an agile and flexible model that serves as a support for the coach rather than the client, it's best to use it in that manner rather than viewing it as a rigid process for the client to follow.

In most cases there are two or three layers to this early conversation when coaching inside an organization. The first conversation most often occurs between the HR partner and the coach to determine whether you, as coach, might be a good fit for the organization and the client. The next conversation likely occurs with the potential client (in most cases, the leader will have an opportunity to interview more than one coach and make a choice), and finally a three- or four-way conversation among you, the coach, the HR partner, the boss, and your client may take place now or once the coaching fully commences.

New coaches may be tempted to view these conversations as largely procedural, covering all of the coaching logistics. Instead, it's important at this early stage to listen carefully and ask thoughtful questions that yield helpful information about how the system works, how all parties view the coaching engagement, and how to work effectively with everyone while managing confidentiality and boundaries appropriately.

Come to an Understanding of Preliminary Goals and Outcomes

This is a very early stage in the coaching process, and while you have not jointly gathered all of the essential elements of the coachee's story (interviews, assessment information, whole person perspective, style, and preference information), it is helpful to come to a preliminary understanding of what the two of you believe the broadest goals will be in the coaching engagement before taking the next step. This first articulation of goals will naturally become more complex and nuanced as you enter the second stage of the coaching engagement, but this becomes a platform for the important steps ahead.

The conversation about broad goals at this early stage might go something like this:

> Carol, we've covered the important elements of this coaching engagement including important details of how often we'll meet, when we'll do so in person, and when we'll conduct sessions via phone. We've talked about how important confidentiality is and the ways I, as your coach, will manage confidentiality. At this stage, we have agreed that you are committed to further development of your leadership skills in order to maximize your current impact and position yourself for any future advancements.
>
> We are going to seek information from key folks you work with as we progress, but for now, we agree that you are interested in increasing your ability to inspire your team, communicate even better with your team, and gain their buy-in to meet new and demanding deadlines with a feeling of team cooperation. Do I describe the broad goals as you see them? And if we were to speculate about how these changes might impact you and your team, you've highlighted three areas: positioning yourself for being considered for upcoming promotion possibilities; building stronger skills in inspiring the best from your team, resulting in better output, retention, and overall satisfaction; and examining any aspects of your communication style and approach that might impede any parts of the above.

The Coach's Checklist

The following checklist sets out some questions for the coach that are useful in this stage:

Stage One Checklist of Questions for the Coach

- ☐ Have I made a good connection with this client and conveyed my interest in working with the client, my respect, and my sense of service in moving forward with this engagement?

- ☐ Am I confident I've explored the coachability factors in this situation and deemed that this client is coachable and that the organization is onboard to fully support this coaching effort?

- ☐ Have I had a preliminary meeting with the HR partner or the boss, or both of them, and ascertained their intentions and cleared their commitment to the success of this leader? (A coach doesn't want to uncover midway into the engagement the reality that a client does not have the true support of his boss and perhaps coaching is being sought as a final step in encouraging this person to leave the company.)

- ☐ Have I adequately shared enough details of the methodology to provide the HR partner and boss with a sense of all aspects of the coaching engagement? (Although the entire methodology is seldom shared with the client, it is very helpful in providing a clear mapping of the process for the organization.)

- ☐ Have we jointly reviewed all of the important details of the coaching contract and the next steps?

- ☐ Do we jointly have a sense of the general coaching goals at this early stage of our work, knowing these goals will be adjusted and refined as we move forward?

- ☐ Have I allowed ample time and access for this client to ask any questions of me that are important in making the decision to move forward in the engagement?

- ☐ Have I attempted to increase the readiness of a potential client who exhibits significant resistance by exploring the benefits of the work to the client and jointly examining what the client knows about the nature of his or her resistance?

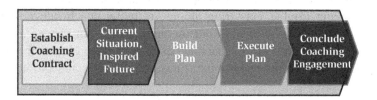

STAGE TWO: UNDERSTAND THE CURRENT SITUATION AND INSPIRED FUTURE

Stage Two lays the groundwork for the success of the entire coaching engagement. This stage necessitates a close partnership with the client in order to develop a thorough perspective on what's currently working and what's not; how other key individuals view the client's strengths, weaknesses, and areas for continued development; and how styles, preferences, and aptitudes inform the overall picture. This stage takes time—often longer than an early coach anticipates. It's not unusual when working at senior leadership levels to spend 25 to 35 percent of the coaching engagement focused on the first two stages in this methodology.

When a coach isn't supported by a sturdy methodology and all that we know about how to facilitate change, there can be a tendency to view the work as aiding the client in fixing a problem, a transactional approach that significantly reduces the power of coaching and the hope for lasting change. In our developmental approach to coaching, the focus is on helping the client to gain a comprehensive understanding of his or her current situation and all that is not working optimally. It's even more important to work with the client to gain clarity about the future the client is reaching for, the changes the client is committed to addressing, and the link these changes have to the broader team and organization in which they are engaged.

Before the client's coaching goals can be fully developed, the coach and client need to gather information from all existing sources that fill in the full picture of what's true today and what goals and behavioral changes will be important for the future. This examination includes valuable information from key stakeholders, information gleaned from assessments, and a holistic view of the client. Once all of this information has been gathered and synthesized, the coach and client, in partnership with the boss and in many cases the HR partner, craft the clear aspirational and supporting behavioral goals that address the client's interests and align with the organization. This is a dynamic and complex process that requires time and diligence on the part of the coach in order to build a true contract for change that is informed by all key parties.

Throughout these early steps in the coaching process, the goal is to shift from a problem orientation about a specific issue to an aspirational future orientation focused on development of the client's capacities. Clients and client systems invariably seek out coaching because they are stuck with something they are having trouble mastering alone. Yet if the coach allows the focus of the work to be on the deficit, and therefore a problem viewed as needing to be solved, the nature of the coaching shifts from deep change to a transactional to-do list, with the coach often in the role of fixer and problem solver.

When the coach shifts the exploration from a problem orientation to an aspirational orientation, the client's ownership of the targeted change and his or her motivation increase. A positive vision of what's possible inspires a client to make changes and adjustments in his or her current state much more than focusing on problems and areas of deficits that need to be adjusted.

This stage in the coaching process requires thoroughness and patience, and each of the key elements in it needs to be addressed in order to build a sound contract that is linked to measurable outcomes easily observed by all of the relevant members of the client's system.

Coaches often want to know how long each of the stages of the coaching methodology takes relative to the overall engagement. Of course, this is quite variable, but if stakeholder interviews are a part of the work, it is quite likely the first two stages of this methodology represent 25 to 35 percent of the overall coaching engagement. While the bulk of the work is in stages three and four (60 to 70 percent), the foundation laid in this and stage one provides the basis for lasting change that in most cases turns out to be quite transformative for the client.

There are four elements in stage two:

1. Data collection
2. Whole person context
3. Commitment
4. Fully developed aspirational and behavioral goals

Data Collection

Effective coaching rarely occurs in a vacuum. Leaders work inside teams and larger systems, and a client's self-perception can often vary considerably from how others at various levels in the company experience the client. That's how systems work: our self-perception is limited by our own beliefs, preferences, and blind spots. Coaches must carefully gain a sense of the current situation of clients from all angles in the leader's system before jointly building a picture of a desired future with the client. Together client and coach create the plan for how they will collect data and from whom it will be collected. The three main areas of data are the client's story, stakeholder interviews, and any additional supplemental information available about the client.

The Client's Story. At this stage, the coach begins to strengthen the working alliance with the client and understand life through the mind, heart, and body of the client, carefully examining what's working and what's not for her. A thorough understanding of the current situation requires more than simple data collection. A coach needs deep listening and connecting skills and the well-honed ability to genuinely connect with the client and convey the all-important message to gain the client's trust and confidence and hear the most important parts of the client's story: "We are on the same team, working together." The ability to step into the client's shoes just long enough to see the situation from her perspective is essential. The ability to step outside the client's life and ask questions, probe, and challenge the client to see her situation from additional perspectives is a key skill in the art of coaching. Human beings live inside long-held stories that are often out of awareness and powerful guiding forces in one's life. A pivotal part of the work of the coach is to be fully present with the client in order to hear these stories and perceive the power and influence of these stories on the client's life, decision making, and thinking. Cross-cultural contexts, gender differences, and age-related nuances will surface at this step in the process if the coach is astute and able to discern these contextual dynamics a client might inhabit.

It's here that you as coach must probe by asking questions and providing mirroring feedback telling the client what you've heard and how you hear it relating to the overall story you are hearing. Listen and contextualize, always with tentativeness, by asking, "Do I have it about right?" It's usually helpful to ask the client to provide examples that typify the current situation. If the client tells a story of feeling ineffective as the leader of her team, inquire about specific examples where she believes she was operating effectively and ineffectively. These stories rapidly engage the client's head and heart and often serve to cultivate the client's commitment to change.

In a short time, a coach will have a picture of the current situation according to how the client views it and her sense of the changes she believes she will need to make in order to move toward a more desirable future. If the gap between the client's current situation and aspirational goals is too wide, the coach may consider how to foster a short-term plan with challenging but not impossible goals. Never tell clients that their desired future is unreachable; ask them what they think and how they would get there, and provide realistic feedback on those details. Let the client stay in charge of the plan. The goal is for the two of you to formulate realistic plans so that the client can freely imagine the future she really wants.

Stakeholder Interviews. When the coaching takes place inside an organization, whether large or small, there are key interviews to consider and plan for with the client in order to gain a global perspective on the client's current situation and the strengths and areas of growth others see as important for her. It's not uncommon to experience some resistance from the client in engaging in these interview conversations, particularly in the many organizational cultures that do not see this as standard in coaching engagements. In those cases, it's helpful to provide the client with the sound rationale and your own experience with the enormous advantages of this approach for your client.

The Key Interview with the Boss and HR Partner. A coach who is working with a leader inside an organization is entering a complex system, and it's important to rapidly gain alignment with the key sponsors of the coaching engagement and facilitate and encourage an open and transparent conversation among client, boss, HR partner, and coach. Careful work facilitating this conversation eliminates backstage conversations (the candid conversations occurring after the explicit conversation), triangulation (indirect conversations where the third person being discussed is not privy or present), and unclear expectations about the goals and the outcomes all parties agree on for the coaching engagement. O'Neill (2007) provides a thorough articulation of the three-way (and potentially four-way) interviews that need to occur at the beginning, often in the middle, and again at the conclusion of the coaching engagement. She emphasizes the need for the coach to bring all key players to the meeting in order to model and create an environment of transparency that allows all parties to share their sense of the current situation, their concerns, and their hopes and goals for the coachee relative to the overall coaching engagement.

The meeting typically begins with the coach explaining that the purpose of this meeting is to make sure all parties are aligned and moving toward the same goal: the client's success. It's important to emphasize the need for frank comments and transparency in order to maximize the opportunity for success. It's also essential to thoroughly discuss confidentiality and create ground rules for how communication will occur as the coaching begins.

The following questions might form a potential agenda in this meeting:

- What would you like to see us accomplish as a result of this coaching?
- What outcomes would you consider success indicators along the way?
- What would the impact be on the team or department if these changes occurred?
- How will the organization benefit from the client's development in these areas?
- What do you, as the client's boss, view as the critical areas of development and change?
- Within what time frame are you hoping this will be accomplished?
- Are there any adjustments you might make to increase this leader's opportunity for success?
- How would you like to have this leader communicate progress to you?

O'Neill stresses the necessity of the coach to be able to see the system at play and recognize the role of the client inside the system. She provides two useful models to illuminate the challenges of understanding the dynamics of a system and coaching effectively inside a system.

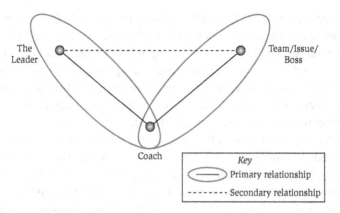

Figure 11.4 Client Rescue Model
Source: O'Neill (2007).

In her first model, termed the rescue model (Figure 11.4), the coach enters the system without sufficient awareness of the system dynamics and the boundaries she has to honor and reinforce in order to empower the client. In the rescue model, the coach becomes the go-between and weakens the link between the client and the boss and team. It can be summed up by an example. Imagine that in a brief conversation you had with the boss prior to this meeting, the boss says to you, "If things don't improve in the next five or six months, she's out of here." When you ask the boss if this has been clearly communicated to your client, he responds, "No way. That's part of what I want you to do!" The coach thus in effect disempowers the client by believing the goal of the coaching is in rescuing the client and satisfying the boss's dilemma. This is precisely the opposite of what a carefully constructed agenda and set of explicit ground rules supports, and it underlines the need for the coach to be fully prepared for this important meeting to set the stage for how the coaching proceeds in a manner that empowers the client and the client's relationship to the boss.

In order to stay away from the rescue model, it will be important for the coach to help the boss view sharing his concerns as his role and support him in sharing this candid information inside the three-way meeting of boss, client, and coach.

O'Neill's client responsibility model (Figure 11.5) illustrates the dynamic that is supported in this wiser approach. Here the coach is aware of the systems dynamics and seeks to empower the client by working with him or her to strengthen connections and communication between client and boss, client and team, and client and peers.

A brief illustration of the two approaches is described here. Let's say that you receive a call from a leader in an organization where you've coached in

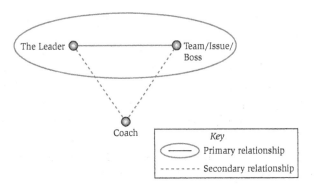

Figure 11.5 Client Responsibility Model of Coaching

Source: O'Neill (2007).

the past. The leader gives you an overview of a coaching situation where, she says, she "needs help right away." She has a team leader who is struggling. She doesn't want to let him go, but something is going to need to change, and fast, if this leader is going to hang on to his job. She says, "I need you to see what you can do in the next thirty to forty-five days." When you ask her what she has said to this leader, she replies, "It's hard. He's a good guy, but he's just not performing up to the level that we need. Frankly, I've said very little to him."

If you were to take the role of the go-between, communicating what's not working and what needs to change to this client, you would be colluding with a system that is not providing frank and useful feedback that allows others to make wise choices about their work and their future. Instead, you want to engage and support the organization leader in a conversation exploring her willingness to speak frankly with her leader and engaging her willingness to be proactive.

The goal at the conclusion of the initial three- or four-way conversation is that all parties are committed to the client's development, all parties have shared the goals that are most important for this leader, aligned with the leader's team and the overall goals and mission of the organization. Everyone is also clear about next steps, how information and progress will be shared, and the parameters of confidentiality. It's optimal at this stage to agree on key measures of success, although this will become clearer when all of the data are gathered and the overall coaching plan is outlined.

Other Stakeholder Interviews. A hallmark of great coaching and an important element in support of getting to results is the work of gathering information about your client's strengths, weaknesses, and areas of development according to other key stakeholders. This approach to seeking stakeholder input is a key differentiator from the work of mentoring or counseling, and it underlines and leverages the systemic nature of change.

These interviews broaden the scope of understanding and provide coach and client with a well-rounded picture. This full picture aids in crafting coaching goals that are most likely to get the results that are most important. Targeting key stakeholders from all levels—boss, peers, direct reports—provides both client and coach with a broader sense of the client's strengths and development goals as viewed by these important sectors in the leader's life.

Clients are often naturally hesitant to engage stakeholders in conversations about themselves. The coach must work jointly and transparently with the client to build a simple set of questions that will elicit relevant and helpful information. When the coach and client develop these together, the client is much more of a participant in the gathering of this information and feedback from others. These interviews and the client's overt request for feedback become sources of support for the final coaching goals.

Research has shown that sharing goals openly within the system provides support for the change and allows others to be more alert to observing it. The content of stakeholder interview questions is usually quite straightforward. A sample agenda and set of questions for stakeholders might include these:

1. A brief introduction including the purpose of the conversation—for example: "Priya is engaged in leadership coaching in order to continue to develop her leadership skills, and your experiences and perspectives relative to her current work will provide us with helpful information as we develop our coaching goals." Ensure the interviewee that all information gathered is confidential and will be shared with the client only in a thematic manner, without any specific attributions.

2. A question asking the individual to provide a context for his or her work relationship with your client, such as, "How long have you worked with Priya?" and, "How would you describe your working relationship?"

3. A question asking the individual to comment on what Priya's strengths are and what she might do to be even more effective.

4. A question linking to the organization's leadership competencies is often helpful in getting at some specific areas of development—for example, "One of your important leadership competencies is developing others. How do you observe Priya on this front?"

5. A final question that allows the individual to share anything he or she believes might be helpful that hasn't been addressed yet.

6. A request for this leader's support as your client develops her coaching goals.

Recall from Chapter Six the discussion on the Johari window as a foundational theory for understanding self as coach. This same model is useful

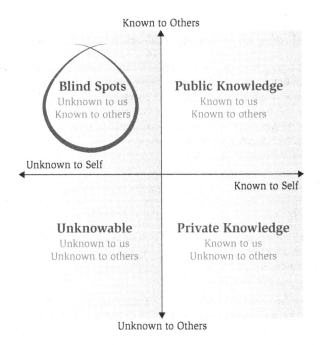

Figure 11.6 Stakeholder Interviews and the Johari Window

here in underlining the value of the information gleaned from the stakeholder interviews (Figure 11.6). The Johari window model illustrates that the client naturally has blind spots outside his or her awareness. The stakeholder interview process allows the coach to surface and collect information about the client's strengths and weaknesses in order to shed more light on the blind spots and craft contracts for change that are on target for the individual leader and of importance to the broader organization's success as well.

The following case example shows the turning point this information creates for a client who is dubious about the need for coaching in spite of his boss viewing it as essential.

Adjusting an Autocratic Leadership Style

Bob has been a successful leader of a sales team for the past five years and takes enormous pride in the fact that his team outperforms all others in the company every year. Bob's boss is pleased with these results too, but he knows that Bob has an autocratic and at times gruff approach that doesn't sit well with his team. Bob's approach results in outstanding sales figures but costs the company in turnover and a lack of well-developed bench strength on his team. Bob's singular focus on exceeding sales numbers made it easy for him to downplay the need to make any adjustments in his leadership style.

(continued)

Adjusting an Autocratic Leadership Style *(continued)*

When Bob's boss convinced him it was time for some coaching, and his coach, in partnership with Bob, collected information from his team of direct reports, his peers, and in a three-way meeting with his boss, Bob couldn't ignore the negative impact his leadership style was having. The good news is that given his drive to succeed, once he saw these data, he was prepared to do the work of making some basic changes in his leadership style. Take a look at what the stakeholder interviews uncovered through the lens of the Johari Window in Table 11.4.

Table 11.4 Johari Window Coaching Example

Bob's Blind Spots	Public Knowledge
• Direct report theme in their interviews: "This guy cares about one thing and one thing only: beating every other team in the company year over year at any cost."	• Bob's team can exceed the sales figures of any other team in the company.
• Peer feedback theme in interviews: "Bob is still around because numbers talk, but he's a jerk and a loner who ultimately costs the culture of our organization."	• Bob's team players are often shifting and changing, and tenure isn't as strong as on other teams in the company.
• Boss's feedback: "Bob is great at driving the numbers, but he will never be able to progress to a larger role because he lacks support within the broader organization, and no one trusts him to consider the longer-term view or the bigger picture."	• Bob is a loner; he doesn't socialize much with fellow sales managers or with his team.

Unknowable	Bob's Private Knowledge
• Strong likelihood that new information useful to Bob will be forthcoming in the coaching work.	• Bob's knowledge of his own internal challenges and obstacles to taking a different approach to leading his team will be uncovered in the coaching engagement.

Additional Supplemental Information. It's useful to request any current assessment information that might be on hand with the client or on file. This might include recent 360-degree feedback reports, along with any additional recent assessment information. It may at times include relevant performance management information. It is always useful to obtain the leadership competencies of the organization as a backdrop for developing strong development goals.

A coach may additionally recommend a specific assessment based on the details of the emerging coaching agreement. For example, a coach working with a leader who demonstrates plenty of success in meeting numbers and deadlines but often does so at the cost of relationships may decide that using an emotional intelligence assessment might provide a helpful lens in the coaching work together. Or if the overriding challenge a client and the client's associates identify is around conflict as it shows up on his team, this might be a signal to the coach that an assessment highlighting key ingredients of successful conflict management might be a good choice.

Two important caveats around assessments include timing and choice. If a coach leads the coaching with an assessment, the work and the coaching goals will be driven by the dimensions of the assessment rather than a holistic and developmental orientation. It's far wiser to first understand the issues through the eyes and heart of the client and then tailor any choice of assessment to fit the needs of the individual client rather than the preferences a coach might have for a favorite assessment. One assessment, model, or tool does not fit all.

Whole Person Context

A holistic and development perspective and understanding of one's client is essential when entering a coaching engagement (see Figure 11.7). This broader perspective encompasses the context in which we all live while simultaneously acknowledging our individual journey in life and the specific and targeted goals of our work together in the coaching engagement. Whether coaching a leader at the peak of her career, an early career person looking to define her own path, or a successful midcareer leader who is burned out and bored with work, it's essential that coaches understand the developmental terrain in a holistic context.

Several important characteristics are inherent in this broader view of adult life. First, a naturally occurring cyclical view portrays life as complex and pluralistic, with ongoing cycles in nature, societies, and people. Familial systems, companies, and nations are all part of a larger, often chaotic flow that can be influenced and shaped but never controlled. Second, the cyclical paradigm assumes life develops through cycles of change and continuity rather than in progressive, linear, straight lines. It concentrates on understanding both what persists throughout our lives and what necessarily changes. Each time we relinquish an old stage of life, we differentiate one more time, and a new level of development and individuation emerges. Third, the cyclical picture honors the polarities in life and in organizations: good times and difficult times are incorporated into our understanding of the undulating rhythm of opportunities and obstacles. Fourth, continuous learning is essential to the constant retooling of our multilayered human systems.

The reality of the world we live in today is more complex than ever before and changing at a tremendous pace. We live in a highly globalized

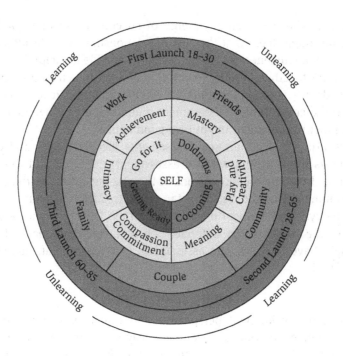

Figure 11.7 Hudson's Whole Person Model

© Hudson Institute of Santa Barbara, 1986.

Note: The outer circle captures the adult journey in three broad phases: first launch, the early transition into the adult years (roughly ages eighteen to thirty); second launch, the middle years (roughly ages twenty-eight to sixty-five); and third launch, the later years (roughly ages sixty to eighty-five). A full description of these stages can be found in McLean and Hudson's *LifeLaunch* (2011).

world requiring adaptability to cultural nuances, time zones, the 24/7 work week demands, shifting business realities, economic uncertainties, and ever-decreasing stability in organizational work settings. Many conditions of our modern life make a whole person context difficult to unearth yet more important than ever before to uncover. A broad developmental perspective of the whole person provides the coach with an understanding of the developmental pathway of the client in the context of the world and simultaneously inspires the client to gain a longer view of his or her overall journey.

All clients come to a coach with challenges and changes they want to explore in their lives. Some arrive at the door with specific targeted behaviors they want to adjust, others have broad goals that will allow them to open bigger doors for themselves, and yet others have been presented with unexpected crises that require adaptation in the moment. No matter what the presenting situation is with a particular client, the coach needs to be able to view the context of the client within a holistic and developmental framework. Several lenses provide this broad context for us and for the client:

- The continuous cycle of change. Is this a stable time or time of major transition for the client?
- The client's sense of purpose and what's most important to him or her.
- The roles and systems relevant to the client's life. Are some roles—work, family, friends, or community—more important than others at this time in life?
- The client's place in the life course. Is this early in life's journey, nearing the end of a dominant work role, or midway on the journey?
- The client's place in the continuous learning journey. Is this a time of important new learning for the client?
- The overall sense of mission and aspiration in the client's life. Is the client clear on what's most important at this time in life?
- The underlying developmental level of the client.

Part Five of this book examines the complexities and interactions of each of the elements in a holistic and developmental perspective in detail.

Commitment

Determining the level of the client's commitment is a pivotal element in a successful coaching engagement, and yet it's easy for a coach to rush through the early contracting phases and miss this key ingredient to success. A coach may find herself in a situation where the coaching goals articulated by the organization or the boss make a whole lot of sense, and she moves ahead with the work before adequately determining whether the client is as interested as she and others are. Commitment is often elusive for both novice and experienced coaches. It's easy enough for a client to early on tell the coach, "Yes, this is important to me," but often as trust builds, a deeper exploration yields a different story and reveals lower levels of motivation that ultimately undermine the ability to reach the goals and the outcomes the coach and client articulated.

It's natural to wonder why it needs to be so complicated. If a client wants to make a change, why not say so and proceed. Yet much of the time, that's not how human nature works. Most people can craft a long list of important changes to make, and in the majority of cases, the items on these lists are not trivial. And yet we do little or nothing to address the changes we wish for ourselves. Perhaps it's something to do with health. A physician sends the clear message, "Lose twenty pounds now, or you are going to have more challenges with your heart and risk the possibility of diabetes." Or maybe it's on the home front: "I keep saying I will make more time for family, find more ways to be at home all weekend and fully present, and yet it seems impossible." Or maybe there have been important signals over the past year or two that the client is not spending enough time connecting with direct reports or members of the team. It turns out that good intentions don't create change; that's where work with a great coach can make a big difference in creating lasting change around important issues and areas of development.

While it's tempting as a coach to gain easy agreement with a client around the coaching contract because it's sensible, others view it as critical to this individual; and it is obvious to the coach that the contract makes good sense for the client to address. The danger in falling into the trap of easy agreement is that a coach may find himself more committed to the work of the contract than the client is.

Change is not easy when all parties are fully committed; it's impossible without these key elements of commitment:

- A sense of urgency
- An understanding of clear and important benefits
- A deep commitment even in the face of hard choices and hard work ahead
- A clear commitment to make the time that will be required to address the change

Take enough time at this step in the contracting journey to thoroughly explore the client's motivations. Challenge the client to examine how important this change will be in her life. Discuss the costs if the client chooses to do nothing and the potential benefits if she decides to move forward. Explore time commitments and the client's ability to make space in her life for the coaching. Emphasize that it takes time, patience, and commitment to make changes in behaviors that have been around for many years.

Two important factors are at play in this step of the coaching process. First, the client is gaining clarity about her willingness to make the time, space, and commitment to this work now. Second, you as coach are finding out how successful this work will be based on the depth of your client's commitment.

Recall from Chapter Eight the work of Kegan and Lahey (2009) that sheds light on the power of the individual system in undermining change and the natural tendency to put one foot on the gas and one foot on the brake when considering change. Their work demonstrates the reality that lasting transformative change demands great commitment on the client's part. Consider one coach's experience:

By the time I met Blake, he had already completed a four-month coaching engagement. The focus had been on improving his communication with his direct reports. Feedback from his team at that time was that he was so severely punitive in his communication style that conversations felt more like interrogations than discussions. At the end of the four-month engagement, Blake had made some real progress, and his team, boss, and HR partner were feeling more confident that Blake could continue to grow in his role. Now, six months later, the company (and in particular this sales division) is under a lot of pressure to produce better sales figures, and Blake has not only reverted to his old habits, but it seems that under more stress, he's gotten even worse.

Blake's return to old habits is a potential signal that some important elements were neglected in the prior coaching engagement. Perhaps the level of commitment wasn't carefully examined, perhaps the benefit of making the change wasn't apparent to Blake, and perhaps the obstacles to change weren't fully uncovered. Change isn't easy for even the most willing, so setting the stage for understanding the benefits of making a change, the costs of remaining the same, the time and effort that will be required, and the competing priorities that will need to be addresses are important part in the conversation about commitment.

Fully Developed Aspirational and Behavior Goals

At this stage, the coach has gathered the essential ingredients of the client's story, the key stakeholder perspectives, additional sources of data, and assessment information. A holistic context of the client's world and an exploration of the client's current level of commitment to making some important changes lead to arriving at the overall work of the coaching. Now it's time to jointly distill all of the information and develop the key goals that will support the client's desired future state.

This stage is central to reaching successful outcomes with the client. You must balance all of the data gathered from key external sources, listening to what the client views as most important in this overall picture, what you jointly understand to be most important to key stakeholders, and factoring in your own assessment to jointly craft the details of the aspirational outcomes and the goals the coaching will address (see Figure 11.8).

The two important steps in this stage are clarifying the big, aspirational goal—that all-important desired future state the client is moving toward—and crafting the two or three behavioral goals that will get the client as close as possible to that desired state. The power of a big, overarching aspirational goal cannot be underestimated in helping to motivate a client to make an important change. If instead of an aspirational vision of what's possible, the focus of the coaching contract is on something the client needs to fix or stop doing, or a crisis the client wants to avoid, the chances for success are significantly reduced. The examples in Table 11.5 are illustrative.

Clients are inspired to make changes that sound appealing, attractive, and doable and, in short, creating a slightly better version of self. Recent research by Boyatzis (2011) finds there is a neural signal when visioning occurs: increased cognitive and perceptual openness that comes from the experience of being inspired. Take a look at the two very different approaches we frame up as a coach in a case example.

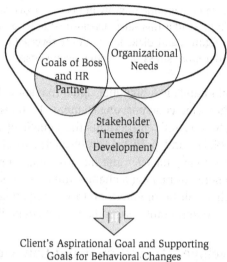

Client's Aspirational Goal and Supporting
Goals for Behavioral Changes

Figure 11.8 Distilling the Aspirational Goal

Table 11.5 Problem Orientation Versus Aspirational Future Orientation

Problem Orientation	Aspirational Future Orientation
Stop taking on the work of my team	Become a strong delegator who empowers team members and strengthens my leadership style
Stop being so self-critical when I'm faced with an important project	Learn to support myself internally and seek support from trusted sources in order to take this next big step
Stop second-guessing my best choices for what I'm going to do when I retire	Fully explore all possibilities that excite me in order to develop a new chapter when I retire that I feel engaged and alive about
I need to find more time in my days	Develop a work/life balance that allows me to do my work effectively and in a timely fashion
I need to stop avoiding conflict and providing feedback to my team	Develop my capacity to provide feedback to my team in a timely manner
Get out of the weeds and learn to think more strategically	Become a strategic leader

Bob's Big Presentation

Bob comes to you because he is a month out from making a major presentation to his board. He knows he doesn't do well in these situations and this presentation is vital for him as a leader. Bob explains to you, as coach, that he gets so anxious about big presentations that he often loses his ability to think clearly and perspires profusely, and all of the work he's done to craft a powerful message seems to vanish.

A Transactional Approach

The coach quickly moves to goal setting with Bob. They establish a coaching contract focused on helping Bob to control his anxiety in preparation for the upcoming presentation.

A Transformational Approach

The coach takes a step back with Bob and examines how he wants to operate as a leader, how he wants others to experience him, and what his overarching goals are for himself as a leader in this organization. The coach then works with Bob to articulate an inspiring vision for how he would like to show up at the board meeting next month and in the future. By the time Bob, with the help of his coach, arrives at his aspirational goal and identifies one or two areas for the coaching work, Bob is feeling fully committed, enthusiastic, and hopeful about making the needed adjustments that will serve his upcoming presentation and his overall role as a leader with a strong and confident presence.

The Coach's Checklist

The following checklist outlines some questions for the coach that are useful in this stage:

Stage Two Checklist of Questions for the Coach

- ☐ Have I carefully laid the groundwork and discussed the approach in a three-way meeting of coach, client, and boss?
- ☐ Have I surfaced all of the concerns and hopes in the three-way meeting, working to increase the connection between boss and client and reduce any tendency for me to play the role of broker?
- ☐ Have I carefully set the stage for stakeholder interviews and jointly built the process with the client?
- ☐ Once all third-party information has been collected and explored, have we jointly developed an overall aspirational goal my client is energized about reaching?
- ☐ If I am working with a leader inside an organization, is the aspirational goal clearly linked to the desires and goals of sponsor and client?

☐ Have we jointly targeted the two or three most important goals that at least for now will get the client closer to the bigger aspirational goal?

☐ Are the top two or three goals truly goals rather than action steps?

☐ Have we taken first steps in making the goals measurable and trackable so that we can map successes and, importantly, provide this information to the client's boss (and in many cases, stakeholders)?

☐ Have I carefully set the frame with stakeholders so that they will become supporters and advocates of my client's progress?

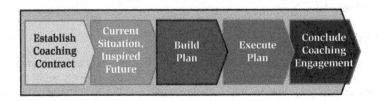

STAGE THREE: BUILD THE PLAN

Remember that this methodology is agile and iterative more than linear. Key elements of the coaching plan are emerging throughout the first two stages, and now, at stage three, the work begins to solidify the coaching plan around the key coaching goals.

Change theory is particularly relevant in highlighting the essential steps in the plan that will ensure lasting and sustainable change. Enduring change happens from the inside out, and this means a plan requires more than a list of action steps. We need to incorporate into the plan the internal dimensions that will support real and observable change.

There are four elements to stage three:

1. Identify obstacles

2. Identify strengths

3. Inner work: Awareness-building practices

4. Outer work: Building new behaviors

Identify Obstacles to Change

Once the top one, two, or three goals have been identified in support of the overarching aspirational goal the client has targeted, it's vital to jointly investigate what's going to make this a challenging change for the client.

This requires more than thinking through important behavioral changes or writing an action plan: neither will provide enough support to ensure change. The coach needs to help the client uncover the predictable obstacles that arise when considering important changes.

No matter how much we commit to ourselves to making an important change, we will still collide with our natural tendency to hang on to our old behaviors and ways of being. If we as coaches ignore this powerful underlying force at play in any change, we will most likely fail in helping our client develop a lasting, sustainable change.

Substantial research and study help to elucidate the power of resistance on the path toward change. Rick Maurer (2010) postulates three levels of resistance that I believe are quite useful to a coach:

The Resistance	Strategies for Coaches
Level 1 resistance: I don't know. I lack the information needed in order to take a step forward.	Recommend links to needed resources.
Level 2 resistance: I don't like it. I understand I need to make a change, I just don't like the thought of making the change.	Join with the client and work to surface the underlying resistance early in the coaching work.
Level 3 resistance: I don't like you. I understand you want me to make the change, and I don't like you because of that!	Lead from behind so you, as coach, do not become the force the client is resisting.

Every coach has the experience of Maurer's level 1 resistance: the client wants to make a change but has no idea what's being asked of him or her. This level of change simply requires adequate information for the client, and then this layer of resistance will vanish. Level 2 is much more frequent in coaching, and it takes skill and patience to tease out the nuances of this deeper layer of resistance. This resistance is deeply rooted in the client's sense of "who I am, how I see myself, and what my comfort zone is." The third level of resistance is a sure sign that as coach, you are leading the charge and your client is now resisting you instead of the change. When the coach gets out in front of the client with his or her own agenda about what changes need to be made and without a close collaboration with the client, the likely outcome is that the client begins to resist the coach. Consider the obstacles for the client in the case example of reaching her important goals. The balance of this section uses the facts in this example:

Identifying Sarah's Obstacles to Speaking with Confidence

Sarah wants to position herself for advancement in her organization. She identifies building her leadership presence as a key goal that will help her move toward the aspirational big goal of becoming a stronger leader. Together we identified the behaviors that would lead to building her leadership presence. The important behaviors on Sarah's list included two key behavioral shifts: speaking with authority and maintaining a strong voice while delivering presentations in key meetings and being viewed as a strong communicator and initiator of key interactions.

We decided to begin with her first goal: speaking confidently and with a strong and authoritative voice. We explored what would be most challenging for Sarah in moving toward this new behavior, and she quickly identified two important areas: she gets nervous when she stands in front of a group, even a small group, and this leads her to speak at a fast, clipped pace in order to be able to sit down as soon as possible. It also makes it hard for Sarah to remember what's most important to highlight and stress in her presentation. The second difficulty is that she notices a critical voice in her head saying something like, "Who are you to be standing in front of these folks telling them the best way to do this?"

These obstacles serve as important information for the coach and client in building the plan for change. The work must start here for several reasons. First, heart and head must be connected in order to create the milieu for change. As Sarah describes the obstacles she encounters when she attempts to stand in front of her team and other teams, she quickly connects her cognitive goals to the palpable emotions that arise in the moment.

Kegan and Lahey (2009) provide another valuable view into the client's natural resistance and focus attention on the client's conflicting concerns. Their work underlines the power of competing priorities in the client's life. So in the case of Sarah, she would like to show up in front of her audience as strong and powerful, and she wants to honor the voice in her head that tells her to "play it smaller, be modest, don't take up too much space, and don't draw too much attention to self." Unless the coach helps the client to tease out these competing priorities, much like Maurer's work on resistance, it's unlikely real change will unfold.

Identify Strengths

When approaching an important change that presents a significant challenge to the client, it's vital to take a step back with the client and identify key strengths that will support this effort. Identifying strengths creates a sense of internal support and hopefulness in the midst of making significant change. Incorporate the strengths that have been identified in stakeholder interviews and in the meeting with the client's boss and HR partner, and take time to help the client surface additional strengths based on past experiences.

In the case of Sarah, she is able to list several strengths that buoy her as she takes on an important shift in her way of being, and together she and her coach build a list of these strengths for continued reference. We can also evidence some of her strengths in a strength-based inventory that highlights her focus on achievement and persistence.

Inner Work: Awareness-Building Practices

All that a coach has diligently attended to and uncovered in partnership with the client up to this point is in the service of building a coaching plan that will hold the promise of deep and lasting change for the client. Let's review what the coach and client have jointly gathered and learned in the early stages of the coaching work:

- As coach, you garnered a thorough sense of what brings the client to coaching and what areas she is targeting for exploration in the coaching.
- If you are coaching a client inside an organization, in most cases you have had a three- or four-way meeting with boss, client, HR partner, and you, and this surfaced important information for the client's consideration.
- If you are coaching a client inside an organization, you'll almost always conduct stakeholder interviews in order to gain additional information and viewpoints relative to how key others in the organization view your client.
- You've reviewed any additional information available, including assessments and relevant performance reviews.
- You've gained a sense of the broader context of your client.
- You've deeply explored the client's level of commitment to the work of coaching and the specific targets articulated.
- Together with your client, you've carefully examined the obstacles and natural resistance to change that will surface when the work begins.
- Together with your client, you've thoroughly outlined client strengths that will support the desired changes.

Now, it's tempting at this juncture to build a plan for Sarah's first goal that includes helping to build a strategy that reduces her stress and gets her fully centered for her next presentation. This is often our tendency: to rush into crafting new behaviors too quickly instead of creating practices and focused intention that allow the client to spend time observing and heightening awareness of the current behavior they are wanting to change. Gestalt theorists often say that awareness is self-correcting, by which they mean that once we create a clear, deep awareness of what we are doing right now, we also create the possibility of new choices for ourselves. Silsbee (2008) frames this same dynamic in his habit loop, wherein the client needs to build heightened awareness before change is possible.

In Sarah's case, it is important to build into the early part of the coaching plan a reflective practice, the *inner work*, that allows Sarah to get more familiar with the nuances of what happens to her when she is "playing it small" and standing in front of her team racing through a slide deck she wants them to take seriously. There are several ways to accomplish this inner work, and a coach is likely to use a combination of approaches that might include these:

- Encourage Sarah to continue as she has and turn up her awareness when she is in front of others, whether the smallest group or a large presentation. Ask her to take some notes on what she notices before, during, and after every presentation she makes over the next two or three weeks.

- Each time Sarah makes an important discovery, it will likely lead to more inner work that will serve the outer behavioral changes. For example, if she notices her slumped posture, a somatic practice that grounds her before a presentation and attends to strong shoulders and a strong vertical line can become a practice of support. If Sarah notices a potent inner critic, this might be examined by "turning up the awareness dial" for two to four weeks and logging the messages in the service of ultimately relinquishing the old critic in exchange for a supportive inner voice.

- Once Sarah has a clear sense of how she shows up in the present, what occurs internally, and what somatic triggers precede the shift in pace and voice, she is in a much stronger position to get deeply committed to making some subtle internal changes that support a stronger self. Once the inner work is under way, it is much easier to clearly identify the specific new behaviors she wants and needs to adjust in order to hit her goal of feeling stronger and being viewed as emanating a leaderly presence.

This all-important work of observing and gaining intimate knowledge of one's current behaviors in order to support relinquishing an old behavior and moving toward the desired behaviors is all part of the coaching plan the coach and client build together and continually and iteratively work over the course of the coaching engagement.

The Outer Work: Building New Behaviors

The inner work supports the outer work, and there is a natural overlap and recurring interplay in these two areas. For example, if Sarah finds that a somatic practice is helpful in grounding her and developing a stronger, more erect presence, there may be outer work that will also support this, including possibilities such as these:

- Identifying a supportive colleague in the meetings who will give her detailed feedback on what she notices about Sarah's presence

- Using videotape to record Sarah's presentations because there is no feedback as powerful as instant replay without interpretation

The focus on both inner and outer work begins the heart of the coaching engagement. At this stage, it's most helpful to develop a coaching plan with the client that serves as an iterative anchor for the engagement. A format might look like Figure 11.9.

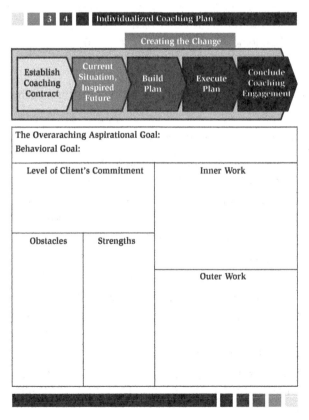

Figure 11.9 Coaching Planning Worksheet

© Hudson Institute of Santa Barbara.

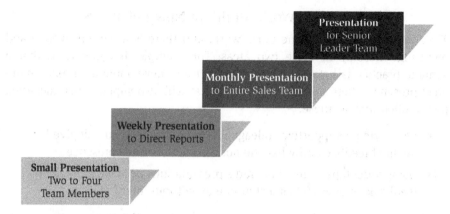

Figure 11.10 Incremental Behavioral Shifts

As the plan develops and the first steps in the outer work of behavioral change are targeted, a coach might find it useful build a ladder of behavioral shifts with the client that range from the easiest to riskiest (scaling it from 1 to 5 or 1 to 10). Sarah's ladder might look something like Figure 11.10.

The Coach's Checklist

The following checklist sets out some questions for the coach that are useful in this stage.

Stage Three Checklist of Questions for the Coach

- ☐ Have we jointly and methodically examined the obstacles and natural resistance that will appear as we move forward?
- ☐ Have we jointly crafted a plan or practice for noticing the behavior the client wants to change just as it is now before making any changes?
- ☐ Have I encouraged the client to find a useful way to log the times when she notices this behavior?
- ☐ Have I taken enough time with this important stage of the coaching work, not rushing to get to building a plan and action steps too soon?
- ☐ Have we jointly built a step-by-step plan that begins with the easiest adjustments and ensures plenty of time for practice before shifting to a progressively more challenging step?
- ☐ Have I given careful thought to resources, tools, and assessments that might be particularly helpful to this client dealing with this challenge or behavior?
- ☐ Have I routinely engaged in my own reflections both following our coaching sessions and prior to the next one, making sure I'm noticing

important nuances in my client, the work, and myself and my own reactions and feelings as coach?

☐ Have I sought the counsel of a peer coach or supervisor if I feel puzzled or concerned about some portion of my work with this client?

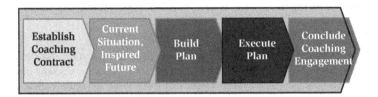

STAGE FOUR: EXECUTE THE PLAN

The foundation of a strong coaching engagement is well in place at this stage, and the execution of the coaching plan becomes an iterative and layered process using the support of key stakeholders and continually recalibrating the coaching goals as progress unfolds.

There are three elements to stage four:

1. Working the coaching goals
2. Periodically checking in with supporters and stakeholders
3. Recalibrating the goals and refining the direction

Working the Coaching Goals

Coach and client are now immersed in executing a fully informed coaching plan. This is the heart of the coaching work, and at each step of your coaching, you've been building a stronger relationship with your client. Now the work of creating real and lasting change begins.

A Step-by-Step Plan. Your plan targets specific areas of development, specific behaviors, and measurable goals that you've jointly agreed to. In a simple plan targeting one or two areas of change, the work will be much easier to stay focused on and track as you progress. In more complex coaching situations where you are working with a leader who is taking on a very big change, the work requires a weaving and layer of several goals over a longer period of time. What follows is an example of a step-by-step plan. As always, what appears quite ordered and linear rarely unfolds in this manner; hence, flexibility and agility are key for the coach.

Becoming an Inspiring Leader

John wants to become a stronger, approachable, and inspiring leader for his team. His aspirational goal is to interact with his team and colleagues in a manner that is both inspiring and inviting to those working with and around him. The step-by-step plan, established after interviews with key stakeholders and a meeting with your client, his boss, your HR partner, and you, will likely include elements such as these.

Step One

Spend time heightening John's awareness of how others view him and how he is interacting with members of his team as well as his colleagues. Take your time. Consider observing as coach and encouraging John to keep a journal or take notes on a regular basis as a way of gaining more awareness of how he currently experiences himself and is viewed by others.

Tools for Step One

You and John might build a spreadsheet or simple log (this depends on how John learns best) that allows him to jot down what he notices about his current behaviors under exploration in the coaching on a daily or regular basis.

Step Two

Once John has gathered adequate information, and he is sufficiently ready to make some changes, it's time to build a ladder of change, or a series of steps that span from the easiest wins to the most challenging changes.

Tools for Step Two

Together you could build a ladder of adjustments from the easiest to most challenging. It might be built similar to Sarah's example in Figure 11.11.

Step Three

Feedback and reinforcement are important for your client. Some feedback occurs in the playbacks that happen in the coaching when your client brings the successes and failures to the sessions. It's also helpful to gain feedback and reinforcement from a few of John's trusted colleagues. This meets two important goals: it provides John with in-the-moment feedback, and it reinforces his commitment to change inside his work system.

Tools for Step Three

Simply tracking feedback provided by colleagues is useful for your client. It's easy to get discouraged when taking on a big and uncomfortable change, and positive feedback from others that John logs provides some visible support for him when the going is tough.

Step Four

Uncover and attend to new awarenesses about self that emerge. While you are working this territory with John, he will naturally become aware of some new layers of himself. There is literally an iterative unfolding that emerges if you are fully joined with him and alert to what gets awakened as he tackles an important change in his behavior.

When Your Client Surfaces New Topics, Emergencies, Tangential Issues, and Surprises. Your client is a whole person, and it's impossible to artificially cordon off all parts of life but the coaching goals, so the unexpected is to be expected. What is important is to maintain a strong enough focus on the goals to accomplish the changes you and your client have agreed are most important. Three broad approaches can be considered when new topics emerge:

- Consider how this new topic links to the current goals. In many cases, there will be a clear link, and creating these connections builds even more momentum for making the change that the two of you have outlined.
- If it's an emergency or big surprise that has captured all of your client's attention, be explicit, take time out from the focused plan, and address the issue.
- If your client brings up a tangential issue and, in fact, has a habit of bringing new and unrelated issues to the coaching, it will be important to address this with your client. This can signal a style worthy of exploration or a form of resistance.

Periodically Checking In with Supporters and Stakeholders

Periodically checking in with the client's key supporters and stakeholders builds important support inside the client's work system relative to the changes under way. These check-ins will sometimes be informal and ongoing, while others will be built into the coaching plans including:

Midpoint Meeting with Boss and HR Partner. Holding a midpoint meeting and a final meeting with the client's boss and, in most cases, your HR partner is important for several reasons. First, it keeps these key players apprised of the work, the progress, and the next steps in the coaching plan. Second, it provides an opportunity to seek feedback about what the client's boss has observed about changes in the client relative to the agreed-on goals. Third, it provides another opportunity to seek support from the client's boss and HR partner in continuing to deepen these adjustments and changes. Fourth, it reminds the whole system that the client is changing; it asks the whole system to notice the new behaviors and adjust their old beliefs and experiences to meet the changes under way.

Midpoint Check-In with Key Stakeholders. If the coach has successfully communicated a transparent message to stakeholders in the first conversation, it is now possible to return to these stakeholders and gain their observations relative to their leader's goals and seek their support in continuing to notice positive changes going forward. This step is important in solidifying a change inside the system. Typically the coach's questions will tie back to the initial interviews. In the case with John, the initial questions yielded the information about John's unapproachable style, so the questions in this midpoint round might include these:

- "What have you observed? During the first conversation, you shared your perception that John is simply not approachable, and as you know, John is focused on developing his approachability. What you might be observing relative to John's goals?"
- "I wonder if you've found opportunities to provide John with feedback about the adjustments you are noticing."
- "As John continues to work this territory, what do you think is going to continue to be important for him to stay focused on?"
- "How do you notice the impact of John's changes and adjustments? Are there any ways you can notice the impact on you, your team, or the team's efforts relative to John's work in becoming more easily approachable?"

A midpoint check-in such as this with key supporters and stakeholders will also often be initiated by the client and supported by coach. This choice in approach is yet another example of building an agile process that accommodates the unique circumstances of the coaching engagement.

Recalibrating the Goals and Refining the Direction

Even the most experienced coaches can be challenged to predict how long it will take a client to make certain changes. Of course the magnitude of the change makes a difference, but so does the inner terrain of the client, and that's never as easy to fully anticipate. Midway along in the coaching engagement, you will inevitably find it important to revisit the progress, the path ahead, and the sense of impact the work is having on your client's behavior and approaches. It's at this point that you'll spend time recalibrating goals and refining direction to best fit the needs of your client and the stated goals of your work. It's not uncommon to reach the first goal or two, only to find the door opens to even more important work in the life of a leader.

In John's case, he made rapid improvements in his ability to stand at the head of the table and maintain a strong and inspiring presence, and about four months into the coaching, he felt he had reached this goal. His trusted colleagues provided feedback that supported his perceptions. However, in the process of getting to this goal, he uncovered another element of his leadership style and behavior: a habit of waiting for the pressure of time to get him moving on a project, a presentation, or even an important conversation. Until now, he hadn't calculated the cost of this habit, and he certainly hadn't seen the connection between a strong presence at the front of the room and a sense of being fully prepared well in advance to deliver a thoughtful message. He believed he would create even stronger traction for himself as a leader if he tackled this newly uncovered layer as well in the course of the coaching. This is when the coach and client together recalibrate and refine the direction in the service of deepening and enhancing the aspirational goal you jointly set out to accomplish.

The Coach's Checklist

The following checklist sets out some questions for the coach that are useful in this stage:

Stage Four Checklist of Questions for the Coach

- ☐ Have I worked with my client to strategize the best approach to seeking feedback providing a midpoint progress and a check-in with the client's boss and, in some cases, HR partner? (We may choose to do this together in some cases, and in others it's optimal for the client to engage in these conversations without my presence.)

- ☐ Have I worked with my client to strategize the best approach to seeking midpoint feedback from the stakeholders and explicitly enlisting their support in their leader's continued work on the stated goals?

- ☐ Have we carefully recalibrated goals, determining where the mission is accomplished and what the next layer of important goals is in support of the overall aspirational target of the client?

- ☐ Have I routinely engaged in my own reflections both following our coaching sessions and prior to the next one, making sure I'm noticing important nuances in my client, the work, and myself and my own reactions and feelings as coach?

- ☐ Have I sought the counsel of a peer coach or supervisor if I feel puzzled or concerned about some portion of my work with this client?

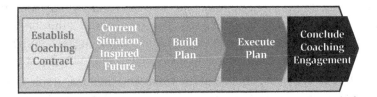

STAGE FIVE: CONCLUDE THE COACHING ENGAGEMENT

As the coaching engagement nears conclusion, it's essential to take a step back and closely examine the effectiveness of the coaching work and the impact of the coaching on the client and the client's systems. It's equally important to take a conscious step with the client to build a bridge for continued growth and support that nurtures and deepens the changes the client has implemented during the engagement.

There are four elements to stage five:

1. Examine overall effectiveness.
2. Develop a long-range plan.
3. Provide follow-up and support.
4. Measure coaching outcomes.

Examine Overall Effectiveness

As the coaching draws to a close, it is important to take a broad view and examine the effectiveness of the coaching engagement. This examination occurs from several angles:

- *The client's sense of accomplishment relative to the goals of the engagement.* Although this is a conversation you and your client are threading throughout the coaching work, there is the opportunity at closure to assess the internal and external efforts of the work from a wider angle.

- *The client's evidence of the accomplishments in the targeted behavioral changes and overall shifts.* If you've done your work well as a coach, you've helped your client gather feedback and input throughout the engagement that tracks how others observe changes in him or her. This external source of evidence is enormously validating and helpful to the client in solidifying the change, and it is also critical to the system in which the client lives. When key colleagues in the client's system have routinely observed and commented on changes your client is making, it further crystallizes the change.

- *The three- or four-way review of results with coach, client, boss, and HR partner to examine one last time the agreed-on goals of the work and the evidence of meeting those goals.* This review tracks the stated and agreed-on goals at the outset of the coaching engagement and the progress that has been made and measured in the following ways:
  - The subjective experience of the client and the measurable markers outlined in the coaching work. This could include, for example,

a commitment to sit down in the office of each team member on a weekly basis or an open-door policy to the client's office with a logging of the shift in how often team members feel comfortable walking into the office.

- The changes observed by team members, colleagues, and boss (much of this has been gathered at the midpoint through interviews as well).
- An exploration of the impact of these changes on all parties.
- In some cases, a 360-degree assessment, administered as a before-and-after measurement. In other cases, a less formal measure is obtained through the stakeholder interviews and the interviews with boss and HR partner at the midpoint and conclusion of the coaching work.

Develop a Long-Range Plan

At the conclusion of a successful coaching engagement, most clients are genuinely surprised and buoyed by the strides they've taken and the shifts and changes they've made. It's often hard to bid farewell to the work of coaching because the changes have been beneficial and the dialogue has opened the client to new ways of thinking and being in his work as a leader and a human being.

It's important to help build a bridge beyond the coaching engagement by developing a long-range plan with the client that is self-guided around supporting the changes the client has made and plotting the course for new paths. Perhaps it is in the form of an ongoing time line or a series of next steps accompanied by a clear plan to support the client's new behaviors and perhaps another layer of goals.

Provide Follow-Up and Support

A follow-up process for support is useful to consider. First, a simple way to stay in touch over the coming months to learn of the client's progress is a natural extension of the coaching. This might consist of short e-mail notes, quick phone calls, or a cup of coffee. These small follow-up gestures following an intense and meaningful coaching engagement provide the client with a sense of connectedness and bridge building.

Second, an open door for future work ought to be addressed before the conclusion of the work. This is a natural outcome of a successful engagement. The understanding that if at some time in the future there is another coaching need, the door is open for reengagement.

Measure Coaching Outcomes

The measurement of coaching outcomes is an essential ingredient in coaching and solutions for measuring outcomes range from anecdotal comments on the part of the client to the highly detailed return-on-investment (ROI) formulas

Table 11.6 Five Levels of Evaluating Coaching Initiatives

Level	Description
Level 1: Reaction	Looks at the initial reaction of the coaching client to coaching received
Level 2: Learning	Captures what the client has learned from the coaching session
Level 3: Application	Evaluates how well the client has applied what he or she learned during the coaching
Level 4: Business impact	Documents impact through output, cost, quality, and time
Level 5: ROI	Tabulates all monetary benefits—factors in the fully loaded cost of coaching and calculates the ROI: ROI = [(Benefits-Cost)/Cost] × 100

requiring significant data collection and analysis. The method a coach uses to measure results of the engagement will vary from setting to setting, but the consistent practice of measuring outcomes should always be a routine part of the engagement.

The early work of Donald Kirkpatrick and James Kirkpatrick (2006) in training and development combined with the contributions of Jack Phillips (1996) relative to measuring the return on investment in coaching provide helpful foundational frameworks for examining the level of outcomes we need to focus on as we coach. Table 11.6 highlights the layers of outcomes from the most superficial, "How did you like our coaching?" to the complex examination of bottom-line business results.

Level 1 evaluation may provide some information about the nature of the coach-client relationship, but it reveals nothing about the effectiveness of the coaching engagement. Level 2 captures the learning from the coaching sessions, but fails to link the client's insights and learning to real behavioral changes. When we move to level 3, we begin to examine the true impact of the coaching by exploring how the client is applying what he or she is learning in the coaching engagement. It is at levels 4 and 5 where we begin to explore the connection among the coaching goals, the outcomes, and the impact on the business.

Let's examine the coaching engagement with John through these levels of evaluation in Table 11.7.

If coaching is going to continue to grow as a viable mechanism for developing leaders and creating the climate for deep change to occur, all levels of outcomes must be routinely examined with all parties involved in supporting the coaching engagement from the boss, to the HR Partner and the stakeholders as well. The coach's job is to help the broader organization gain a sense of the wider impact of the coaching engagement in measurable terms that impact the bottom line.

Table 11.7 Levels of Evaluation in John's Case

Level of Evaluation of John's Coaching Engagement	Evidence of Outcomes
Level 1: John's reaction to the coaching	John's reaction to the coaching was positive.
Level 2: John's learning from the coaching	John felt he learned some important things about himself in the coaching.
Level 3: John's application of the coaching	John was able to articulate how he applied the learnings from coaching. He consciously and regularly initiated conversations with team members, walked into their offices, adopted an open-door policy, and tracked his own physical manifestations of not being approachable in an effort to shift his stance, including more smiling and less folded arms.
Level 4: Business impact of John's coaching	The business (including the HR partner and John's boss) has observed behavioral changes that make a positive impact on all parties and potentially connect to the bottom line at multiple levels.
Level 5: ROI, monetary benefits	Stronger retention of John's team members.
	Development of John's leadership skills in this area results in the organization's being able to continue to promote John and use him effectively as a member of the leadership cadre.
	Better output and efficiency on John's team. The stronger communication and adjustment in John's emotional intelligence and approachability created a team culture that promotes better work, more willingness to go the extra mile, and a team solidarity that produces better results.

The Coach's Checklist

The following checklist sets out some questions for the coach that are useful in this stage:

Stage Five Checklist of Questions for the Coach

- ☐ Have we thoroughly examined the effectiveness of our coaching engagement, mapping our work to the stated goals and the overall aspirational goal and tracking the progress and feedback from the client's boss, HR partner, and the stakeholders?
- ☐ Have we carefully crafted a long-range plan that will ensure a continued pathway of support and development for the client for the next six to twelve months?
- ☐ Have I worked with my client to arrange follow-up that is optimally suited to this client's situation?
- ☐ Have we engaged in measuring the impact of the coaching outcomes on the client, the client's team, and the overall organization?
- ☐ Have I worked with the HR partner to map the coaching outcomes to the impact on the organization's bottom line and culture?
- ☐ Have I routinely engaged in my own reflections both following our coaching sessions and prior to the next one, making sure I'm noticing important nuances in my client, the work, and myself and my own reactions and feelings as coach?
- ☐ Have I sought the counsel of a peer coach or supervisor if I feel puzzled or concerned about some portion of my work with this client?

Remember, a sound coaching methodology provides a map to guide the way through the coaching process, ensuring that all of the essential ingredients for a successful coaching engagement have been explored and examined. Yet a useful methodology is not intended to be lockstep and linear; coaching never unfolds in quite that way. Every coaching situation dictates the need for flexibility, and some elements of the methodology will be more important in some situations than in others. What's most important is mapping a coaching process and plan that guides the coaching engagement from beginning to end and ensures sustainable and lasting change for the client.

PART FIVE

THE CLIENT'S LIFE

Coaching Through Transitions,
Human Systems, and Values

To keep alive and effective, you anticipate difficulties
and opportunities. You adapt, changing and
growing as the individuals and the world around you
change, and you periodically recommit yourself to
your mission.
—Charles Garfield

CHAPTER 12

THE CLIENT'S LIFE: AN INTRODUCTION

A well-rounded coach operates at multiple layers and needs more than theory and skill-based competencies, a coaching methodology, an ability to use self as coach, and a tool kit. A great coach needs to be grounded in the broader context of the human being in today's world. A holistic and developmental perspective transcends any singular coachable issue or pressing challenge in the life of the client and provides a deeper context for the client embedded in the complex layers and systems of life. This more expansive lens allows a coach to thread singular issues into the broader themes of the client's life and articulate aspirational goals that resonate with both the challenges of the day and the broader complexities of life.

When we talk about a developmental perspective, there are two distinct and important realms for our consideration. The first is found in the concepts of constructivism (the notion that as individuals we construct our own reality) and the second in developmentalism (the notion that as individuals, we evolve through time as we weave through transition and change in our lives). The origins of constructivism emerged in the early work of object relations (relationship of self to other) theorists, including Donald Winnicott (1990) and Otto Kernberg (1995). Kegan's (1982) work linked Jean Piaget's cognitive development framework to the field of object relations, thereby providing a foundation for our understanding of the stages of development in our self-other constructions or our ability to make meaning out of any given situation in our lives.

Kegan's contributions are particularly germane to the work of coaching, because he draws attention to the shifts in how adults make meaning of their world over the course of their lives. His original work outlines five levels of development in the adult's life, representing new levels of consciousness as the individual moves through each stage, growing in complexity and allowing the adult to wrestle with more complex understandings and situations.

Kegan and Lahey's recent book, *Immunity to Change* (2009), condenses these stages into three broad levels of development. The first is the socialized mind, characterized by individuals who want to live within a set of rules in their life and in their work. Their decisions about how to behave in the world are shaped by what they believe other people in authority roles expect of them in their role. They live their lives according to a specific set of rules handed down to them by a person or institution in a position of authority. People at this stage of development make excellent team members because they adhere to the rules and remain extremely loyal. According to Kegan and Lahey, about 20 percent of the adult population is at this stage or striving for this phase.

Jamie is an example of this level. He has just completed his law degree, and he's eager to take his first step into the legal profession and launch his career. His parents are particularly proud of him because he's followed in the footsteps of his father and his grandfather, and he's now about to join his father's firm. Jamie readily admits there is a sense of pressure around getting it right and wanting to secure his family's approval at this important juncture, and he also confesses that there is comfort in having a clear pathway to the future that others have helped him create at this stage in life.

The second level, the self-authoring mind, is characterized by individuals who set their own goals and work hard to achieve what they've targeted for themselves. They are clear about their own internal set of values and guided by their own compass rather than an external set of rules. They are comfortable taking a stand that might be different from those of others around them. They are very focused and driven by their own goals and work hard to get others to adopt the same agenda. According to Kegan and Lahey, about 75 percent of the adult population is at this stage or striving for this phase.

Barbara, age fifty-two, with a solid record of work success behind her, is an example. She has taken some traditional paths over the past three decades and now is ready to step off the safe road and try something quite new and different. Some of her friends and family think she is crazy to bid farewell to a corporate career that is secure and prestigious, but Barbara is ready. She is clear about her sense of purpose at this stage in her life, and she's ready for a bold challenge.

The self-transforming mind is the third level, characterized by individuals who are clear about their own inner set of values and simultaneously able to

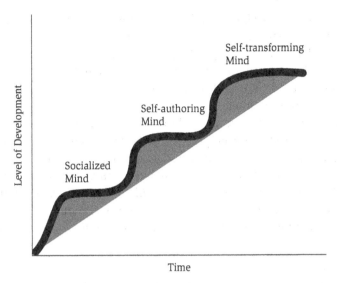

Figure 12.1 Kegan and Lahey's Levels of Development
Source: Kegan (1982).

step back and explore other perspectives and consider the limitations of their own values and goals. They are willing to freely invite feedback, contemplate other points of view, and generally explore the complexities and contradictions of life's issues and dilemmas.

According to Kegan and Lahey (2009), few of us reach this level of development, so perhaps we can see this evolved state of being best in an iconic figure such as Nelson Mandela. Mandela is a powerful example of a human being with clarity of vision forged under the most trying of times and a continual ability to step back and view perspectives differing radically from his own.

Individuals, write Kegan and Lahey (2009), are able to move to higher levels of development as they become able to consider broader perspectives about themselves and others (as shown in Figure 12.1). As long as the individual is trapped in viewing his or her own experience as "the real experience," this person's capacity to fully operate in the world is limited.

Kegan and Lahey's (2009) work becomes more complex and doubly relevant to coaches when we consider the combination of coach and client wherein the client is operating at one level while the coach is potentially operating at another. It's easy to see that if a coach operates at the level of the socialized mind, it will be almost impossible to provide useful coaching to a client who is operating at the level of the self-authoring mind or beyond.

Otto Laske (2006b) applies Kegan and Lahey's (2009) work specifically to the field of coaching and asserts that a coach cannot successfully coach an individual who is at a higher level of development than his or her own. Our way of making meaning within each stage is so engrained that it's impossible to consider that there might be a different, higher state view. Laske has developed an instrument to measure one's individual level of development and believes it could be useful in training coaches to examine the individual level of the coach in training.

This deeper meaning-making level of development in our social maturity is one important aspect of development that is woven into a broader examination of the whole person and the unfolding development that occurs over time and through periods of transition and change throughout our adult years.

At Hudson, we've developed a series of lenses into each of the important elements of understanding a whole person in a framework that captures our meaning-making capacities and examines a holistic and developmental perspective.

CHAPTER 13

COACHING THROUGH TRANSITION AND CHANGE IN THE CLIENT'S LIFE

C hange is the crucible for development in our lives. Sometimes we plan to make changes, but more often, change finds its way to our door and leaves us no choice but to greet it and make sense out of how this change will affect our life. As a coach it's essential to gain a sense of what level of change is afoot in the life of a client. Is it a small adjustment or a major upheaval? Big changes reverberate throughout our whole being, whereas small adjustments often allow us to make minor modifications and keep moving. This broader perspective on the client's life and the level of potential change is outlined throughout Part Five as we address the central elements of a holistic and developmental perspective. These include an awareness of the client's values at this time in life, the roles and systems the client is embedded in and balancing in his or her life, the intricacies and volume of change the client is currently experiencing, the all-important overlay of the client's position on the adult journey, and the inevitable learning and unlearning that are incumbent on the client at this time in his life.

Much as Kegan (1982) suggests, change creates the possibility for new layers of development. Change of one sort or another, big or small, is what brings most clients to a coach. Change can be triggered by internal forces or by external surprises and crisis events in our lives. It can come in the form of a promotion, a firing, or a major shift in roles with new demands at hand. It may simply be a performance review that requires some adjustments, a long-sought-after promotion that requires a move to another continent, a first career position or the final capstone, a death, or a challenging illness on the

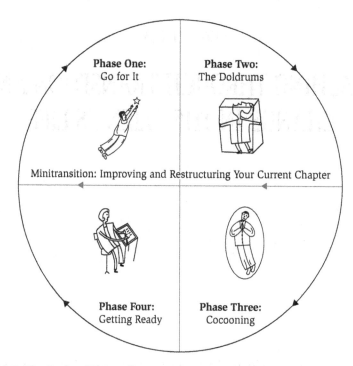

Figure 13.1 The Cycle of Renewal
© Hudson Institute of Santa Barbara, 1986.

home front. All of these changes catch us off guard, and as life would have it, the bigger the surprise, the greater the opportunity and invitation for one's own development. Through years of field research and application, we have developed a model we term the cycle of renewal to provide a framework for viewing a cyclical and normative cycle of ongoing change that intersects with all of the human systems at play at any point in our adult journey. Unlike the older and mostly linear models tied to specific ages and stages, we view development throughout the adult years as continuous and full of growth.

While the focus of coaching will not be guided by the cycle of renewal, it's helpful to step back and consider where you might locate your client on the cycle in order to fully comprehend and acknowledge the degree and intensity of the change she is experiencing and to gauge as well the pace of the coaching. Figure 13.1 provides a visual of the cyclical nature of change.

HOW CHANGE IS EXPERIENCED

We are at all times putting our lives together and taking them apart. But when we are mainly putting ourselves together, we are in a chapter: an era of relative stability, predictability, and challenge. When we are mainly dismantling our roles and story lines, we are in transition: an era of instability, shedding, and new discovery.

Life chapters are about accomplishing something important with your life—having a career, raising a family, reaching a goal—that knits your life together in a meaningful way. For example, four years in college might be a chapter, or ten years working in a corporate setting, or a divorce and being single again, or moving from full-time work to retirement. Life chapters vary in time spans. Some are long, and others are not.

Life chapters are externalizations of the self, doings, and happenings, with explicit goals and objectives. Life transitions are a pulling away from a chapter and an opportunity to turn inward, soul-search, find a new sense of self, to spiritual vitality and meaning, envision new ways to be you in the years ahead.

Some life transitions are triggered by an external event, such as being terminated from a job, moving to a new location, returning to school, being in an accident, or developing a serious disease. Other life transitions are triggered from within through boredom, emotional distress, bodily changes, or powerful new callings. Life transitions are about letting go of roles, unraveling your identity, and discovering new dimensions of yourself from the inside out. They produce renewal, vitality, and resilience. Although few people want a transition to last long, they are seldom short. It takes time to process the metamorphosis from who you were to the person you're becoming. It is largely an emotional and reflective process that can take many months or even years. People in transitions continue to work and remain active; however, more often their energy and attention draws them inward for a bit. "There are two central qualities in our experience of change: a sense of chaotic power beyond our control and a sense of never-ending adventure" (Hudson, 1999, p. 109).

Good coaches should take into account that adults experience their lives in these two general and basic patterns: they are in either a life chapter or a life transition. Both are experienced as cycles of change that are repeated over and over throughout our lives.

Coaching in Life Chapters

In a life chapter, life seems basically stable, with opportunities to grow and with positive challenges on the horizon. A person's dominant behavior pattern is most likely to be upbeat, high energy, and optimistic. Change seems like a reliable flow of resources and opportunities for fulfilling life's purpose. Performing certain action steps seems to be a way to serve those purposes and reach those goals.

For a client in a life chapter, the flow of change provides opportunities to soar. Coaching those in a life chapter is often highly focused on crafting new behaviors and skills that will allow the individual to adapt and prosper in his or her current role or in new opportunities. Performing, doing, and achieving well are at the top of the list when a client is in this phase of a life chapter.

Coaching Through Life Transitions

In a life transition, clients experience the world as much less reliable; it is at times chaotic and even punishing. They are likely to feel discouraged, have low energy, and be pessimistic. For example, when a leader experiences abrupt change—loses a job, life partner, or health—he could also lose his moorings and find himself withdrawing from his usual coping mechanisms. He may envelop himself in a full-time life review. His effort then goes to finding new resources and tools for managing his life.

A person in a life transition turns inward and disengages from as much busyness as possible; inner voices begin to seem more reliable than outer signals. The inner journey of a life transition deconstructs the former chapter; a person then matures and eventually grows into a new chapter, much as Kegan's work suggests the slow unfolding of the levels of development in adulthood allows us to construct yet another layer of understanding about ourselves in the world. We term this cocooning because it is a time filled with opportunities for transformation, amazing growth, and deep renewal.

This model views change and continuity as continuous, positive forces in adult life. We learn from all places in the change cycle, and the most important lesson of this model is that there are no permanent arrival points, only a continuous journey as we navigate continuous change. Coaches help clients understand how to manage change wherever they are in the cycle, and the client's general location in the cycle provides useful information for the coach relative to the pace of the coaching, the depth of the work, and sometimes the length of the engagement.

PHASES WITHIN LIFE CHAPTERS AND TRANSITIONS

In the cycle of renewal, each life chapter has two phases: Go for It (working for goals and experiencing success) and the Doldrums (managing disenchantment and restlessness). Each life transition also has two phases: Cocooning (reconstructing the self) and Getting Ready for the Next Chapter (training, experimenting, and networking). These are four phases of adult life that coaches should understand if they are to coach their adult clients effectively. Figure 13.2 illustrates the behavioral characteristics within each phase of the change cycle.

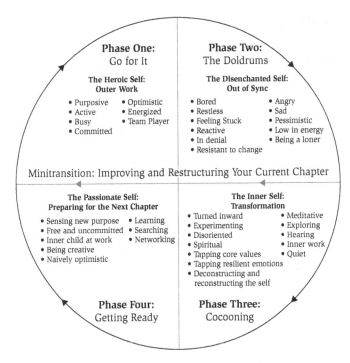

Figure 13.2 The Cycle of Renewal: Behavioral Characteristics

© Hudson Institute of Santa Barbara, 1986.

Life Chapter: Phases One and Two

Phase One (Figure 13.3) is a period of success and stability. The elements and forces of change cohere in what seems to be a linear and permanent life chapter. Coaches need to know how to work with clients who are in Phase One and typically highly motivated and focused on specific targeted goals while working to maintain a sense of balance in their life.

Phase Two is marked by a period of boredom and restlessness. It ends with either a minitransition that serves to improve life in Phase One or with a longer life transition that leads a person to seek new directions.

In Phase Two (Figure 13.4), the elements and forces that seemed so promising at the beginning of Phase One now seem heavy, less promising, and a burden. A person has a been there, done that feeling of ennui and often wonders, "Is this all there is?" In fact, often the career the person imagined for so long as the dream career has lost its luster. Whatever the specific circumstance, coaches need to know how to work with clients who are stuck in Phase Two to build new coping strategies and seek out new options. Coaching strategies for people in Phase Two are very different from the ones that work with clients in Phase One. The best choice for Phase Two clients is for the

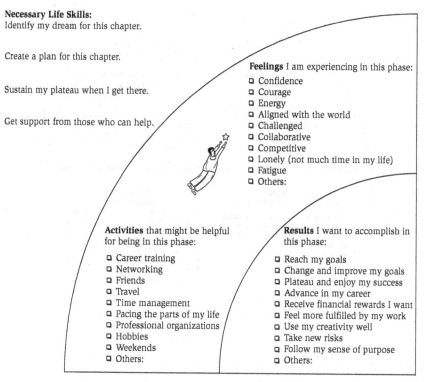

Necessary Life Skills:
Identify my dream for this chapter.

Create a plan for this chapter.

Sustain my plateau when I get there.

Get support from those who can help.

Feelings I am experiencing in this phase:
- ❏ Confidence
- ❏ Courage
- ❏ Energy
- ❏ Aligned with the world
- ❏ Challenged
- ❏ Collaborative
- ❏ Competitive
- ❏ Lonely (not much time in my life)
- ❏ Fatigue
- ❏ Others:

Activities that might be helpful for being in this phase:
- ❏ Career training
- ❏ Networking
- ❏ Friends
- ❏ Travel
- ❏ Time management
- ❏ Pacing the parts of my life
- ❏ Professional organizations
- ❏ Hobbies
- ❏ Weekends
- ❏ Others:

Results I want to accomplish in this phase:
- ❏ Reach my goals
- ❏ Change and improve my goals
- ❏ Plateau and enjoy my success
- ❏ Advance in my career
- ❏ Receive financial rewards I want
- ❏ Feel more fulfilled by my work
- ❏ Use my creativity well
- ❏ Take new risks
- ❏ Follow my sense of purpose
- ❏ Others:

Figure 13.3 Clients in Phase One: Go for It

© Hudson Institute of Santa Barbara, 1986.

coach to facilitate designing an exit plan and departing from Phase Two to either a minitransition or to a life transition in Phase Three.

A Minitransition

When people in Phase Two choose to leave, they almost always choose to make a minitransition, which is some minor revision in the chapter they are already in: change of geographical location, change of job, a divorce, a marriage, or a return to school. A minitransition is a time of strategic planning, renewing the chapter of life with new strategies to improve what's working and change what's not, introducing new options, and getting launched again. Minitransitions are a restructuring of what already exists in the service of improving it. They are not of less value than life transitions. They are simply different and serve to renew the chapter a person is in, whereas a life transition renews and transforms the person.

Life Transition: Phases Three and Four

Major life transitions don't occur very often in the adult journey. At most we'll likely encounter only a handful of crises and opportunities that lead us to this

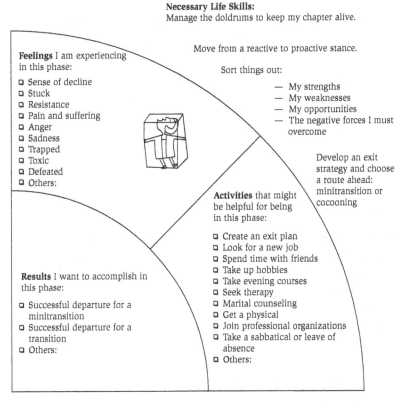

Necessary Life Skills:
Manage the doldrums to keep my chapter alive.

Move from a reactive to proactive stance.

Feelings I am experiencing
in this phase:

- ❑ Sense of decline
- ❑ Stuck
- ❑ Resistance
- ❑ Pain and suffering
- ❑ Anger
- ❑ Sadness
- ❑ Trapped
- ❑ Toxic
- ❑ Defeated
- ❑ Others:

Sort things out:

- — My strengths
- — My weaknesses
- — My opportunities
- — The negative forces I must
  overcome

Develop an exit
strategy and choose
a route ahead:
minitransition or
cocooning

Activities that might
be helpful for being
in this phase:

- ❑ Create an exit plan
- ❑ Look for a new job
- ❑ Spend time with friends
- ❑ Take up hobbies
- ❑ Take evening courses
- ❑ Seek therapy
- ❑ Marital counseling
- ❑ Get a physical
- ❑ Join professional organizations
- ❑ Take a sabbatical or leave of
  absence
- ❑ Others:

Results I want to accomplish in
this phase:

- ❑ Successful departure for a
  minitransition
- ❑ Successful departure for a
  transition
- ❑ Others:

Figure 13.4 Clients in Phase Two: The Doldrums

© Hudson Institute of Santa Barbara, 1986.

place. It is here that the self is explored at a deeper level through introspection and thrashing about; a person searches for deep meaning as well as a sense of new direction for the future. This is a transition space and time for starting over while deepening the maturity of the self and one's dreams. Coaches need to be able to work with clients in transition, fostering transformation and offering possible directions for where they are with their lives. Coaches with a focus on transition work will feel at home exploring coaching and getting to core values and beliefs.

Some people arrive at Phase Three (Figure 13.5) not by choice but by emotional default. Some life crises trigger an emotional response that feels like an uninvited ending has happened—a little death. People who cocoon come to terms with who they are without their previous roles dominating them. They work through an identity crisis and take time out, psychologically speaking, for soul searching. Little by little, out of solitude grows a more resilient self, anchored in a revised set of core values and sense of peace, all the while challenged by new purpose and passion. Life is transformed. Coaching Phase

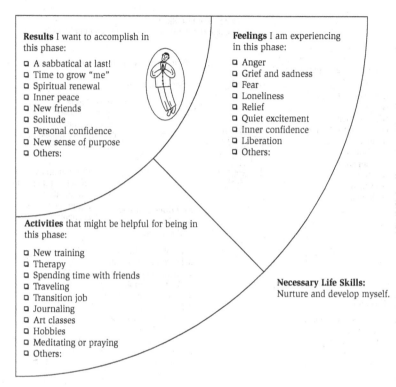

Results I want to accomplish in this phase:

- ❏ A sabbatical at last!
- ❏ Time to grow "me"
- ❏ Spiritual renewal
- ❏ Inner peace
- ❏ New friends
- ❏ Solitude
- ❏ Personal confidence
- ❏ New sense of purpose
- ❏ Others:

Feelings I am experiencing in this phase:

- ❏ Anger
- ❏ Grief and sadness
- ❏ Fear
- ❏ Loneliness
- ❏ Relief
- ❏ Quiet excitement
- ❏ Inner confidence
- ❏ Liberation
- ❏ Others:

Activities that might be helpful for being in this phase:

- ❏ New training
- ❏ Therapy
- ❏ Spending time with friends
- ❏ Traveling
- ❏ Transition job
- ❏ Journaling
- ❏ Art classes
- ❏ Hobbies
- ❏ Meditating or praying
- ❏ Others:

Necessary Life Skills:
Nurture and develop myself.

Figure 13.5 Clients in Phase Three: Cocooning

© Hudson Institute of Santa Barbara, 1986.

Three people is ontological and transformative. People leave this phase when they are anchored to deep meaning within themselves.

The major products of Phase Three are a new layer of self with renewed self-esteem, self-renewing resilience, the courage to be, and a trust in a force beyond one's ego. In fact, just as the person in Phase One turns to doing as the primary vehicle for fulfillment, the person in Phase Three turns to being. Being seeks doing for its own fulfillment, and doing seeks being for its own sustenance; this is the forceful dynamic of the continuous cycle.

In Phase Four, Getting Ready (Figure 13.6), clients are slowly moving out of the deep transition space and devoting their time to getting ready for new challenges. They usually have amazing energy and thirst for creative activities, exploration, networking, and learning. Although clients who have cocooned for some time feel ready to move on, they don't want to be exactly who they were before and doing what they did then. They want new directions, with significant changes from past ways of living and being, so they set about investigating options, investing in learning, experimenting with ideas, networking, and getting trained. It's a fun, busy, optimistic time, but it is lacking

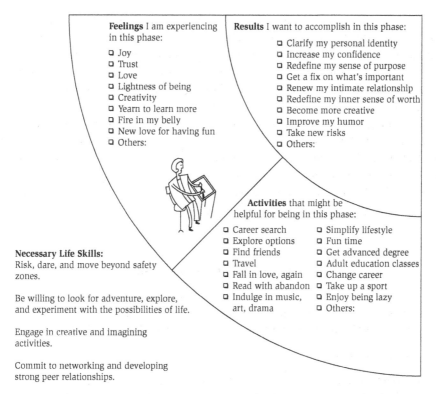

Feelings I am experiencing in this phase:

- ❑ Joy
- ❑ Trust
- ❑ Love
- ❑ Lightness of being
- ❑ Creativity
- ❑ Yearn to learn more
- ❑ Fire in my belly
- ❑ New love for having fun
- ❑ Others:

Results I want to accomplish in this phase:

- ❑ Clarify my personal identity
- ❑ Increase my confidence
- ❑ Redefine my sense of purpose
- ❑ Get a fix on what's important
- ❑ Renew my intimate relationship
- ❑ Redefine my inner sense of worth
- ❑ Become more creative
- ❑ Improve my humor
- ❑ Take new risks
- ❑ Others:

Activities that might be helpful for being in this phase:

- ❑ Career search
- ❑ Explore options
- ❑ Find friends
- ❑ Travel
- ❑ Fall in love, again
- ❑ Read with abandon
- ❑ Indulge in music, art, drama
- ❑ Simplify lifestyle
- ❑ Fun time
- ❑ Get advanced degree
- ❑ Adult education classes
- ❑ Change career
- ❑ Take up a sport
- ❑ Enjoy being lazy
- ❑ Others:

Necessary Life Skills:
Risk, dare, and move beyond safety zones.

Be willing to look for adventure, explore, and experiment with the possibilities of life.

Engage in creative and imagining activities.

Commit to networking and developing strong peer relationships.

Figure 13.6 Clients in Phase Four: Getting Ready

© Hudson Institute of Santa Barbara, 1986.

in clear goals. It's helpful for a coach to remember that a major life transition takes time; he or she needs to understand the nuances of a major life transition and resistant rushing the process.

The cycle of change is a never-ending process throughout the adult years. This cycle is explained in full detail in Hudson's *The Adult Years* (2000) and McLean and Hudson's *LifeLaunch* (2011). Here's a brief walk through the cycle with two very different client situations: one in a stable chapter of life making minor adjustments and another in a major transition time.

Most clients arrive at the door of the coach in the quadrant termed The Doldrums. They have a vague sense of ennui, and as they move further down the arc, the sense of discontent grows in intensity. It might be the leader who finds herself promoted into a position that suits her pocketbook and status but not her heart, skills, and dreams, or the fifty-five-year old who thought his job was secure and lived accordingly, only to find it all go up in smoke overnight. People in these situations feel discouraged. They have a sense of hopelessness, big or small, and may languish in the doldrums with no wind to help them move in one direction or another.

There are only a handful of choices when we find ourselves in this place. Of course, we can dig in our heels, get angry, and refuse to take action. Nonaction typically results in more of the same, and eventually even this stance is impossible to maintain. To move out of this quadrant, we need to make some changes—either small adjustments (a minitransition) or deeper changes that result in developmental shifts of the transformative kind. We tend to make the decision about whether to make a small adjustment and keep moving ahead or take the longer road based on how big the change is that we face. Big endings and beginnings offer (and, just as often, force) us to make some major changes in our lives or larger systems.

Consider Steve's situation. He had been leading a large health care organization with great success for fifteen years.

Beyond the Succession Plan

Steve had planned for his retirement, and he and the board were in agreement about the timing and the important next steps. Yet Steve had made no plans for the shift and instead worked at his usual breakneck speed right up through his final day on the job.

The Doldrums Phase

A month later, when he assumed he would be enjoying his new sense of freedom, he found himself instead in a very lonely and dark place: no more tight schedule and constant demands, no more global travel, no more administrative support at his side, no more title and identity. Most of all, he was completely surprised by his own sense of loss and unexpected reaction to this new place. For Steve, the change was enormous, and no number of small adjustments would bring him back to equilibrium. He was faced with peeling away an identity, a mask of sorts, and uncovering a new layer of self and identity: repurposing.

The Big Transition: The Cocooning Phase

As organizations and individuals, we spend very little time in this repurposing quadrant, and it's likely that we'll move into this transformative space only a handful of times in our lives. Yet each time we find ourselves here, whether it's a loss or a new beginning, we inevitably face parts of our self that we haven't known much about. Steve had been a successful leader, but he had paid the price of single-mindedness, and now the one-string guitar wasn't enough for him. He had to do the hard work of creating a new layer of self, and this is not a comfortable place. It requires self-reflection of significant dimensions, letting go of old identities, and some grieving, and it all takes time—more time that we'd like.

When we've traveled the quadrant of repurposing, we say good-bye to what we no longer need on the journey ahead. For Steve, the work seemed enormous: he was genuinely surprised by how much his role as head of an organization defined who he was, what he did, and how others responded to him. Creating a new sense of himself without his organization took time, space, and self-reflection, and he found some solace in writing as well.

The Getting Ready Phase

Finally after nearly a year of sabbatical-like living, Steve was ready to venture into new territory and try some new ways of being. This is the quadrant we term "Getting Ready": the territory that requires new thinking, experimenting, and exploring new ways of being. At some points in the journey, it's likely to include forms of learning—maybe an advanced degree or more training. At other times, as in Steve's case, it's a time to harvest all of life's skills and talents and test new ventures with fewer stakes and plenty of pleasure. We are a doer-addicted culture, and it's our tendency to jump on the first experiment we try and often miss out on the value of real experimenting at this juncture.

Steve found himself tempted to try out the first idea that stumbled on him: a call from a well-respected nonprofit agency in his community. But with the help of his coach, he stepped back and allowed himself to take a broader look at his options before settling on his next steps. Ultimately Steve decided to test out a dream he had many years ago: starting a small business of his own.

A Return to the Go for It Phase

Once Steve moved into this new decisional place, he was in the first quadrant—that place where we feel most alive, most aligned with our sense of what's most important at this time in life. Steve's stay in this place could be a long while, and it will inevitably lead him to that out-of-sync place a few times and require some adjustments in order to maximize this chapter. Then at some point, it won't be enough anymore, or some major external change will rip him out of this chapter and require another longer journey through repurposing.

A Leadership Passage

Jill's story is quite different.

Making Changes Inside a Life Chapter

This story begins when, at age forty-two, Jill moved into a leadership role following the sudden death of a colleague. She was honored to have the position offered to her and willingly agreed to accept it. But once in the position, she was overwhelmed with the challenges coming from both her leadership team and her own personal sense of inadequate capacity to do the job. What's more, she found herself questioning her decision and the wisdom of the big leap she had signed on for. Her new role demanded a toughness and an in-the-moment decision-making style that was well outside her comfort zone. And in the language of the cycle of renewal, Jill had been happily engaged in her old role and likely enjoying a long stay in the Go for It quadrant until this big change

(continued)

> ### Making Changes Inside a Life Chapter *(continued)*
>
> came along, catapulting her into that out-of-sync place where things don't feel right and there's worry about what's to come. Jill could have refused the promotion and dodged these challenges. Instead, she willingly took it on, and her success required some significant shifts in her perception of self and concomitant capacities.
>
> **From Doldrums to a Minitransition**
>
> In the end, Jill succeeded, and she would be the first to say she's a far better leader. She has developed new capacities and confidence that didn't exist at the same levels before this change was thrust on her. Jill is more alive and engaged than ever before: no longer second-guessing decisions, taking remarks too personally, or deliberating on strategies too long. Jill's journey required what we term a minitransition: a series of adjustments that enabled her to operate effectively at a new level of leadership in her organization. Her identity hasn't fundamentally changed; rather, she has deepened her skills in order to be fully equipped to step into this new role.

Levels of Change: Transformational and Adaptive

Steve's journey was likely transformational for him: it required letting go of an old identity, coming to terms with a new time in his life, and creating a new way of being in the world—all the work of the lower half of the circle on the cycle of renewal, uncovering a new level of differentiation and a new stage in the adult journey. Jill's journey included a series of smaller changes that required not an overhaul of self but an increased capacity in her leadership role.

Life today breeds endless change, and our clients' abilities to map the way are aided by our understanding of an ongoing and normative change process that is always present in our lives. A normative and cyclical view of change allows us to make far more intentional choices. Simply put, change is a ubiquitous force in today's world. Leaders and organizations have only a handful of choices in this new terrain: to react, resist, or leverage the inevitable change as an opportunity for development, allowing us to reinvent ourselves and our systems as we remain engaged, agile, and vibrant.

The central function of coaching is facilitating development in individuals and systems. Leveraging change to foster development is the domain of coaching in today's change-dominated world.

ASSESSING CLIENTS RELATIVE TO THE CYCLE OF CHANGE

By listening carefully, a coach can tell whether a client is in a relatively stable chapter and wants help improving it or whether a transition is taking place and the client seeks help in managing that transition creatively. All of this becomes the life script of the individual, who is moving from chapter to transition to chapter to transition over and over again.

It won't be immediately obvious to a coach which phase of the change cycle a client is in. Considering these questions is likely to be useful:

- Is my client in a more or less stable time of life or in a less stable transition?
- Is it a minitransition or a life transition [if the client seems to be in a transition of some sort]?
- Which of the four phases illustrated in the model is my client in? What specific life skills can I encourage my client to consider at this time?
- What critical developmental activities would promote growth and discovery for this client?
- What is my client's resistance to moving ahead in the renewal cycle, and what do we need to address in order to make big aspirational goals more compelling?
- What strengths does my client have that might be vehicles for growth and development at this time?
- What is my client's vision of the future—dreams, expectations, aspirations? Does my client have a sense of purpose or mission? Where does the client want to be five years from now?
- If my client is committed to a minitransition or restructuring, how can I assist in promoting an accurate evaluation of what to hold on to, let go of, or take on?
- Are there external sources of change triggering a transition in my client? If so, how do I encourage self-management at this time?
- What planning items has my client identified for his or her next chapter of life?
- What follow-up coaching or referral items has my client identified for his or her next chapter of life?

CHAPTER 14

COACHING FOR CORE VALUES

T he previous chapter was about understanding how coaches can help clients manage their experience of change. Now we turn to the importance of understanding the client's core values. My colleagues and I have examined 250 biographies of successful adults over the past twenty-five years, searching for the dominant inner anchors that guide people toward realizing their own greatness. We found that most successful leaders and professionals tend to measure their lives with one or more of six basic core values, and most often in some combination:

1. *Personal power*, or claiming oneself: Self-esteem, confidence, identity, inner motivation, a positive sense of self, clear ego boundaries, self-love, courage

2. *Achievement*, or proving oneself: Reaching goals, conducting projects, working, winning, playing in organized sports, having ambition, getting results and recognition, being purposive, doing

3. *Intimacy*, or sharing oneself: Loving, bonding, caring, being intimate, making relationships work, feeling close, nesting, coupling, parenting, being a good friend, reaching out to others, seeking companionship

4. *Play and creativity*, or expressing oneself: Being imaginative, intuitive, playful, spontaneous, original, expressive, humorous, artistic, creative, curious

5. *Search for meaning*, or integrating oneself: Finding wholeness, unity, integrity, peace, an inner connection to all things, spirituality, trust in the flow of life, inner wisdom, a sense of transcendence

6. *Compassion and contribution*, or giving of oneself: Improving, helping, feeding, reforming, leaving the world a better place, bequeathing, being generative, serving, social and environmental caring, institution building, volunteering

These six core values compete for our loyalty and passionate commitment throughout the adult journey, and we often shift gears throughout the adult years from familiar, accomplished value areas to new, challenging ones.

Most of those whom we studied combined two or three of these values (rarely more than three) to form an alliance that produced energy and direction for living and sustaining their sense of purpose, chapter by chapter. In a life transition, individuals (or organizations) go through a reevaluation of core values, making a conscious selection based on the reconstructed self at the end of the cocooning process. This choice of values in the middle of a transition generates immense energy and sense of purpose, which join together to prepare persons to evolve as they move on successfully into the creation of new visions and plans. Coaches are most likely to facilitate this process of values clarification, commitment, and action when their clients are sorting emerging core values in a major life transition. Each core value or passion draws on a different aspect of our human abilities, but every adult has the capacity to tap all six passions at various times in the adult journey by way of sustaining vitality and purpose. Too often we lock ourselves into the passions and values of our young adult years and burn out on them during midlife. A better approach is to keep evaluating our priorities and preferences to be sure that at any time in our lives, we are marching to our own drumbeats, empowered by the values we honor in our hearts at any given time.

HELPING A CLIENT ASSESS CORE VALUES

A coach won't necessarily know from casual conversation what values a client holds dear. The following questions for a coach to consider will help focus his or her approach to dealing with values:

- Which of the six passions does my client feel drawn toward?
- Which of the passions seem to produce energy for life in my client?
- Which of the six passions are negative or neutral for my client at this time?
- What are the core values that my client is struggling with?

- What are some passionate destinations (goals or results) that my client would like to reach with his or her top three passions?
- How can I enable my client to move from an articulation of values to a statement of purpose for the next chapter of life?

COACHING THE SIX CORE VALUES

Often clients are not sure how they feel about values. Following are questions pertaining to each of the six values that a coach could ask a client to consider. With each set of questions, I suggest some goals a coach might reach for in the questioning process.

Core Value One: Personal Power

Basic Questions

- Who am I?
- What do I like most about being me?
- What are my boundaries?
- What is my sense of purpose?
- Where am I going?
- Who is going with me?
- How will I get there?
- Will I have a place in it?
- What do I need to learn?
- What is my work?
- How shall I measure my success?
- How am I evolving as a person?

Possible Coaching Goals

Increasing self-confidence or self-esteem	Improving personal performance
Developing better relationships	Managing conflict
Increasing trust in the future	Embracing the maturation process
Developing leadership and spiritual awareness	Wellness planning
Financial planning	Developing a career
Becoming more introspective	Deepening a sense of self
Increasing self-esteem and confidence	Maintaining clear boundaries
Becoming more assertive	Using solitude time creatively
Spending time alone in nature	Joining a vision quest

Core Value Two: Achievement

Basic Questions

- What are my gifts?
- What is my compelling sense of purpose?
- If I could leave a mark, what would it look like?
- If I reach my goals, what would I do next?
- What rewards am I really seeking?
- What training do I need to be at my best?
- How much is enough?
- How do I count what counts?
- What is my legacy?

Possible Coaching Goals

Promoting personal vision	Reaching goals
Getting results	Being dependable
Collaborating	Gaining leadership skills
Pursuing continuous training	Motivating others
Knowing how to make and conduct	Obtaining business skills
strategic plans	Learning time management skills

Core Value Three: Intimacy

Basic Questions

- What matters most to me?
- How do I love myself and remain my own best friend?
- What are the bonds I honor most in my life?
- How am I investing in those bonds this year?
- How do I attach to others?
- How do I want others to attach to me?
- Am I a good friend to others?
- Are my friends available to me in ways I want them to be?
- How is my love evolving and growing?
- What would add value to my expressions of intimacy?

Possible Coaching Goals

Maintaining healthy self-love	Sustaining affective bonds
Knowing how to maintain healthy love relationships	Investing in friendships
	Succeeding in father-mother-helper roles
Sustaining a high level of empathy for others	

Core Value Four: Play and Creativity

Basic Questions

- How often does my mind wander to imaginative domains?
- How do I have fun being me?
- What are my favorite forms of spontaneous expression?
- How am I creative?
- How am I playful?
- What learning would deepen my creativity?
- With which friends am I most naturally playful and creative?

Possible Coaching Goals

Eliciting intuition	Processing client dreams
Future visioning with clients	Indulging in nonsense
Laughing	Risk taking
Being playful	Allowing spontaneous laughing
Being inventive	Creating new forms of things or ideas
Being spontaneous	Having fun
Finding flow in everyday life	

Core Value Five: Search for Meaning

Basic Questions

- What am I doing here?
- What is my ultimate concern?
- What can I rely on?
- How do I arrive at inner peace?

- What are my basic beliefs, and how do I express them?
- What are the settings that help me experience the unity of all things?
- What forms of caring are part of my spiritual beliefs?
- What do I feel called to do with my life?
- How do I express reverence for life?

Possible Coaching Goals

Looking for connections and unities	Purpose
Inner peace	Profound spirituality
Tapping the soulful part of a client (not the ego)	

Core Value Six: Compassion and Contribution

Basic Questions

- What is my legacy?
- What will live on long after I am gone?
- How can I support the needs of others, not merely my own needs?
- What are the important contributions I want to make?
- How can I express the compassion I feel?
- What causes am I willing to support?
- How can I volunteer my time to make a difference?

Possible Coaching Goals

Finding meaningful ways to express social caring	Becoming compassionate
	Wanting to leave a legacy
Becoming concerned beyond oneself	Becoming socially active or politically
Seeking fairness in treatment of all people	connected

CHAPTER 15

THE CLIENT EMBEDDED
IN HUMAN SYSTEMS

A coach comprehends the broader context of the client when he understands how the client interacts with and prioritizes within each life system, which encompasses self, couple, family, friends, work, and community. All of these groups give context to life. Adults need to be and to feel effective within the systems that surround and support life. Just as fish cannot live without water to swim in, we cannot live without the systems we're in and the environments they provide. In fact, our lives are embedded in systems through the roles we have in them. Systems shape the way we think and feel, provide us with arenas for our own fulfillment, and program us with roles and expectations.

During our adult years, we can define the roles we prefer and choose how to leave or diminish the roles that become burdensome. Sometimes coaches can help clients gain a broader perspective and transcend system roles temporarily by reflecting on the roles the clients prefer in the years ahead. Specifically, coaches can help clients see what their own roles are within a system, gain perspective on their involvement, and identify ways to change roles if they are no longer satisfying. And clients might want to improve an unhappy situation by rearranging priorities and achieving balance. Another possibility is to move on, either inside or outside the system, when roles no longer satisfy or remain available. Coaches can help clients understand their options and feel empowered to pursue newly found goals. This chapter is organized around six human systems: self, couple, family, friends, work, and community.

Coaches must first determine their clients' status in and feelings about the system or systems they're in that are of concern. Considering these questions can be useful:

- Which of the six systems (self, couple, family, friends, work, community) concerns my client the most?
- To what extent is my client helped and supported by this system, and to what extent is the system dominating my client's life?
- To what extent is my client contained by, defined by, and driven by the rules and values of one or more of the human systems in which he or she is embedded?
- If my client is role bound, how can I provoke a dialogue with the real self without being perceived as being against the role?
- How do the system concerns of my client correlate with the information I have about his or her place in the cycle of change?
- How do my client's system concerns correlate with the information I have about his or her commitments to core values? Are the major positive system concerns related to the top three or four core values?
- Is my client experiencing role overload? If so, what steps might I imagine to reduce investment in this role and get control of it?
- Is my client experiencing a hunger to explore a different system or role?
- Is my client experiencing a conflict between or among the roles and systems of life?
- What is the balance my client would like with roles and systems in the next chapter of life?

THE SELF SYSTEM

Self-care often emerges as foundational to great leadership in the work of coaching, and it is directed to fostering holistic, balanced self-care. The better clients do with this system, the more likely they are to do well with the other five. Managing personal roles effectively prepares clients for managing larger roles.

Basic Questions for a Coach to Consider

- Does my client have a healthy lifestyle?
- Does my client have health challenges?
- Does my client engage in regular physical exercise?
- What sort of balance does my client seem to have relative to work life and home life?

- Does my client create time alone for himself or herself?
- Does my client seem to manage finances in a manner that supports self-care?

THE COUPLE SYSTEM

The couple is probably the most neglected human system in adult life. Typically we give more attention and have more professional assistance for work roles and family roles than we do for couple roles. Coaches should look for what is working in a client's life as part of a couple and promote that. A coach should look for the ties that bind currently. Be ready to refer a couple to a trained therapist if that seems appropriate.

Basic Questions for a Coach to Consider

- Where does the couple role fit into my client's life?
- How does my client attend to the couple's relationship?
- How does my client view the importance of this relationship?
- If my client is not in a long-term relationship, what is the impact on my client?

THE FAMILY SYSTEM

Coaches are not family therapists, yet when a leader's life includes a dynamic family, the natural crises and challenges that surface at the most unexpected times in this system will undoubtedly surface in one way or another inside the coaching engagement.

Basic Questions for a Coach to Consider

- If my client has a family, how does he or she view the family's level of priority in his life?
- How does my client interact with his or her family?
- How does my client manage the balance of work and family when a family crisis develops?

THE FRIENDS SYSTEM

The important role of friends in our adult lives tends to provide a sense of balance between work and life and a sense of continuity. More than men, women typically have more friends in general and more life friends in particular, that is, the friendships aren't based on work or career. Men tend to develop friendships around work- or career-related contacts and around sports interests. But as men and women move into their fifties and sixties, friends play more important roles in their lives.

Basic Questions for a Coach to Consider

- Does my client engage in maintaining active friendships?
- How do friendships fit into my client's life? Are they, for example, central or peripheral?
- If my client has few friends, what is the impact on him or her?
- How might the cultivation of new friendships change my client?

THE WORK SYSTEM

Because few linear careers are left, adults have to learn throughout the life cycle how to reevaluate their work roles and preferred rewards for work in order to formulate a personal business plan that extends their overall responsibilities into a challenging future.

Basic Questions for a Coach to Consider

- How central is the role of work in my client's life?
- How dominant is the work identity to my client?

THE COMMUNITY SYSTEM

A coach might help a client evaluate his or her social system connections, including involvement in community organizations and activities.

Basic Questions for a Coach to Consider

- How involved in community (local and global) is my client?
- To what extent does my client value contributions to his or her community?

CHAPTER 16

THE CLIENT'S VISION AND PURPOSE

The ultimate function of coaches, no matter what their particular specialty or immediate issue, is to help people and organizations find their purpose, vision, and plans for the immediate future. Purpose is of ultimate concern. Purpose is a deep source of meaning, the reason we are alive; it generates energy and life direction. Vision is the way we see our lives or organizations being at some future time; it is a visual snapshot we can pursue. Scenario development incorporates purpose, vision, and planning into a living framework for inventing the future. Planning is a day-by-day measuring stick for linking today to a visionary tomorrow. Coaches help clients plan ways get to their future vision with a high probability of success, all the while honoring their clients' purpose.

Purpose, vision, and planning are equally important and work together. Coaches weave these themes in and around each other as they work with their clients, using the coaching methodology and inviting clients to envision an inspiring future. To create an inspired future, the purpose must become a dream, and the dream must become a plan. The dreamer becomes, in effect, a planner. But planning is more than a bunch of skills; it is an inner force, a felt competence, a strength within. The planner pushes forward with logical, informed steps, like choosing reliable stepping stones to cross a stream. Through strategic thinking, the planner embroiders the dreamer's vision with the complexity of the world, weaving together technical and human resources that are required to bring the life structure into reality. The possible dream becomes a probable plan.

FINDING PURPOSE

Finding purpose is more than pursuing a goal. A person with purpose has a compelling reason for being alive—an ontological pull, a motivational push, a calling. Purpose is the most important quality for each of us to possess experientially, consciously, and with words. It tells us what we want most to be about. At different times in the life cycle, we reformulate our sense of purpose, that is, our sense of what matters most to us. Quite often our sense of purpose changes as we mature. Most often it evolves from ways to be successful to ways to be.

Purpose produces passion or positive energy. On-purpose people have passion in their lives, and tapping the passion a client has for constructing a future direction is a coaching challenge. A coach should ask, "What emotional resources does my client have for generating sustained motivation for inventing the future he or she wants?"

VISIONING

A vision is a snapshot in our mind's eye of how we want to be, look, act, achieve, and interface with others at some given date in the future. It is more than visual. It includes hearing, sensing, feeling, and being. The more we can feel viscerally the excellence we are pursuing, the more likely we are to approximate it.

The future is not something waiting for us but something we create. It is time and potential resources waiting for form, the not-yet waiting to be programmed. And if we don't create our own future, someone else will fit us into theirs. Life is a series of collisions with the future, said one Spanish writer. Tomorrow is either the sum of our pasts or the sum of our yearnings for what we may become. If we are creating our own future, we almost always begin with a dream. "I have a dream," yearned Martin Luther King Jr. in Washington, D.C., as he painted a picture of equality and fairness in America. The dream comes first. Reality chases after the dream, to make it happen.

A vision or dream, then, has these characteristics:

- A simple picture of what the future means. It declares what is important, purposive, and valuable for our lives ahead.
- A poetic picture, not a literal statement.
- A visceral yearning, not a wish list. It is not a vision or dream to want a new car, an exotic vacation, or even a new career. A vision is an all-encompassing picture for our lives, not a simple wanting of something that would be nice to have.

- A spiritual promise of a new quality of life, a deeper sense of being. The vision within us is a yearning for an improved (not ideal or perfect) state of affairs, a promise for human betterment that is just beyond our reach but worth reaching for and possible to approximate.

- A promise that is convincing. To think it is to go for it. It feels right, and it's going to happen. It's a Promise (with a capital "P"), and it pops into our minds frequently. It is a Promise happening. It feels that simple.

- A pull toward it from without and a push toward it from within. Its pull is the perception it gives to our priorities, and its push is high-level motivation within us.

- Energy as much as anything else. We know we have a vision when we get positive energy every time we think of it.

- Like a haunting refrain. We know we have a vision when it won't let us go and others are attracted to it. We know we have a vision when it is already guiding us ahead, and we instinctively trust it and don't feel we have to explain it to anyone.

- An inspiration and motivation that doesn't order us around. Human beings are the only creatures on earth capable of envisioning a future and then setting about to make it happen.

We dream and imagine, expect and plan, invent and create. Almost always when we are alive and happy, we create our future to be different from the present. Then we set about to make it happen. This is how new companies get born, poems get conceived, Olympic races get won, music gets written, and better mouse traps get invented.

Much of the dreaming that we do takes place in childhood and adolescence. We encourage children and young adults to dream and to launch plans to achieve those dreams. In the midlife and midcareer years, however, when life is complicated by many commitments and responsibilities, dreaming tends to diminish or to be limited and episodic. A midlife dream may be for a trip to Hawaii or a move into a new house.

Fundamentally a vision or dream is holistic, encompassing all of life and unleashing enormous energy for a sense of personal mission. It feels deep and earth-shaking. The greatest power in our lives is our capacity to imagine, vision, or dream, not only when we are young but over and over again throughout the life cycle. It is an essential lifestyle ingredient for the self-renewing adult. The more we can create a sense of how we want the next few years to be, with continuities and change from the way we are today, the more we can and will make our futures happen.

CHAPTER 17

THE CLIENT'S LEARNING AGENDA

Continuous learning is the secret weapon of adult empowerment in our age of constant change. This is true no matter which part of adulthood a person is in. Unfortunately, few use it to full advantage. It is all too easy to lock oneself into the assumptions born of youthful schooling as the world spins on with new paradigms and technologies. It is just as easy to lose the learning edge in a mellowed-out midlife, leaving leadership to others.

Adults at any age who fail to stay abreast of our ever accelerating learning curve are at risk. Younger adults miss opportunities; older adults take on stereotypical "old" behaviors: they seem over the hill, passive, resigned. But adults who keep pushing into new learning of any type are questioning, imaginative, and daring. Continuous learning keeps a person vital, awake, and forward looking. As many parts of the world become a grayer culture, it must also become a continuous learning society if it wants to remain a leader among nations.

People in their twenties haven't yet launched their first life chapter. Many are busy going to school to get ready for the great adventure ahead—the grown-up years: earning degrees, getting work experience, learning to manage in many settings, becoming experts in something. Many imagine settling down after all this for the long haul.

Those who are now older adults remember that early period well when training for their first adult life chapter took more than twenty years. When they launched their first dreams, they may have lacked experience, but they didn't lack careful preparation and powerful determination. During the rest of their lives, they gained lots of experience but probably never again had such intense learning preparation. They now must engage in whatever learning they need if they are to sustain the great adventure of adulthood.

UNDERTAKING A NEW LEARNING AGENDA

Coaches should ask themselves these questions about a client who seems ready to undertake a new learning agenda:

- What does my client need to unlearn, and how can I help build this agenda into the follow-up plan? What must he unlearn if he is to master the future he truly wants? What patterns of thinking that served him well earlier in life are now in the way of what he really wants to do and become?

- What new information does my client need to learn, and how can I help build this agenda into a follow-up plan? What new information and knowledge does he need in order to be at his best?

- What new technical skills does my client need, and how can I help build this agenda into the follow-up plan?

- How can I help my client find the best learning environments for the next chapter of his life?

- How can I help my client identify the best teachers and mentors for this learning agenda?

- What can I do to enable my client to network successfully?

CONSTRUCTING A LEARNING AGENDA

To begin discussion of a learning program with clients, a coach should ask, in one way or another, the following eight questions to encourage clients to begin constructing their own learning agenda:

1. What do I need to unlearn?
2. What new information do I need?
3. How do I increase my personal competence?
4. What new technical skills do I need?
5. How can I deepen and clarify my own values?
6. Where are my best learning environments?
7. Who are my real teachers and mentors?
8. How will I execute and evaluate my current learning program?

Because abundant learning resources are available not only through recognized educational institutions but through informal learning groups and the Internet, it is possible for all adults to be committed to a continuous learning agenda that evolves and changes throughout the adult life cycle.

WHERE ADULTS LEARN

The whole global village is an adult's campus. We can choose our own learning environments and formats: seminars, mentors, conferences, books, study groups, certification programs, advanced degrees, and ways to get connected. There is no paucity of adult learning opportunities near and far.

Adults do not want to sit at the feet of mere knowledge experts; we want to learn from masters of our fields—others who have applied the knowledge they are espousing to themselves and their professions. That is why so many conventional college professors do not appeal to midlife adults as appropriate teachers. The new adult teacher is a mentor, mensch, or master—someone who lives and breathes what the learner wants to learn. Many such experts are available around the world today. Each of us has to find them and hire them. We may not find them at conventional learning institutions, although some can be found there too.

PART SIX

COACHING IN ORGANIZATIONS

It could be argued that all leadership is appreciative leadership. It's the capacity to see the best in the world around us, in our colleagues, and in the groups we are trying to lead. It's the capacity to see with an appreciative eye to the true and the good, the better and the possible.
—David L. Cooperrider

CHAPTER 18

BUILDING A COACHING CULTURE

L eadership coaching has become a mainstream approach for developing today's best leaders in organizations large and small across the globe. In 2010 it was a $2 billion industry and growing. Today, as organizations experience the positive impact of executive coaching, there is increased interest in developing a coaching culture that supports a coaching mind-set throughout the organization and equips managers with coaching skills and a simple methodology that allows for what we can call just-in-time coaching—an intentional approach to developing team members on the spot when it matters most.

Clutterbuck and Megginson (2005) offer a definition of a coaching culture: "Coaching is the predominant style of working together, and where a commitment to grow the organization is embedded in a parallel commitment to grow the people in the organization" (p. 19). Recent studies have examined the key ingredients in developing a coaching culture in an effort to extend the power of coaching well beyond the commonly used external executive coach approach. The Center for Creative Leadership conducted a benchmarking study in 2008 analyzing the trends in coaching inside organizations and based on the input of 347 leaders across industries. It concluded that the development of a strategic initiative to create a coaching culture requires a deliberate approach using five strategies:

1. Seed the organization with leaders and managers who can role-model coaching approaches.

2. Link coaching outcomes to the success of the business. Develop a competency model with strategic coaching goals, tactics, and measures around coaching behavior.

3. Coach senior leadership teams in creating a culture change. Over twice as many leaders wanted team coaching as those who said they were receiving it.

4. Recognize and reward coaching-culture behaviors. Highlight role models and the positive outcomes produced by these new behaviors.

5. Integrate coaching with other people management processes.

Hawkins and Smith (2006) carefully examined the path in developing a coaching culture and articulated seven stages in developing a coaching culture:

1. The organization employs coaches for some of its executives.

2. The organization develops its own coaching and mentoring capacity.

3. The organization actively supports coaching endeavors.

4. Coaching becomes a norm for individuals, teams, and the whole organization.

5. Coaching becomes embedded in the organization's human resource (HR) and performance management processes.

6. Coaching becomes the predominant style of managing throughout the organization.

7. Coaching becomes how we do business with all of our stakeholders.

Hawkins and Smith highlight the importance of evaluation at each stage in this process in order to support the shift in culture, stressing the reality that a shift to a coaching culture must not be an end in itself but rather a means to a stronger and more successful organization.

A CASE STUDY ON DEVELOPING A COACHING CULTURE

In our work with organizations focused on developing a coaching culture, we've had an opportunity to engage with organizations that develop a strategic approach in building a coaching culture from the ground up. TaylorMade-adidas Golf Company is one of those organizations (McHenry, Harrah, and Berry, 2008). Over the course of several years, TaylorMade's coaching culture has evolved from a handful of executive coaching engagements to a full-blown coaching culture achieving impressive success in the marketplace and fast becoming a best-place-to-work environment in Southern California. Here we chronicle both the strategies it created at the outset and its pathway through the stages of development similar to those that Hawkins and Smith (2006) articulated.

In the year 2000, the leadership team of the TaylorMade-adidas Golf Company was fractured and frustrated. There was an absence of trust, meaningful collaboration, and camaraderie. The CEO first tried unofficially disbanding the senior team and discontinuing regular staff meetings that had been unproductive and often devolved into conflict. In a sense, he sent the team members "to their corners." Having tried different tactics and methods to pull the group together, he determined that the one area yet to be explored was team and individual development. He decided it was time for the group to take a hard look at their ineffective working relationships and explore how to develop greater awareness, tolerance, and understanding as individuals and as a team.

Having reached a plateau of $300 million in sales, TaylorMade-adidas Golf Company was no longer a small enterprise. It was clear that what had worked before was no longer effective if the team was to move past the plateau and into a significant expansion of market influence and leadership. Not surprisingly, the primary challenge was one of communication and collaboration. The team had grown larger in order to reach the $300 million mark, but what had not grown was its ability to share more, understand more, and work together in new ways. Team members were stuck in silos, splitting off one another to protect their turf, living in a daily mind-set of individual rather than company success. The challenge was one of competition versus collaboration. The CEO understood that for the company to take the next step in its development, his leadership team had to develop as well.

Having experienced the impact of professional coaching and leadership consulting before, the CEO understood the potential impact an intervention could have. With the advice and counsel of both his HR leader and an outside consultant and executive coach, he decided to step into this new endeavor, believing that this focus on communication and collaboration would illuminate a way forward. With the personalities and conflicts that existed previously, he tasked his consulting partners with pulling the group together through a leadership assessment tool and demonstrated his own willingness to hear some tough messages about his dysfunctional team. Participation came with significant resistance. However, the CEO led by sharing his own values, strengths, and challenges. Team members followed his example, and the pattern of internal competition slowly began to change.

Early in his tenure, the CEO recognized that to change the dysfunctional pattern of the executive team, collaboration would have to take priority over competition. The CEO rejected the notion of quick fixes to deeply challenging problems. At an early off-site meeting, the team was given a choice to continue in the old pattern of surface relating or change the pattern to foster greater depth. A useful metaphor was born at the meeting. The difference was identified as "diving rather than surfing." It is a striking example that fits the Hudson cycle of renewal. The team was out of sync, and instead of moving forward through a series of small tweaks and adjustments, the CEO enabled and instructed the team to do something quite different. He challenged them to take a deeper look in order to repurpose and redirect the group's effectiveness for one another and for the business.

Out of the team's initial interactions with the assessment and the challenge to dive rather than surf, it became clear that a small percentage of the team members were ready to challenge themselves to become more effective leaders of the business. Equally clear was that a larger proportion of the group wanted nothing to do with activities that required confronting and exploring the hard and personal questions raised through both personal assessment and the team discussions that followed. Those few who wanted to go further were offered the chance to work individually with a professional coach. These early adopters made a decision that continues to resonate in the organization today.

Lesson 1: Crisis Is a Catalyst for Change

The CEO made a decision to explore a new way to get at the old problems he and his team were facing. To use Freud's analogy from archaeology, he saw that a beautiful layer has to be destroyed in order to get to the next level. There was a significant desire to change on the part of the CEO that flowed from him to his team and eventually out into the wider organization. As painful as it had become, it took courage to destroy what had worked for so long based on the promise of something that could not yet be seen.

A series of interventions, off-site meetings, and individual consulting and coaching were undertaken to help individuals and the group deal more effectively with existing and recurring conflict (competition versus collaboration). What was clear early on was that the group rarely, if ever, took time to reflect, think, absorb, and discuss what was going on with them as individual leaders and as a team. The people themselves were never the subject matter of their discussions; rather it was always about the actions necessary to move the business forward. This orientation toward action, absent reflection, was the working style of the team members and represented their most significant challenge. The success of this period was both the sharing of a slowly evolving common language of development (the values, strengths, and challenges mentioned earlier) and the ability to remain in the tension of action versus reflection in spite of some vocal and ongoing resistance to the work.

Lesson 2: Executive Permission and Support Is Imperative

While the coaching initiative appeared to many as an organic outgrowth of the work of the senior team, this initiative was, significantly, an aligned decision by the CEO and the HR leader to optimize and extend into the organization the development work that the senior executives were engaged in. They believed that individuals who hold leadership positions in the company needed to be better equipped to lead their teams and functions well and, in some cases, prepare themselves for more senior roles. In hindsight, this is both an obvious and simple directive, but in the context of the time, it marked a significant shift in the attitude of the organization that it would now take responsibility for developing the leaders of the organization. With that responsibility came the permission and support to extend coaching into the ranks. The absence of reflection and the need to safely and creatively explore new possibilities for old problems existed in the wider leadership group, beyond the executive team. In this way, coaching has provided a safe harbor for the affected, and the opportunity for repair is now built into the culture.

Lesson 3: The Value of Context Is Massive

After attending the coach training program at the Hudson Institute and inviting some of that organization's alumni to begin coaching relationships with senior leaders, the HR leader at TaylorMade-adidas Golf Company decided to expand the number of internal coaches by sending seven members of his team to the same training program over a three-year period. This decision, made in 2004, led to an equal number of internal and external coaches serving the business. This would shift permanently in 2006 when the senior team decided that, with the internal capacity now at a sustainable threshold, external coaching relationships would be discontinued below the executive level in order to take full advantage of the investment made in an internal coaching group.

With some limited but important experience with external coaches, the senior team determined that the value of cultural learning and awareness held by the internal outweighed the pure coaching technique and experience of the external coaches. The team discovered that internal coaches with both competence and the context of living day-to-day inside the organization are more effective, get more buy-in, and have more intuitive initial empathy than external coaches.

There were also challenges to this decision: confidentiality and objectivity might been lessened because of the decision. For a variety of both positive and negative reasons—a leader wanting to set the agenda for a direct report's work with a coach, the reliance on coaching as a way to help someone be more effective, the pressures from the business to get someone or something "fixed"—there are stated and unstated efforts to influence the coaches. After all, these individuals are peers of other company leaders and, in most cases, direct reports of executive team members. It is not uncommon for the coaches to hear something along the lines of, "I know you're coaching so and so and you can't say anything, but . . ." Another challenge is that living in the organizational dynamic, there is a predisposition, tied to objectivity, to want to commiserate or collude with clients about the most recent conflict, reorganization, market shift, or something else.

In addition, the risk existed that an internal coach would decide to leave the organization or, due to the demands of the business, reduce the amount of time dedicated to coaching. As this risk became reality, it became clear that the best approach was to maintain a balance of internal and external coaches, allowing the company to leverage the best of both worlds.

Ultimately the value of context overwhelmed these challenges, partially because the coach, whether internal or external, maintained the idea that "the self is the best tool for help" and set the stage for the self of the client to do the heavy lifting in the relationship, thereby making it more effective.

Lesson 4: Effective Coach Selection Is Essential

How should the coaches be selected? How many internal coaches are enough? The first and most obvious group to invite into this new role was the leadership group within the HR department. These individuals were closest to the new initiative given their daily involvement with the HR leader and, as stewards of the company culture, were already proven to be trustworthy and reliable in supporting employees and maintaining confidences.

In addition, and in support of the mandate to develop leaders from within the company, non-HR business leaders were invited and considered to take on the additional responsibility of professional coaching. It was understood that qualified line managers serving as coaches would allow the effort to reach a broader and deeper population of employees. These candidates had to have the willingness to enter a long and continuing involvement, and their capability was assessed by personal interaction, assessment, and feedback from organizational follow-up. It was a formula of self-selection with both peer and management feedback.

Missing from the equation, however, was a formal vetting process or a set of standards to guide coach selection. The invitation was opened to the company leadership because of the belief that those who stepped forward would come from a place of conviction and that with the addition of competence, both existing and learned, there would be a strong and compelling cadre of coaches to offer to the company. Although this turned out to be true in most cases, we didn't realize that the political dimensions that would lead someone to declare interest in becoming a coach (to gain organizational power, increase prestige, or be a distraction from his or her functional job responsibilities) would naturally surface. After several graduating classes of coaches, additional criteria became clear and have been put into place. For the purpose of preparation and selection, a minimum of fifty hours of experience as a client is required. Also, a demonstrated ability to coach as a manager, even in short, unscheduled sessions, is now a prerequisite. This type of informal coaching is evidence of the manager's ability to distribute responsibility and create accountability among direct reports.

One key challenge has been building a business case for the process. Whether the coaching is for skill, performance, or development, the target needs to be business relevant, translating appropriately to the overall company goals as well as the needs of the individual. When the overt support of bosses or supervisors is lacking, coaches have been denied a supportive framework for the important work of challenging the client's purpose, intent, and patterns of behavior. Conversely, when the boss is included in the discussion of the client's goals, business relevance is a likely outcome, and accountability can be a regular part of the coaching experience. A more robust and thorough client application process, inclusive of the manager's sign-off, has been put into practice and continues to evolve in an effort to solidify the necessary supportive framework for success in the relationship.

A second challenge is the fast cycle of change, allowing minimal time for reflection at the group level. Coaching has become a touchstone for those in the midst of a high-intensity, "move first, ask later" environment. Not infrequently, coaching is used to restore reflection and understanding when clients feel challenged by the corporate rhythm. As much as reflection is needed, the idea of "going slow to go fast" it is not easily described in terms that are understood by the dominant culture or the parent company. This requires an ongoing and intensive effort on the part of the coaching advocates to translate and interpret the importance and impact of coaching for the business.

Lesson 5: Coach Training Is a First Step

Preparation for the coaching initiative was important in at least two major aspects. Initial and ongoing coach education was necessary for the best practice of coaching technique and ethical standards. The education of the coaching clients about appropriate expectations for themselves, their direct reports, and bosses was essential.

To maximize the training experience of new coaches, the HR leader and the director of coaching and leadership development determined that coaching experience needed to be a priority. When they enter their training program, the new coaches are asked to coach as part of a coaching internship. In addition, a coach supervision group exists to challenge and encourage the ongoing development of the coaches. The group, which meets about eight times each year, is a forum for both skill development and the exploration of depth through connection, the discussion of coaching case studies, and learning about organizational and individual dynamics present in the coaching work. It allows a discussion of the current organizational context and themes critical in helping to serve clients from a place of significant awareness and understanding.

The following standards for coach development and continuous learning were created out of this group:

- *A continuous relationship with the best possible coach.* This stems from the belief that the best way to learn how to be an effective coach is through active participation and learning as a client. The coaches are not asked to focus this relationship on their work as coach but to make it about their own development as an individual and as a professional.

- *An understanding of the key coaching competencies and an explicit ethical practice orientation.* The coaching group meetings are the forum in which discussion and practice of the coaching core competencies and ethical standards take place. This is done through a combination of teaching, discussion, triad coaching practice (coach, client, and observer), feedback, and debriefing.

- *A consistent and simple coaching methodology tied to business outcomes.* Use of a consistent and straightforward methodology by all members of the internal coaching team provides the basis for measuring quality and tracking outcomes in a more predictable and meaningful way.

- *Consistent participation in one-to-one supervision.* Building on the concept of the coach supervision group, the coaches can explore their individual work with clients at a more intense and useful level through a one-on-one relationship with a supervisor or mentor coach.

- *Annual participation in outside learning events.* It is an expectation that the coaches will continue their learning outside the organization by attending at least one coaching conference or something of related and relevant subject matter each year. The coaches are asked to bring their learning from these events back to the group and to assimilate them into their coaching practice.

Mirroring experiences of other organizations growing a coaching culture, once TaylorMade invested adequate resources and the necessary internal support for developing a strong coaching culture, it was motivated to take another step. It provided training in coaching skills along with a simple methodology for its managers in order to provide leaders at all levels in the organization with enough skills to engage in regular development conversations among all members of their teams.

Two years into this next wave of coaching, TaylorMade-adidas Golf Company continues to experience the positive impact in its culture and on the bottom line.

EMERGING BEST PRACTICES

Building a coaching culture takes time and intention, and best practices and processes are beginning to consolidate as more organizations experience the value in coaching from the corner office to the team leader. Based on our experiences and confirmed by current research, we have identified these emerging best practices:

- *A thorough screening and education process for external executive coaches.* As Hawkins and Smith (2006) noted, the use of external executive coaches is often the informal beginnings of a coaching culture. Just as in the case of TaylorMade-adidas Golf Company, an organization hires an executive coach or two, has a positive experience that links to business results and the leader's development, and a shift toward a coaching approach begins. Today many organizations have sophisticated vetting processes for their external coaches, resulting in an approved panel of coaches, along with an education process for external coaches to ensure they understand the organization's mission, the leadership competencies, and the culture.

- *A system for measuring the value of the coaching on the bottom line.* Organizations are becoming increasingly skilled in standardizing systems and processes to measure the value of the coaching on the leader, the team, the organization, and the bottom line. This growing sophistication is good for the coach, the field of coaching, and the organization. The work of coaching must track the results that matter to the business and the bottom line if coaching is going to be viable over the long haul. Jack Phillips and Merrill Andersen (2008) provide tools for measuring ROI that range from self-observations to complex predictive formulas, but in the end, it's usually the simpler methodologies that get utilized. Lisa Edwards (quoted in Phillips and Edwards, 2008) concurs and makes a case for keeping it simple, suggesting that key stakeholders are much more interested in what was actually accomplished in the coaching engagement and how these accomplishments meet the organization's bigger goals.

- *Development of well-trained internal coaches across lines of business.* As the impact of coaching at the senior levels becomes more apparent, there is typically a heightened interest in the power of coaching beyond the executive level, and this leads to coaching high-potential leaders and providing coaching skills for high-level leaders to use in their role as leaders of their organization. TaylorMade-adidas Golf Company's investment beyond external coaches began by providing comprehensive coach training to a series of leaders in HR and subsequently in other divisions in the company. This layering occurred over three years and ultimately paved the way to another layer of a coaching culture.

- *Coaching supervision and support inside the organization.* In the most mature stages of a coaching culture such as TaylorMade-adidas Golf Company, there is attention to providing internal coaches with supervision in order to hone and develop mature coaching skills and craft procedures for continually examining the impact of a coaching approach on the bottom line of an organization.

DEVELOPMENT OF COACHING SKILLS FOR MANAGERS

The natural evolution of a coaching culture reaches into the managerial layers of the organization, providing a set of skills for managers to operate in the manager-as-coach realms and adopt a coaching mind-set in their work. Mink, Owen, and Mink (1993) foreshadowed this evolution when they wrote about coaching as a major advancement over the traditional management styles of command, control and dominance. Even in the early 1990s, they viewed the effective manager as the one able to acknowledge and empower others by using a coaching approach. Today's research supports their early suppositions. The Corporate Executive Board (2009) examined the main factors in driving leadership bench strength inside organizations and found that coaching provided by the leader's direct manager drives bench strength more than any other factors, including 360-degree feedback, peer mentoring, external executive education, action learning, or in-house classroom-based education.

A highly publicized 2011 study by Google aligns with that study. Google spent two years analyzing what the key indicators are in a successful manager in its own organization by examining over ten thousand manager observations to determine and prioritize the key traits. In 2011 it produced the results and reported the top trait as "being a good coach." Another finding was that one-on-one coaching with problem managers led to a 75 percent improvement in the manager's performance ("Google's Eight-Point Plan to Help Managers Improve," 2011).

CHAPTER 19

MANAGER AS COACH: THE NEW FRONTIER OF COACHING INSIDE ORGANIZATIONS

The focus on building coaching skills at the managerial level—what is often termed manager as coach—is a new frontier for coaching inside an organization. This next wave of coaching democratizes an approach that was once seen as an executive perk for accelerating development. Today organizations experience a rapid payoff when they equip managers with a set of skills and simple methodology that allows even first-time managers to quickly build skills in developing others.

A review of current research supports the view that equipping a manager with coaching skills pays off for the team and the organization. Mink, Owen, and Mink (1993) early on envisioned coaching at the managerial level as a process that encourages development and improves performance on the manager's team. Ellinger and Bostrom (1999) conducted an extensive study to examine the specific behaviors of a manager that shift this person's orientation from the model of control–dominate–prescribe to a facilitator of learning. Their findings identified two clusters of behaviors: empowering and facilitating.

- Empowering behaviors
  - Question framing to encourage employees to think through issues
  - Transferring ownership to employees
  - Holding back instead of providing the answers

- Facilitating behaviors
  - Providing feedback to employees
  - Talking things through
  - Promoting a learning environment
  - Setting and communicating expectations
  - Fitting into the bigger picture
  - Stepping into another role to shift perspective

These clusters of behaviors closely resemble coaching skills.

Ellinger and Bostrom's study provides the field of coaching with important direction in articulating what is needed in order for managers to develop a coaching mind-set and a coaching approach. The clusters of behaviors developed over a decade ago closely resemble many of the coaching skills required for the manager as coach to successfully engage team members in their own development.

LADYSHEWSKY'S STARTING BLOCK FOR MANAGERS

Ladyshewsky's (2010) recent study, "The Manager as Coach as a Driver of Organizational Development," is a natural extension of Ellinger and Bostrom's earlier work. Ladyshewsky examines success and failure factors for the manager as coach and provides a thumbnail sketch of what's required in the training of managers to equip them with the necessary skills to engage their team members in coaching and hold a coaching mind-set in their work. We set out his findings in the following sections.

Begin with a Coaching Mind-Set

Mind-set precedes change, and a good starting block for any manager of people is to reflect on the current beliefs and practices employed when managing others. Often the manager believes his job is to direct and problem-solve for others instead of developing and delegating. A coaching mind-set focuses on empowering team members by providing support in the growth and development of others in areas important to the worker, the manager, and the team.

Hargrove (1999) highlights some of the common obstacles that get in the way of a manager who is adopting a coaching mind-set, including a view that coaching is something that someone else does and takes too much time away from the work of managing. Hargrove urges managers to take a different view of their role and highlights the reality that "coaching lies at the heart of management, not the edges. Coaching is everything you do to produce extraordinary results in your business with colleagues amid change, complexity, and

Figure 19.1 Managing-Coaching Continuum
© Hudson Institute of Santa Barbara.

competition" (p. 8). He believes in the importance of helping managers view their role as much more than a checker or a cop; they are coaches and collaborators. Developing a coaching mind-set is an important step in organizations today.

In our work providing coaching skills to managers, we often place butcher paper on the wall with arrows going in both directions from highly directive to facilitative (see Figure 19.1) and ask a group of managers to stand where their current approach is best represented.

Almost without fail, the largest cluster of managers is at the far left end of the continuum, where the focus is on a highly directive approach of telling a direct report exactly what he or she needs to do or, in cases where a problem develops, moving in, taking over, and doing whatever needs to be corrected themselves. When we ask managers how it is to spend much of their time at the directive end of the continuum, they offer candid comments like these:

> "I find myself frustrated when a team member doesn't do it the way I think it ought to be done, and instead of taking the time it would require to get it back on track, I often just take over and do it my way—not a good long-term solution!"

> "I guess I worry about whether or not some of my team members are capable of coming up with good solutions, so instead of taking a risk, I just opt to give detailed instructions and tell them what to do. Problem is, they just keep coming back for my instructions!"

At the other end of the continuum, where coaching occurs, the manager deliberately finds the right times to develop team members by asking questions, supporting and empowering good thinking, and challenging team members to come up with their own solutions (when the risks aren't too high).

This coaching mind-set is a paradigm shift in the manager's approach to working with teams and individuals. Instead of being overly committed to solving everyone's problems and listening to complaints, the coaching mind-set creates a framework for ongoing development, collaboration, and empowerment among teams, direct reports. and peers.

Too often managers find themselves in the time-consuming role of mediator, problem solver, solution builder, and driver of the latest initiatives and

Table 19.1 Managing Versus Coaching Mind-Set

Managing Mind-Set	Coaching Mind-Set
Creates a quick solution	Helps team members develop their own solutions
Mediates staff differences	Queries team members about their role in a given challenge
Tells team members how to manage	Queries and listens to the issue
A step ahead of the team-building solutions to strategies	Asks questions before creating solutions and strategies. Seeks to empower team members to develop a sense of their contribution.
Gets it done!	Gets it done collaboratively
Managing can be the best approach in many situations, particularly when time pressure is intense.	Coaching builds skills while developing strategies and solutions designed to strengthen the organization but takes time

deadlines—all roles that generally result in predictable tensions (and often disempowerment) with a short-term solution often being drawn into a long-term issue. By developing a coaching mind-set, the manager has another way of approaching the development of a team member. This new approach produces a sense of empowerment and encourages the employee to contribute to developing solutions and approaches to any number of issues and challenges. For the manager with a coaching mind-set, team tensions become an opportunity for individual and group development, as well as the chance for members to take a role in resolving friction.

An important step in developing this skill is to build awareness of the differences between a managing mind-set and the coaching mind-set. Table 19.1 provides a brief comparison.

Use a Sound and Simple Step-by-Step Methodology

We have developed the spot coaching approach (Figure 19.2) to allow managers to use coaching skills at the appropriate times to engage in ongoing development of team members and direct reports. This three-stage approach provides a simple structure and reliable methodology for successfully coaching people on the spot in their day-to-day work.

Twenty- to thirty-minute spot coaching sessions can rapidly yield measurable results, maximizing employee performance as well as laying a foundation for longer-term development. These sessions apply a proven and sound methodology:

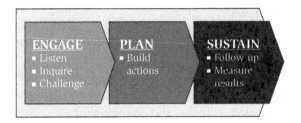

Figure 19.2 Hudson Spot Coaching Approach
© Hudson Institute of Santa Barbara.

Engage

- Listen and build rapport.
- Move from a chat or complaint to a coaching discussion focusing on the issue.
- Address the change required to move the issue in a new direction.
- Obtain a clear commitment to that change.

Plan

- Develop a set of action steps with specific times and agreements.

Sustain

- Provide follow-up support and measure for the impact.

Although the comprehensive set of skills needed for a manager to engage in just-in-time spot coaching conversations is beyond the scope of this chapter, we offer a brief examination of what's required at each step in this simple process.

Engaging. The manager's coaching tool kit needs to contain some essential skills in order to engage in a just-in-time coaching conversation. Given the tendencies of many managers to move quickly into the tell-and-fix approach when a problem surfaces, the first work is in changing old habits that don't serve the manager's ultimate goal and the development of a team member. A fix-and-tell approach may be called for in emergencies and high-risk situations, but when it's time to develop and nurture the capacities of a member of the team, it's time for a coaching mind-set and a coaching approach.

These are the key skills:

- *Building rapport* to create a coaching relationship that is trusting and respectful.

- *Listening.* This sounds simple, but listening without an intent to fix a problem, beyond the actual words, and beyond one's own set of experiences requires skill, practice, and commitment.

- *Asking questions.* This is easy when we are asking questions that lead to the answers we have in mind. But when the purpose of the question is to seek clarification, deeper understanding, and new awareness for the other, it is a much more challenging skill to develop.

- *Challenging thinking.* Instead of moving to offer a solution, challenge the thinking of the other to explore new possibilities and uncover what might be getting in the way.

- *Getting an agreement for change.* Once the good listening, open questions, and challenges have occurred and the client is clear about the change he or she needs to tackle, it's time to get a clear agreement that supports the desired change and holds this person accountable to self and manager.

PLAN

Building a Plan and Action Steps. It takes a plan with clear action steps to support any change. At this stage in spot coaching, it's important to get specific about when, where, what, and how a change will start to unfold.

Change happens through a combination of support and holding the other accountable for making the agreed-on and necessary adjustments. The employee can identify action steps that can be taken, and the manager can help identify building blocks that will lead to sustainable change in the future. The manager can support a member of the team in simple ways after this commitment through a follow-up conversation, a check-in e-mail, or whatever else will best support the other. Support creates another level of accountability because it is clear that there will be some follow-up on the progress and agreed-on action steps. A manager's investment in coaching team members needs to be aligned with the organization and boost the bottom line of the team and the organization.

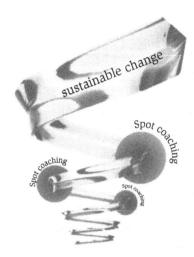

Figure 19.3 Spot Coaching Spiral

Sustaining. Sustainable change is the goal in all coaching, and in a manager's just-in-time coaching, it most often takes several coaching conversations to create deep and long-term sustainability. It is useful to think of the impact of spot coaching as a spiraling dynamic (Figure 19.3) that continues to build momentum and lasting change through time and repetition:

- *Follow up.* The manager's routine follow-up is important to build into each spot coaching conversation in order to underline the importance of the conversation and provide both support and recognition for changes that are under way. This might include a phone call, stopping into the office for a moment, sending an e-mail with notes of progress or success, or whatever else best suits both parties.

- *Measure results.* Crucial to any coaching inside the organization, the work of measuring results may span from observations that other key stakeholders note to careful work tying to the business metrics that a new behavior will affect, such as productivity, sales, or retention.

A SPOT COACHING TRANSCRIPT

In this transcript, Steve wants to strengthen his delegation skills.

Connect and Listen

COACH: Good morning. Steve, How are you?

STEVE: I'm good. How are you?

COACH: Really good! So what's going on? You said you wanted to chat for a few minutes.

STEVE: I was wondering if you might be able to help me out with an issue I'm having. I'd like some help around delegation. I have the opportunity to really use somebody in a position, and I feel that I don't have the skills quite yet to do that.

COACH: Okay. Is this a good time for a little coaching on this right now?

STEVE: Sounds good.

Ask Questions

COACH: So tell me a little bit more about what's going on.

STEVE: Well, I have a person coming in a couple of times a week who's helping me on some specific projects. I don't have a lot of experience delegating, so I'm having trouble focusing on my own tasks and handing stuff off.

COACH: Okay. And is it generally an issue with delegation, or do you think it's particular with this individual?

STEVE: That's a good question. I think it's a general issue.

COACH: Okay. So what success have you had in the past, if any, in this area?

STEVE: Well, I'm really good at preparing specific tasks for the individual—figuring out what is something that I should pass off. That's a strength, I think. I've found success there.

COACH: So where does the challenge come in?

STEVE: I find myself going over their work even after it's been completed, and I feel that's kind of micromanaging, as well as a certain amount of discomfort with delegating. I don't feel completely comfortable telling people what to do.

Challenge Thinking

COACH: Do you feel like you are telling people what to do or perhaps helping people be more successful in their role on the team?

STEVE: Well, I guess I hadn't thought of it in that way. Instead of helping them, I've always thought of delegating as bossing others around, and that's very uncomfortable for me.

COACH: And when I mention the possibility that you are helping someone be more successful . . .

STEVE: It's good! It really turns the whole thing upside down for me, and instead of being bossy, I can imagine I'm actually doing a favor for them.

COACH: Perhaps helping to develop them?

STEVE: Yeah. That's really a great way of thinking about this—very freeing actually!

Get a Contract for Change

COACH: So if you were to create an ideal situation, what is your goal here? How would you want it to work?

STEVE: Ideally, I would appreciate someone in that position coming to me when they have questions, so I don't feel as if I have to keep a close eye and go through everything that they produce with a fine-toothed comb.

COACH: That makes a lot of sense. So if I understand this correctly, you want to be better and more effective at delegating, you don't want to be micromanaging this person, and you want to have some confidence that if they bump into something, they're going to come and initiate the contact with you.

STEVE: Yeah.

COACH: So if you were to think about what you're doing with this person that is working well, what specifically would that be?

STEVE: I think it's useful to have a very specific set of items prepared and be able to sit down briefly. Sometime I go into too much detail when I say exactly what I want done. But being able to take that time just initially to go through what I expect and what I need is useful.

COACH: So a strength of yours right now that you're using is you're pretty clear about what you need done, and you have, more or less, the list of things and some details connected to it, and you're clear about what you expect. Do you take the time each week or each day when she comes in to have this conversation with her about what's expected that day?

STEVE: Yeah, generally when she first comes in.

COACH: So what is problematic for you? Is she not getting the work done in the way that you want? Tell me where the gap is for you.

STEVE: I think at this point, because she's new to the projects, she needs a lot of clarification. So switching gears between what I'm working on and managing the projects that I'm hoping she will accomplish without much supervision is challenging.

COACH: It sounds to me as if she is able to do some of what you want, but it doesn't sound like she is doing everything that you want her to be doing. So if you were to identify for yourself, what would you need to do differently to get more from her?

STEVE: Rather than looking at it from a day-to-day basis is having things laid out either weekly or monthly that could be standardized and put into a format that she could track, without my having to hand over projects on a daily basis. That would be useful for both of us.

PLAN

Build a Plan and Action Steps

COACH: So for you right now, you've got the daily tasks more or less outlined and handled, and you're thinking that if you were to step back and do this more on a project or give her a longer view than just that day to day, it might be useful. So for you, what would that require?

STEVE: Maybe just taking a little more time to better define the position and really giving boundaries to what that position entails and what projects she could take over.

COACH: So what I'm hearing you say is rather than having it just be a daily "here's the list of things I want you to do today," you would take a step back and look at the projects you would want her involved in more closely and give her more of a project view of this. Have you done any of that at this point with her?

STEVE: Very little, I would say. It's been more of specific tasks, closer to the ground.

COACH: So for you, when you think about that being the ideal, her stepping up and being better able to come to you when she has a challenge, trusting that she will able to do that, is it your sense that if you give her a bigger view in the project orientation, she's more likely to do that with you?

STEVE: I think so. I sure know for me it is easier to understand the day-to-day stuff if I can see the bigger picture. That might be the case for her as well.

COACH: Okay. Are there any other perspectives that we might consider here?

STEVE: Yes. I'm also wondering what I can do in my attitude toward delegating, in that it's unnatural for me to direct someone so directly. It's very direct to say, "Do this, do that." I'd like to maybe soften that, but I'm not really sure how.

COACH: So what is it when you think of yourself as delegating and telling someone what to do? What's challenging about that for you?

STEVE: It's the bossy thing again, like I'm putting myself at a higher level, and that's uncomfortable. I feel like it's not necessarily good for the relationship.

COACH: Interesting. So you would like to experience a more collaborative relationship with her, and I'm wondering, in the position you're in, what is your sense of what the organization needs from you?

STEVE: I think at this point, efficiency is important. Being able to add things to my plate, and that's part of being able to hand things off.

COACH: So more is expected of you here because you're learning more and they want you to take on some additional things, so in order to that, you have to be able to pass some things on to someone else. So you're caught in that transition, so to speak, right now. And part of that transition is learning how to inform and support and get other folks to get the job done.

STEVE: Yeah, absolutely.

COACH: So as you grow into this, is this something you want to learn for yourself?

STEVE: I do. I think it's very important and something that will be useful for the rest of my career.

COACH: So it's a good practice place, this relationship with this individual? I have a thought for you. Are you interested in hearing my thought on this?

STEVE: Yeah, definitely.

COACH: I'm wondering if a conversation with this individual would be helpful, because right now, she's getting daily tasks from you, and you're thinking of giving her things on more of a project basis. I wonder how she experiences you, because your concern is that you don't want to be bossy or come across as if you're higher than her. What's your sense of how she experiences you?

STEVE: I would imagine that if you're constantly being handed things of that nature by one person, it might—this is probably part of my bias as well—feel like one thing after another is being shot at you without really getting that whole perspective.

COACH: Okay. So as you think about moving forward and reaching more of your ideal, what are some of the things that we've talked about that you might do with her to support this for you?

STEVE: I think having a conversation around how she sees me and how she feels about the way she's been presented tasks and projects, and explore new ways of working with her that would fit better for her. And maybe present to her the idea of coming up with something for her that's longer term rather than just that initial meeting of the day— something for the week or the month. Maybe a certain format or spreadsheet would be useful and a good place to start.

COACH: Okay. So what is it that I might do to support you in having a conversation? Is there anything else we could talk about that would facilitate it?

STEVE: It might be helpful if you have any ideas around how to initiate that conversation.

COACH: One of the things that you talked about when we started is that this is new for you, and it's something you really want to do well, and you also want to support her. Given that those are your objectives for becoming more effective at this, would this be a good way to start the conversation? You want to be a more effective delegator; you want to do it in a way that really supports her and in a way that has you feeling like coworkers versus maybe her treated in a way that isn't effective for her. When would you like to have this conversation with her?

STEVE: Well, today even. Why not?

Sustain

COACH: Okay! Great! So you'll have the conversation today, and how about, if after you do that, you'll let me know how it goes, and maybe then determine what we can do for the next steps.

STEVE: Absolutely. That'd be great.

COACH: All right, good luck!

STEVE: Thanks!

COACH: Well done!

The three-step process of spot coaching is evidenced throughout this coaching dialogue. What's also clear is that a good methodology is not meant to be a lockstep linear process. At some points in this fifteen-minute just-in-time coaching session, the coach moves into building a plan with Steve.

When she finds herself once again exploring Steve's challenges around delegating, she quickly steps back and returns to the work of challenging Steve's thinking and feelings and gaining more clarity about how Steve wants to adjust his current approach.

Sustainability is developed over time for managers as they engage in a just-in-time coaching approach and follow-up. Even the briefest follow-up creates the foundation for sustainable change, one conversation at a time.

PART SEVEN

JOURNEY TO COACH MASTERY

Learning any new skill involves relatively brief spurts of progress, each of which is followed by a slight decline to a plateau somewhat higher than that which preceded it. . . . To take the master's journey, you have to practice diligently, striving to hone your skills, to attain new levels of competence. But while doing so—and this is the inexorable fact of the journey—you also have to be willing to spend most of your time on a plateau, to keep practicing even when you seem to be getting nowhere.
—George Leonard

CHAPTER 20

JOURNEY TO COACH MASTERY: AN INTRODUCTION

W hat makes a coach masterful? What methods and techniques are evidenced at the mastery level that are simply too complex to develop in the early stages of the coach's development? One thing we know is that mastery is an endless journey that involves far more than logging hundreds of hours of coaching. It would be possible for any coach to continue to practice the same missteps hour after hour without awareness of the shortcomings of the approach or in the absence of experiential learning and development.

The development of mastery has been thoroughly studied in several fields, and useful models have evolved that prove helpful in understanding the coach's pathway to mastery. The role of supervision has long played an important role in the development of mastery in many professions as well, and research in this area underscores the tremendous value supervision provides in the coach's development.

In this concluding part of the book, Chapter Twenty-One examines what we know about the developmental journey to mastery—the pathway from novice to expert—using two well-known theories as a backdrop for understanding this journey along with specific evidence-based applications to the role of the coach. Chapter Twenty-Two explores the role of supervision in coaching, the types of supervision a coach might use, and a model of group supervision in support of the coach's development. The final chapter briefly returns to the basic tenets of the book and a summons to all coaches to continually cultivate the journey to mastery.

CHAPTER 21

THE DEVELOPMENTAL JOURNEY
TO MASTERY

Mastery is an arduous journey for any coach. It requires conscious attention to the cultivation of self; demands continual learning about useful and relevant theories, concepts, and tools; and necessitates regular and consistent practice in the art and science of coaching. For each of us as coaches and for the field of coaching, this is our challenge and our goal: the ongoing quest for mastery.

THE WORK OF HOWELL

Howell (1982) provides a launching point for understanding the journey to mastery in his well-known model mapping the journey from unconscious incompetence to conscious competence. In his study of the progression from novice to master, Howell identifies four stages:

- *Unconscious incompetence.* The unconscious incompetent lacks the skills and knowledge-based competencies needed in a particular area of study and is completely unaware of this insufficiency.

- *Conscious incompetence.* The conscious incompetent is aware he lacks the skills required to perform at a high level in a particular area. This revelation of incompetence is usually unnerving for most of us in our adult years when we've already achieved competence in several areas.

- *Conscious competence*. This stage takes time, and the more sophisticated and demanding the skill set, the longer the time spent here, with peaks and valleys and finally a sense of reaching a meaningful skill level. At this stage, the individual is still highly alert to each part of the process he or she has learned to execute.

- *Unconscious competence*. This fourth stage is the level of mastery that no longer requires focused attention, but now comes so naturally that the elements are elusive and intuitive. Many (Leonard, 1992; Ericsson, Prietua, and Cokely, 2007; Gladwell, 2008) cite ten thousand hours of time and practice as required to reach a meaningful level of mastery in any complex task.

In Coaching. Because many professionals become interested in adding a coaching approach and skill set to their practice when they have already achieved significant milestones as leaders, Howell's model is particularly useful in helping to frame a new learning journey (see Table 21.1). Many experienced leaders sense that coaching will be a very useful skill set to add, and many, in fact, believe they are already acting as coaches. However, within a short time of their examining the skill- and theory-based

Table 21.1 Coaching Examples of Howell's Model

Unconscious Incompetence	*Conscious Incompetence*	*Conscious Competence*	*Unconscious Competence*
An experienced manager who believes he coaches every day, but whose style is only directive and "telling."	The novice coach who understands all that is required to become a coach and is hyperalert to all he has yet to learn.	The coach who has engaged in enough practice and skill building to begin to feel confident about his level of competence, but remains highly alert to all of the skills and uses of self that he deploys at each step of the way in his coaching.	The coach well on the journey to mastery no longer monitoring each intervention, each use of self, and all that informs any particular approach. At this stage, the coach is fully present and so skilled that the work feels almost intuitive.

competencies and watching masterful coaching at work, their transition from the unconscious incompetent to the conscious incompetent occurs. The journey through conscious competence is a long one. It requires far more than a year of coach training or hundreds of hours of solo coaching in order to accelerate one's skills on the path to unconscious competence. Continual development, reflection in action, and supervision experiences accelerate the progression.

THE WORK OF DREYFUS AND DREYFUS

The path to mastery is not for the faint-hearted. The Dreyfus brothers (1980), Hubert and Stuart, researched the stages of the journey to mastery with a goal of understanding how to best support a student's development. They distilled the stages of skill acquisition in complex learning in a study conducted for the U.S. Air Force Office of Scientific Research. Their model and findings were subsequently and successfully applied to the process involved in learning a foreign language, chess playing, and flight instruction.

Today the Dreyfus model is widely used as a means of supporting the development of skills in education, medicine, nursing, and a variety of other professions, most recently in the study of the acquisition of coaching skills. Dreyfus and Dreyfus proposed five stages of development with specific definitions for each:

- *Novice*—strict adherence to the rules. The novice learns the steps taught and practices in a highly formulaic manner.

- *Advanced beginner*—a limited situational perspective. The advanced beginner still evidences very limited situational perspective and gives all parts of the process equal weight and importance.

- *Competent*—coping with crowdedness (many activities and layers of knowledge). The competent copes with crowdedness (the accumulation of information) through thoughtful deliberation and careful planning.

- *Proficient*—holistic view emerging. Proficiency comes with a more holistic view of the entire scenario, and a situational perspective relative to the nuances is now possible.

- *Expert*—intuitive grasp transcending rules. The expert is able to creatively work alone, relying on all that's been learned along the path, able to naturally balance the layers of knowledge and situational features while transcending formulas and operating in the present.

Catherine Robinson-Walker (1999) overlaid the Dreyfus model on the progression of a coach's skills in Figure 21.1. Several of her interpretations are valuable for the developing coach, addressing several areas, including these:

- The tremendous focus on oneself in the novice stage and the need for reassurance that anxiety and self-consciousness are a normal part of the learning journey.
- The importance of modeling great coaching at the advanced beginner level when there is more capacity to learn from good role modeling of experts.
- The reality that at the expert level, the coach may indeed skip steps because of her level of mastery. At this level of development, it requires the coach's keen attention to his or her own coaching process in order to communicate this in a helpful way to novice coaches.

Robinson-Walker's work overlaying coaching on the Dreyfus pathway from novice to expert also links the stages with Howell's model in a helpful and integrative manner. Bennett and Rogers (2011) take this a step further in their study with twenty-six coaches representing four categories of coaches: beginner, skilled, practiced, and seasoned. They conducted semistructured interviews comparing advanced beginners with experts in order to test the applicability of the Dreyfus model in coaching. They found distinguishable differences between advanced beginner coaches and expert coaches, thus validating the Dreyfus model as applicable to the work of coaching. Specific findings affirmed the usefulness of the model in understanding the journey to mastery for the coach:

- Awareness of self increases with skill level.
- A client-centered focus grows with skill level.
- The coaching role becomes clearer with skill level.
- The coach's presence becomes more confident with skill level.
- Similar skill-based competencies appear differently as skill progresses.

In Coaching. The developmental progression that Dreyfus and Dreyfus outlined provides a pathway and a source of encouragement for leaders who enter the field of coaching. It is reassuring to know that in the initial stages of development, a hyperfocus on balancing skills, use of self, and a sturdy methodology is often awkward and challenging. The developmental pathway is particularly helpful in providing a broad lens for the natural progression that evolves through time and practice for the coach.

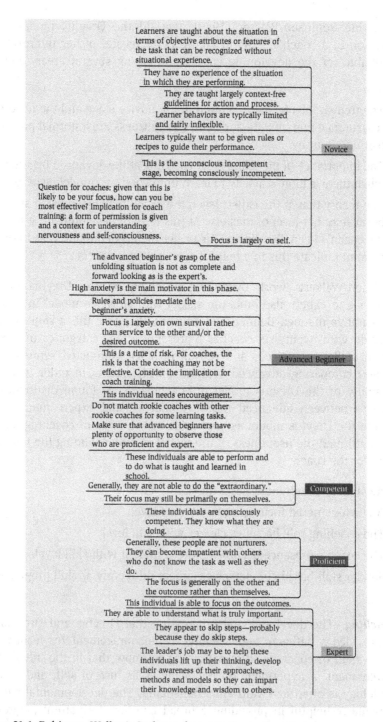

Figure 21.1 Robinson-Walker's Pathway from Novice to Expert

Source: Robinson-Walker (1999).

THE INSPIRATION OF CZIKSENTMIHALYI

Finally, the work of Mihaly Cziksentmihalyi (1997) provides yet another perspective on one's learning journey with a particular focus on what is required in order to maintain a state of flow when a practitioner has reached a state of mastery (see his model in Figure 21.2).

Cziksentmihalyi's model maps the natural progression of skill development relative to the feeling state of the individual. When skills are low and the challenge is high, as is the case for the novice or the conscious incompetent, anxiety and worry are pervasive. When one moves to Dreyfus and Dreyfus's stage of proficiency or Howell's conscious competent, it likely aligns with Cziksentmihalyi's arousal state. The well-known flow state comes with mastery when intuition and a sense of unconscious competence dominate. An additional element in this model is the waning side of the cycle, when the challenge of the work is no longer sufficient to keep the individual fully alive and engaged. This can easily happen to any coach who continues to coach without challenging her own development through structured supervision, peer supervision, coaching, and ongoing development.

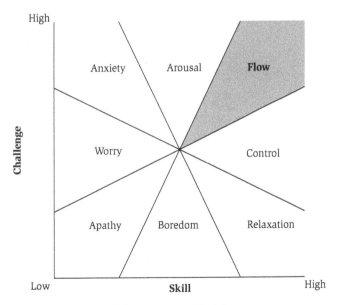

Figure 21.2 Cziksentmihalyi's Skill Progression Model

Source: Cziksentmihalyi (1997).

In Coaching. This model is equally helpful to novice coaches because it high-lights the normative nature of worry and anxiety when skills are low and motivation is high. Cziksentmihalyi's model is equally useful on the waning side where the skills are at a peak and the challenge is waning. The coach who reaches this plateau needs to be able to easily identify this (not at all unlike the doldrums of the cycle of renewal) and use this as a signal to make some adjustments in order to get into flow.

CHAPTER 22

SUPERVISION IN COACHING

Supervision has been an important staple in the developmental trajectory of professionals in several prominent fields of study, including psychology, medicine, counseling, and social work, providing a structured approach to ongoing development. The ten thousand–hour rule of mastery seems to be a simple enough equation, but it's not merely the accumulation of hours of practice that creates mastery. Rather, it is the continuing work of reflecting on one's skills, linking skills and practice to helpful theories and concepts, and tracking one's developmental edges at each stage in the journey. Coaching supervision—the process of working with a masterful coach in order to take a step back and reflect on the ongoing development of the coach's skills, the dynamics of the coaching session, the client dynamics relative to larger systems, and the coaching outcomes—serves an important role in the journey to mastery.

Korotov, Florent-Treacy, Kets de Vries, and Bernhardt (2012) note in their recent book on coaching that "no coach has a monopoly on wisdom. Many coaches still work without supervision, and many encounter similar coaching challenges." We all need the support of a mirror to see our self and our work with more clarity. Supervision both supports and holds the coach's feet to the fire, driving ongoing development, uncovering blind spots, examining failures as well as successes, and experiencing the parallel process at play in supervision that mirrors the coaching work.

Supervision can provide enormous value to a coach at several levels:

- Continuing to learn about one's self as coach
- Intentionally remaining on a path of self-development
- Continually challenging one's capacity as coach
- Understanding one's client and the client's context
- Exploring approaches, interventions, and tools most useful with each client
- Understanding the key elements associated with the client's work system
- Ultimately seeking to ensure the best possible outcomes for the client

Most coaches practice in a predominantly one-on-one format, and this can be a lonely experience for a coach over time. Supervision not only builds capacity for the coach, but it represents a form of self-care for the practitioner as well. In Cziksentmihalyi's terminology, supervision serves to keep the coach in flow, continually cultivating new territory for capacity building. In Howell's model, supervision serves to move the coach more rapidly toward the state of unconscious competence.

Supervision spans a broad spectrum of activities:

- Focus on use of self and continual capacity building as coach
- Thoughtful attention to the developmental edges of the coach and continual tracking of progress and advancement relative to those edges
- Attention to the working alliance between coach and client and between coach and supervisor (in some cases, this may include a supervision group)
- Attention to transference and countertransference in coaching cases and in the coaching supervision relationship
- Use of reflection-in-action during supervision and reflective processes in general
- Linkage of each coaching case to the underlying coaching methodology—from working alliances to aspirational contracts to key coaching goals to measureable outcomes
- Linkage to key theories, concepts, and best practices relative to each coaching case
- Examination of ethical issues and challenges that arise
- Careful attention to coaching outcomes and measures that best support these outcomes

The models previously covered in this book relative to self-as-coach domains (Figure 4.3), coach methodology (Figure 11.3), and the elements of masterful coaching (Figure 4.1) provide foundational reference points for the supervision work.

TYPES OF SUPERVISION

There are several types of supervision a coach can use, and we explore them next.

Solo Supervision

Solo supervision is essentially a practice of reflecting on each coaching session in a methodical manner that aligns with the development goals of the coach. It tracks the progress of the coaching work, including the rough edges and the difficult spots that need further exploration. Every coach ought to regularly engage in this first layer of supervision with self at all times. Portions of Clutterbuck's seven conversations model (Figure 7.5) for reflection before, during, and after dialogue are particularly useful for solo supervision.

These questions are useful to consider in solo supervision:

- What did I feel best about in this coaching session?
- What did I observe about myself as coach relative to my own areas of continued development?
- What did I observe about my own level of presence throughout the session?
- What did I notice relative to my own reactions and feelings toward this client?
- Where did I feel lost in the coaching session?
- In retrospect, how did my session track to the methodology?
- In retrospect, what theories and concepts are most relevant to my work with this client or myself as coach in this session?
- How am I gaining the client's input relative to our coaching engagement?
- How am I working with my client to continually link our work to the overall coaching goals in a manner that demonstrates coaching outcomes relevant to all levels of the client's system?

Peer Supervision

Peer supervision could be in the form of a regular coaching buddy or a small group that meets on a regular basis. Many of the questions addressed in solo supervision prove equally useful here. These two additional questions take advantage of the presence of other coaches:

- Given what you know about my development goals as a coach, what stands out for you in this case as I describe my work?
- What might you consider that I'm not addressing?

Formal Individualized Supervision

There is a growing trend toward formalized individual coach supervision. The U.K. coaching community has led the way on this front, and it is rapidly spreading to other parts of the globe. The process of individual coach supervision typically includes a regular meeting between supervisor (master coach) and coach, with a focus on examining coaching engagement relative to the coach's development goals and all of the essential elements required to reach mastery.

Formal Group Supervision

All forms of supervision serve an important function in the journey to mastery, but in my estimation, group supervision has the potential to be the most effective. The group supervision model ideally runs the course of one to two years with a consistent group of participants. Group supervision has several unique advantages that I believe make it a particularly potent approach:

- The ability of group members to track the coach's development goals and learning edges relative to the coaching case under discussion
- The ability of group members to observe parallel processes at work for the coach relative to the work with a particular client, the supervision group, and the coach supervisor
- The opportunity for group members to practice their own skills in staying present, providing helpful feedback, challenging at the appropriate times, and sharing observations relative to themes and patterns
- The experience of learning from one another, observing vulnerabilities in fellow coach colleagues, and the insight and reassurance that we are all humans with failings and failures along the way

Spot Supervision

Once a coach has engaged in regular supervision over the course of one to two years, it can prove helpful to have a relationship with a supervisor that allows spot supervision when a particularly challenging situation emerges with a client. Spot supervision is a focused session, lasting fifteen to twenty minutes, in which the coach brings a specific coaching dilemma to a short just-in-time supervision session.

Internal Coach Supervision Groups

As organizations continue to create internal cadres of coaches, the use of external supervisors becomes more common in an effort to provide continued support and development for the coaching cadre and track the impact of the coaching on the overall organizational needs and goals.

MODELS FOR SUPERVISION

Models of supervision are well developed in the field of psychology, and coach experts and researchers in the United Kingdom have adapted several of these models for use in the emerging field of coaching including Hawkins and Smith's (2006) seven-eyed process model, Hay's (2007) reflective practices in supervision, and Hawkins and Shohet's (2006) developmental approach to supervision that all provide a useful support in supervision. Interestingly enough, while the United States was an early adopter of a supervision model in the field of psychology, we have been slow to research and adopt relevant models in the work of coaching.

At Hudson, we have developed an early model for coaching supervision (Figure 22.1) that specifically pertains to supervision within a group setting. In this model, the foundation of supervision rests on all that has been covered in this book: self as coach, skill-based competencies, theory-based competencies, sound methodology, and the tools and assessments that might apply to any particular situation. The ultimate goal of a successful coaching engagement is to create sufficient change so that the goals of the work are achieved in a sustainable fashion. This is also the final goal of all coach supervision. The coach in supervision is at the center of the model, and the dynamics of supervision are focused in three constellations. We use the term *supervisor* in this model to refer to the internal or external master coach who serves as the supervisor for the coach, *client* refers to the individual seeking coaching, and *client system* refers to the organization or environment in which the client works.

Coach–Client–Client System Constellation

The coach's understanding of this primary system—the coach's role in the interface between coach, client, and client's organization and the tension points and complexities found in this constellation—is at the heart of the work in supervision.

Questions for the coach in supervision relative to this constellation might include these:

- What role might you be drawn into in this larger system that would create challenges and limit your effectiveness?

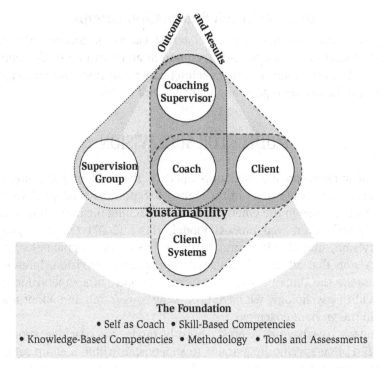

Figure 22.1 The Hudson Coach Supervision Model
© Hudson Institute of Santa Barbara.

- What are the signals you notice when you have entered the client's system in the coach-client work?

- What do you notice about your own internal experiences relative to this client? Is this experience unique to this particular client?

This vignette highlights the natural dynamics that occur within the coach–client–client system triangle and in the context of the supervision group provides ample opportunity to explore the situation through these lenses:

- Theories and concepts: Systems thinking and systems dynamics

- Self as coach: Ability to observe and manage boundaries, ability to challenge at the appropriate times, ability to be fully present to what is occurring in the moment

- Coach methodology: Revisiting the early contracting conversations, the ground rules relative to communication within the system, confidentiality, boundaries, and transparency

A Coach–Client–Client System Example

Bob, a member of a group supervision experience, brings a case to the group that highlights this essential triangle. He tells the group he met a professional colleague, a human resource professional (HR), at a learning event in his community a couple of months ago at which time this former colleague (Bob explains that this colleague was never a personal friend) and Bob exchange business cards. Bob talks about his current coaching practice, and his former colleague remarks, "Boy, you could be helpful to us in our organization. I'll give you a call next week."

The call comes to Bob the next week, and he proceeds to take all of the right steps, meeting with his former colleague, the boss, and the prospective client and then convening a four-way meeting with all parties to clarify the hopes each member has for the coaching work. Goals are clear, all parties understand how the coaching will proceed, and Bob is ready to develop a strong working alliance with his client and embark on a series of stakeholder interviews.

Before he is ten days into this work, he receives a call from his former colleague, who says to him, "Off the record, some things have changed. Your client really blew yet another presentation this week, and if something doesn't change within the next two weeks, he's out of here. What can you do?"

Coach–Client–Coach Supervisor Constellation

The coach and the supervisor's understanding of this essential system—the nature of the working alliance with the client, the awareness of transference and countertransference dynamics in this constellation, and the ultimate outcomes that have an impact on the client's success—is the next important layer in the supervision work.

Questions for both the supervisor and the coach in this constellation include these:

- What do you notice about the nature of the challenges you bring to the supervisor?

- What are you aware of leaving out of the discussion with your supervisor?

This is only a first step in Marge's work (see the following case example), but it points out the power of the coach–client–coach supervisor in uncovering new layers of awareness that will help the coach's work with clients. Each member of a supervision group has a development plan, and if the themes of pace and presence weren't already on Marge's plan, they will become an important part of it going forward.

The Coach–Client–Coach Supervisor Example

Marge has spent years as a consultant and facilitator, traveling about 70 percent of the time and attempting to do her best to balance her family's needs and her work life. She is the first to admit it's a tough act. Now Marge has added coaching to her repertoire of offerings. She is in her second year of coaching when she brings to supervision a theme she has become aware of in her coaching engagements. She brings this up during our supervision and notes, "For some reason, I seem to create coaching contracts with a lot of clients who don't seem to take coaching very seriously or don't seem really motivated to make any changes." Marge wants to explore what she could be doing differently to build contracts that are more productive.

As Marge and the coach supervisor explored the challenge, they uncovered one common denominator: Marge's rapid-fire pace and her drive to get her clients to a solution. The discussion then moved to two other areas: Marge's awareness of her own presence and the impact this has on her work in building a strong working alliance with her clients. When the coach supervisor asked Marge how she experienced their working alliance in the moment and how this alliance made it possible to jointly uncover this important awareness around Marge's pace and presence, Marge became tearful and said, "I feel your support, your focus, and your willingness to challenge me. I haven't built this relationship with my clients, and I wasn't even aware of this. I clearly see where I need to focus my attention."

Coach–Coach Supervisor–Supervision Group Constellation

The final layer of the supervision constellation lies in the awareness and use of the dynamics at play in the supervision group as it relates to themes for both the members of the group and the supervisor.

Questions for the coach-in-supervision might include these:

- What do you notice about parallels that might show up in supervision and in the coaching engagement?
- What can you learn from the keen observations of fellow group members?

This next-level layering of Marge's awareness relative to the triangle of the supervision group and coach supervisor creates a powerful epiphany for Marge in the moment. It also provides the entire group with an in-the-moment experience of the power of sharing observations, providing feedback to one another, and attending to one's internal experience and using it in the service of the coaching work.

A Coach–Coach Supervisor–Supervision Group Example

Returning to Marge's challenge around developing a stronger working alliance with her clients and managing her pace and noticing her own presence, the triangle of coach (in this case, Marge), coach supervisor, and supervision group becomes a particularly potent combination. Once Marge and the coach supervisor fully explored Marge's coaching challenge, the exploration expanded to the entire supervision group with an inquiry to all members relative to what they noticed and heard in the interaction.

Some members of the group returned to Marge's development plan and recalled her wish to be more present and commended her for working the territory that she has at the top of her own development list. Two of the group members exercised a bit more courage and transparency and shared their experience of Marge's pace and presence relative to the supervision group and how that affects each of them. One group member provided specific data about how often Marge comes to the supervision group several minutes late and how often she is unable to make it a priority because of her travel schedule. The group member shared with Marge the impact this has on her and how in this current supervision session, she has a heightened awareness of the negative impact this has on her sense of connectedness to Marge.

These brief vignettes provide a glimpse into the potent capacity for development that a supervision group provides for all members of the group and the impact the supervision work has on the ultimate effectiveness of the coaching with the client and the larger systems of the client. In essence, supervision becomes a dynamic process for providing quality control to the client and client organizations through the continual focus of the coach's development.

CHAPTER 23

STAYING THE COURSE ON THE JOURNEY TO MASTERY

S enge (2006) reminds us that staying the course on the perpetual road to mastery is perhaps one of the greatest goals of any accomplished and conscientious professional: "People with a high degree of personal mastery are able to consistently realize the results that matter most deeply to them. In effect, they approach their life as an artist would approach a work of art. They do that by becoming committed to their own life long learning."

The work of coaching is both art and science, and there is no one right way or a final arrival point of mastery marked by a degree or credential for any of us. Instead, the mastery journey is fraught with challenges and failures along the way and the sheer exhilaration that comes with growing mastery. Beware of the coach who has a singular method, technique, or categorization of behaviors that he or she uses to understand and approach work with every client. This is not mastery; it is clinging to a singular perspective in a world and field of study that has much more depth and complexity.

Practitioners on the mastery journey will find that continued cultivation and practice in the basic areas evidenced in the elements of masterful coaching (Figure 4.1)—self as coach, knowledge and skill-based competencies, and coaching methodology—are inextricably interwoven with each layer of development and mastery uncovering another layer of subtle intricacies: with self, the working alliance, or the growing ability to facilitate lasting change.

It is helpful for coach practitioners to overlay the developmental progression outlined by both Howell (1982) and Dreyfus and Dreyfus (1980) relative to the key areas covered in this book in order to map their own developmental pathway. Consider Chapter Eleven on coach methodology, including the thorough discussion of the Hudson coaching methodology (Figure 11.3).

For novice coaches, this chapter will likely appear both formulaic and a soothing source of a step-by-step process. However, any good methodology is meant to be an agile and flexible framework that provides support for coach and client on the path to reaching reliable outcomes. Experienced practitioners will quickly see that rather than a step-by-step process, a methodology represents a general flow to the coaching engagement that includes essential elements that may occur and reoccur in a much less predictable fashion in real life than the model suggests. Part Two on the self as coach and the model for the self-as-coach domains (Figure 4.3) can be viewed in the same manner.

Novice coaches will interpret the domains of the self as coach as more simplistic and concrete than experienced coaches will, and the progression from the simplistic to the complex is part of the joy of the journey to mastery that Senge (2006) refers to in the quotation at the start of this chapter. It's only when we've experienced a failure in our coaching because we didn't attend to or notice an important boundary that we begin to viscerally understand the layers at play in the development of our boundary awareness. Range of feelings appears straightforward to coaches, but as the journey progresses and the conscientious coach engages in a reflective practice, she might begin to notice how often she moves away from certain feelings—angry, sadness, tears—with her clients and contemplates the limitations her own range of feelings creates in the coaching work. And of course, we could continue around the wheel and peel the layers of complexities found in each of the domains.

Embrace the path you are on, and view it as an ever-unfolding process. Perhaps the following strategies will support you on this journey to mastery:

Ten Strategies to Stay on the Journey to Mastery

1. *Know yourself.* Inscribed on the Temple of Apollo at Delphi, this wisdom has been passed along through the ages from Plato, to Hobbes, to Benjamin Franklin. Leaders and thinkers through the ages have imparted this sound maxim that we must always start at home with self-knowledge before we seek to know and understand others.

2. *Develop yourself.* Continual development is an important ethic and mind-set for every coach. Coaches from novice to experienced are well served by routinely setting development priorities, seeking feedback to uncover the most important areas of development, and creating mechanisms for accountability. It's hard to grow alone, so support yourself by seeking coaching, creating collegial development groups, or joining a supervision experience.

3. *Take care of yourself.* The work of coaching inevitably leads us into difficult terrain—sometimes painful, other times deeply challenging—and it's likely you'll leave some sessions and engagements feeling discouraged, lost, and at times inadequate. This is unavoidable, and it requires a thoughtful plan for regular self-care. Self-care will include different practices for each of us. Perhaps it is the ability to reach out and sit in conversation with a fellow colleague, or the ability to say no when it matters most, or the routine of setting aside time for leisure or cordoning off space in life without technology at our side. Learning to take care of self is a perpetual challenge for many of us. Set routine goals in areas of self-care that are most important and engage in your own self-coaching to stay the course.

4. *Engage in reflection.* Schön (1983) taught us about the power of reflection-in-action—that ability to think and reflect while we are engaged in the act of doing, and Clutterbuck's work covered in Chapter Seven examines seven layers of reflective conversations a coach might engage in from the moments before a coaching session until well after the coaching concludes. Reflection is foundational to learning: learning about self (feelings, biases, reactions), learning about others, and learning about the world around us. Experiment with a reflective practice that works for you, and engage in this practice on a regular basis. Maybe it's time alone in nature, a long walk in a restorative setting, a meditation practice, a yoga practice, time alone in a sacred space, or regular journaling—and stay the course.

5. *Know your fields of study.* Coaching is far more than a set of skills; it's an emerging field built on the shoulders of giants (many of them discussed throughout this book) with an ever-increasing volume of research and writing specifically focused on coaching. As coaches, we must be literate in the fields that inform our work and remain up-to-date with research and writing in coaching, as well as peripheral fields that are relevant to our work. Make a list of key relevant readings at the beginning of each new year, and stay the course.

6. *Read outside your field of expertise.* We learn about the vicissitudes of life and our universal human dilemmas through literature, history, fiction, poetry, art, and more. Branch out, and expand your thinking, your emotional terrain, and your being.

7. *Regularly engage in a form of supervision.* Whether you are at the early stages on the journey to mastery or are an experienced coach, you will inevitably encounter moments of doubt, coaching failures, coaching dilemmas, and ethical puzzles in your work. A coach without a supervision relationship in one form or another is left to make sense of

these situations using only his or her own frame of reference, experiences, knowledge, and understanding of self. Such a choice is perhaps how we might define arrogance, and it surely speaks to a cautionary comment by Manfred Kets de Vries (Kets de Vries, Korotov, and Florent-Treacy, 2007): "I have come to believe that any coach who does not take supervision is bordering on irresponsible. No coach has the monopoly on wisdom and an experienced coach is a sine qua non, an extra mirror to the work." So whether you find a respected colleague or join a formal supervision group, if you want to provide the highest-quality service to your clients and simultaneously build your own capacity, this is an essential part of the journey.

8. *Respect your clients.* Our clients are often our best teachers. If you find it difficult to maintain a respectful position about a client, you probably shouldn't be engaged as that person's coach. A fundamental respect for those we are working with is at the core of the working alliance and essential for great coaching to occur.

9. *Maintain hope and optimism.* Richard Davidson says, "Hope is the comforting, energizing, elevating feeling that you experience when you project in your mind a positive future" (quoted in Groopman, 2003, p. 193). A growing body of research in the area of hope and positivity teaches us that hope rapidly leads to other positive emotions that have a direct impact on our behavior and the way we think and act. Monitor yourself for a week or two, and pay close attention to the level of hope and optimism present in your life on a daily basis. If your findings surprise you, make some adjustments in order to build a stronger reservoir of optimism and hope.

10. *Humility matters.* Humility fosters the working alliance, and it empowers the client's ownership of change. Robert Quinn (2004) speaks to it in this way: "Being humble is often associated with weakness or lack of power. Real humility comes when we see the world as it really is. The real world is a world of connectedness, of moving flows of power. When we transcend our own egos, when our outer self and our inner self connect, we experience increased integrity, increased oneness, greater connectedness. At such moments, we feel greatness."

As coaches, we all find ourselves drifting toward arrogance from time to time when we get too attached to models, concepts, assessments, and more, sending a message to our client that we know better than the client what the best next step is or what the accurate interpretation might be. Yet the work of fostering humility happens when we are engaged in a conscious journey to mastery knowing we'll never arrive because that's not the goal. The goal is the journey.

REFERENCES AND ADDITIONAL READING RECOMMENDATIONS

Anderson, M., Frankovelgia, C., and Hernez-Broome, G. (2008). *Creating coaching cultures: What business leaders expect and strategies to get there.* Greensboro, NC: Center for Creative Leadership. www.ccl.org/leadership/pdf/research /CoachingCultures.pdf.

Anderson, D., and Anderson, M. (2005). *Coaching that counts.* Burlington, MA: Elsevier Butterworth-Heinemann.

Argyris, C. (1982). *Reasoning, learning and action.* San Francisco: Jossey-Bass.

Argyris, C. (1991, May). Teaching smart people how to learn. *Harvard Business Review,* pp. 14–28.

Bacon, T. R., and Spear, K. I. (2003). *Adaptive coaching: The art and practice of a client-centered approach to performance improvement.* Boston: Nicholas Brealey Publishing.

Bar-On, R. (1997). *Bar-On Emotional Quotient Inventory (EQ-i): Technical manual.* Toronto: Multi-Health Systems.

Benner, P. (2001). *From novice to expert: Excellence and power in clinical nursing practice* (Commemorative ed.). Upper Saddle River, NJ: Prentice Hall.

Bennett, J. L., and Rogers, D. B. (2011). *Skill acquisition of executive coaches: A journey toward mastery.* Charlotte, NC: McColl School of Business, Queens University.

Berne, E. (1961). *Transactional analysis in psychotherapy.* New York: Grove Press.

Berne, E. (1964). *Games people play.* New York: Grove Press.

Bordin, E. (1979). The generalizability of the psychoanalytic concept of the working alliance. *Psychotherapy: Theory, Research and Practice, 16,* 252–260.

Bowen, M. (1978). *Family therapy in clinical practice.* Northvale, NJ: Aronson.

Boyatzis, R. (2011, October). Presentation at the Harvard Medical School Coaching in Medicine and Health Conference, McLean Hospital, Belmont, MA.

Boyatzis, R., Goleman, D., and McKee, A. (2002). *Primal leadership.* Boston: Harvard Business School Press.

Boyatzis, R., and McKee, A. (2005). *Resonant leadership: Renewing yourself and connecting with others through mindfulness, hope and compassion.* Boston: Harvard Business School Press.

Center for Creative Leadership. (2008). *Creating coaching cultures.* http://www.ccl .org/leadership/pdf/research/CoachingCultures.pdf.

Clutterbuck, D. (2011, June). *Using the seven conversations of coaching in supervision.* Presentation to the First Annual Coach Supervision Conference, Oxford University, Oxford, UK.

Clutterbuck, D., and Megginson, D. (2005). *Techniques for coaching and mentoring.* Burlington, MA: Elsevier Butterworth-Heinemann.

Corporate Executive Board. (2009, March). Learning and Development Roundtable.

Csikszentmihalyi, M. (1997). *Finding flow: The psychology of engagement with everyday life.* New York: Basic Books.

de Haan, E. (2008). *Relational coaching: Journeys toward mastering one-to-one learning.* San Francisco: Jossey-Bass.

Drake, D. B. (2009). Coaching is dead. Long live coaching! *International Journal of Coaching in Organizations, 1,* 138–150.

Dreyfus, H., and Dreyfus, S. (1980). *A five stage model of the mental activities involved in direct skill acquisition.* Arlington, VA: Air Force Office of Scientific Research.

Egan, G. (2009). *The skilled helper.* Florence, KY: Cengage Learning.

Ellinger, A. D., and Bostrom, R. P. (1999). Managerial coaching behaviors in learning organizations. *Journal of Management Development, 18,* 752–772.

Ericsson, K. A., Prietua, M. J., & Cokely, E. T. (2007, July-August). The making of an expert. *Harvard Business Review,* 1–6.

Flaherty. J. (2010). *Coaching: Evoking excellence in others* (3rd ed.). Burlington, MA: Butterworth.

Fogel, A. (2009). *The psychophysiology of self awareness: Rediscovering the lost art of body sense.* New York: Norton.

Gardner, H. (1983). *Frames of mind.* New York: Basic Books.

Gilligan, C. (1992). *In a different voice.* Cambridge, MA: Harvard University Press.

Gladwell, M. (2008). *Outliers.* New York: Little, Brown.

Goleman, D. (1998). *Working with emotional intelligence.* New York: Bantam Books.

Google's eight-point plan to help managers improve. (2011, March 12). *New York Times.*

Groopman, J. (2003). *The anatomy of hope*. New York: Random House.

Hargrove, R. (1999). *Masterful coaching fieldbook: Grow your business, multiply your profits, win the talent war*. San Francisco: Jossey-Bass/Pfeiffer.

Halpern, B. L., and Lubar, K. (2003). *Leadership presence*. New York: Gotham Books.

Hawkins, P. (2011, July). *Coaching supervision*. Presentation to the First Annual Coach Supervision Conference, Oxford University, Oxford, UK.

Hawkins, P., and Shohet, R. (2006). *Supervision in the helping professions*. New York: McGraw-Hill.

Hawkins, P., and Smith, N. (2006). *Coaching, mentoring and organizational consultancy*. New York: Open University Press.

Hays, J. (2007). *Reflective practice and supervision for coaches*. New York: Open University Press.

Horney, K. (1945). *Our inner conflicts*. New York: Norton.

Howell, W. S. (1982). *The empathic communicator*. Belmont, CA: Wadsworth.

Hudson, F. (1999). *Handbook of coaching*. San Francisco: Jossey-Bass.

Hudson, F. (2000). *The adult years*. San Francisco: Jossey-Bass.

Jones, B., and Brazzel, M. (2006). *The NTL handbook of organizational development and change: Principles, practices and perspectives*. San Francisco: Jossey-Bass/Pfeiffer.

Kegan, R. (1982). *The evolving self*. Cambridge, MA: Harvard University Press.

Kegan, R., and Lahey, L. (2009). *Immunity to change: How to overcome it and unlock the potential in yourself and your organization*. Boston: Harvard Business School Press.

Kernberg, O. (1995). *Object relations theory and clinical psychoanalysis*. New York: Jason Aronson.

Kets de Vries, M., Korotov, K., and Florent-Treacy, E. (2007). *Coach and couch: The psychology of making better leaders*. London: Palgrave Macmillan.

Kimsey-House, H., and Kimsey-House, K. (2011). *Co-active coaching: Changing business, transforming lives* (3rd ed.). Boston: Nicholas Brealey Publishing.

Kirkpatrick, D., and Kirkpatrick, J. (2006). *Evaluating training programs: The four levels*. San Francisco: Berrett-Koehler.

Korotov, K., Florent-Treacy, E., Kets de Vries, M., and Bernhardt, A. (Eds.). (2012). *Tricky coaching*. London: Palgrave Macmillan.

Ladyshewsky, R. K. (2010). The manager as coach as a driver of organizational development. *Leadership and Organization Development Journal, 31*, 292–306.

Landsberg, M. (1999). *The Tao of coaching: Boost your effectiveness at work by inspiring and developing those around you*. New York: HarperCollins.

Laske, O. (2006a). *Measuring hidden dimensions: The art and science of fully engaging adults*. Medford, MA: IDM Press.

Laske, O. (2006b). From coach training to coach education. *International Journal of Evidence-Based Coaching and Mentoring, 4*(1), 45–57.

Learning in Action Technologies. (N.d.). *EQ in action*. Seattle: Learning in Action Technologies. http://www.learninginaction.com/.

Leonard, G. (1992). *Mastery: The keys to success and long term fulfillment*. New York: Penguin.

Levinson, D. (1986). *The seasons of a man's life*. New York: Random House.

Levinson, D., and Levinson, M. (1997). *The seasons of a woman's life*. New York: Random House.

Lewin, K. (1997). *Resolving social conflicts and field theory in social science*. Washington, DC: American Psychological Association.

Luft, J. (1970). *Group processes: An introduction to group dynamics*. Palo Alto, CA: National Press Books.

Mandela, N. (1994). *Long walk to freedom*. New York: Little, Brown.

Maurer, R. (2010). *Beyond the wall of resistance: Why 70% of all changes still fail—and what you can do about it*. Austin, TX: Bard Press.

Mayer, J. D., and Salovey, P. (1997). What is emotional intelligence? In P. Salovey and D. Sluyter (Eds.), *Emotional development and emotional intelligence: Implications for educators*. New York: Basic Books.

McHenry, B., Harrah, C., and Berry, D. (2008). Developing a coaching culture at TaylorMade-adidas Golf: An exploration of lessons learned. *International Journal of Coaching in Organizations*, no. 3, 75–89.

McLean, P., and Hudson, F. (2011). *LifeLaunch: A passionate guide to the rest of your life*. Santa Barbara, CA: Hudson Press.

Mink, B., Owen, K., and Mink, O. (1993). *Developing high performance people: The art of coaching*. New York: Perseus.

Neugarten, B., and Neugarten, D. (1996). *The meanings of age: Selected papers*. Chicago: University of Chicago Press.

O'Neill, M. B. (2007). *Executive coaching with backbone and heart: A systems approach to engaging leaders with their challenges* (2nd ed.). San Francisco: Jossey-Bass.

Phillips, J. (1996, April). Measuring ROI: The fifth level of evaluation. *Technical and Skills Training*, 10–13.

Phillips, J. (2003). *Return on investment*. Burlington, MA: Elsevier.

Phillips, J. J., and Edwards, L. (2008). *Managing talent retention: An ROI approach*. San Francisco: Jossey-Bass.

Prochaska, J. O., and DiClemente, C. C. (1982). Transtheoretical therapy: Toward a more integrative model of change. *Psychotherapy: Theory, Research and Practice*, 19, 276–288.

Prochaska, J. O., DiClemente, C. C., and Norcross, J. C. (2002). *Changing for good: A revolutionary six-stage program for overcoming bad habits and moving your life positively forward*. New York: Quill.

Quinn, R. E. (2004). *Building the bridge as you walk on it: A guide for leading change*. San Francisco: Jossey-Bass.

Robinson-Walker, C. (1999). *Women and leadership in health care: The journey to authenticity and power*. San Francisco: Jossey-Bass.

Rogers, J. (2004). *Coaching skills: A handbook*. New York: McGraw-Hill.

Satir, V. (1988). *The new peoplemaking*. Palo Alto, CA: Science and Behavior Books.

Schön, D. A. (1983). *The reflective practitioner: How professionals think in action*. New York: Basic Books.

Scott, S. (2002). *Fierce conversations*. New York: Berkeley.

Senge, P. M. (2006). *The fifth discipline*. New York: Doubleday.

Short, R. (1998). *Learning in relationship*. Bellevue, WA: Learning in Action Technologies.

Siegel, D. (2001). *The developing mind*. New York: Guilford Press.

Siegel, D. J. (2007). *The mindful brain: Reflection and attunement in the cultivation of well-being*. New York: Norton.

Siegel, D. J. (2010). *Mindsight: The new science of personal transformation*. New York: Bantam.

Silsbee, D. (2008). *Presence-based coaching: Cultivating self-generative leaders through mind, body, and heart*. San Francisco: Jossey-Bass.

Strozzi-Heckler, R. (2007). *The leadership dojo*. Berkeley, CA: Frog Books.

Tolbert, M.A.R., and Hanafin, J. (2006). *The NTL handbook of organization development and change*. San Francisco: Jossey-Bass/Pfeiffer.

Whitmore, J. (2009). *Coaching for performance* (4th ed.). London: Brealey.

Whitworth, L., Kimsey-House, H., and Sandahl, P. *Co-Active Coaching*. Mountain View, CA: Davies-Black Publishing, 2007.

Winnicott, D. (1990). *Home is where we start from*. New York: Norton.

Wolfe, B. E., and Goldfried, M. R. (1988). Research on psychotherapy integration and conclusions from an NIMH workshop. *Journal of Consulting and Clinical Psychology, 56*, 448–451.

ADDITIONAL READING RECOMMENDATIONS

Erikson, E. (1997). *The life cycle completed*. New York: Norton.

Goleman, D. (1995). *Emotional intelligence: Why it can matter more than IQ*. London: Bloomsbury.

Goulding, R., and Goulding, M. (1997). *Changing lives through redecision therapy*. New York: Brunner Mazel.

Kahler, T. (1978). *Transactional analysis revisited*. Little Rock, AR: Human Development Publications.

Knowles, M. (1988). *The modern practice of adult education: From pedagogy to andragogy*. Boston: Cambridge Book Company.

Knowles, M., Holton, E. F., and Swanson, R. (2005). *The adult learner: The definitive classic in adult education and human resource development* (6th ed.). Boston: Elsevier.

Moss, R. (2007). *The mandala of being: Discovering the power of awareness.* Novato, CA: New World Library.

Neugarten, B., Havighurst, R., and Tobin S. (1968). *Personality and patterns of aging.* Chicago: University of Chicago Press.

Nevis, E. C. (1987). *Organizational consulting: A gestalt approach.* New York: Gardner Press.

Phillips, J. J., and Phillips, P. P. (2007). *Show me the money: How to determine ROI in people, projects, and programs.* San Francisco: Berrett-Koehler.

Polster, E., and Polster, M. (1974). *Gestalt therapy integrated.* New York: Vintage Books.

Schein, E. H. (1995). *Kurt Lewin's change theory in the field and in the classroom.* http://www.solonline.org/res/wp/10006.html.

Williams, P., and Menendez, D. S. (2007). *Becoming a professional life coach: Lessons from the institute of life coach training.* New York: Norton.

Wilber, K. (1998). *The essential Ken Wilber: An introductory reader.* Boston: Shambhala Press.

INDEX